A WHOLE WORLD BLIND

Nish Nalbandian

Cofounders: Taj Forer and Michael Itkoff
Creative Director: Ursula Damm
Copy editor: Elizabeth Bell
Editorial Assistant: Dasha Kabanova

ISBN 978-1-942084-25-9

Printed by OFSET YAPIMEVI, Istanbul

Daylight Books
E-mail: info@daylightbooks.org
Web: www.daylightbooks.org

ALEPPO STRUGGLES ON

Nish Nalbandian

A note about group nomenclature: I have used the following convention in referring to combatant groups. Due to the difficulty of distinguishing between differing Opposition groups, unless I am sure of the name of the group I refer to them all as "Opposition Forces" or "Opposition Fighters." In general, they told me they were "Free Army (FSA)," but that was an umbrella term. Opposition is an accurate descriptor, so I have chosen to go with that.

For any Syrian Government or Regime action I refer to "Syrian Government Forces." It is very difficult to know which branch of the service was active, or even if it was the Syrian Army, since many supporting Militias were and are active.

Finally, when referring to damage done by incoming fire, I have used the generic "Bombing" or "Shelling," since unless I witnessed the event myself I do not know whether it was an air strike, a missile, a rocket, or something else.

PART 1

Standing in front of Dar Al-Shifa hospital in Aleppo, Syria, I hear the distinct punch of artillery shells fired by Syrian Government forces from the airport a few miles away. Within seconds, I cringe at the explosions as the shells impact less than half a mile from where I'm standing. The people on the street around me continue going about their business. They have been through this before. They know what to expect. I do not.

Cars and trucks race up to the front of the hospital. People begin to gather and watch. Armed Opposition fighters work to keep the street in front of the hospital clear for the vehicles, but it's hard to keep onlookers and helpers out of the way. A man rushes into the hospital carrying a bleeding boy in his arms. Another man struggles to walk into the hospital, his shirt and pants peppered with bloody holes, as others reach over to help him.

Even in the midst of chaos, it is still fairly calm on the street. Bystanders and workers pull a third man out of a white pickup and roll him onto a gurney, his body smeared with blood from half a dozen wounds. My heart races and my instinct kicks in, and while I can't ignore the intrinsic horror of what I'm seeing, I keep my focus and continue to take pictures. That is why I am here. I frame the images and shoot. At the same time, the people at the hospital kick into high gear and bustle people out of vehicles in whatever way they can. I stop trying to count the arrivals and become a part of the press of people coming and going.

I've been looking to a kid for information about what's happening. Mohammed is 16. He works at the hospital because he wants to support the revolution peacefully. He's been working for three days straight, with no more than an hour or two of sleep snatched here and there. This is a constant for him, he says. The gurney comes back out for its next passenger, smeared with the blood of those who've already ridden on it. Mohammed leaves me to get back to work. Blood pools on the ground and people walk right through it. It's hard to tell who works for the hospital, and who is just trying to help, or watch.

In the mounting turmoil a truck pulls up, and Mohammed motions me toward it. A crowd gathers, arguing and jostling. Whatever is in the back of the truck is covered by a tarp. One of the fighters angrily jumps up into the back of the truck. The crowd is yelling, but quiets as the man yanks the tarps aside. He is yelling, quivering with rage, as he motions down at the pile of meat below him, the torn remains of a man killed by one of those artillery shells: "Look at what Bashar al Assad is doing to you!" The air is electric, the rage palpable, and I feel sick seeing the bloodstains on the street as they haul what amounts to a torso into the morgue.

Another man is unloaded with a gaping hole in his face, blood pouring down the front of his body as he dazedly looks around, motioning at the bloody wound as if to say, "Hey, guys, is there something on my face?" They carry him in past a confused, bleeding man rolling around on a gurney. Again I lose count as the crowd thickens and people scramble to help. The bloody yellow gurney is back, whisking away a crying, bleeding woman this time.

Again a white truck with tarps pulls up and Mohammed points toward it. The dead are here again. This time there is no shouting, no yelling, only the crying and wailing of women. They carry in five or six wrapped-up bodies and place them in the garage next door, which now acts as a makeshift morgue. The crowd presses forward, anxious to find out who is there.

Off to the side, Mohammed motions me over and guides me down a corridor in the hospital, through a side door, and into the morgue. He wants me to go in and photograph the bodies so that people can see what happens here.

I do not hesitate, I just follow. We walk in, and there is a stack of bloody blankets. Mohammed pulls some blankets aside to reveal a pile of bodies and body parts, all of young girls. I have never imagined anything so horrifying. But I take the exposure, frame the shots and take the pictures. Headless bodies, limbs literally exploded apart, feet and hands separated from bodies. But it's the eyes that I won't forget. They still look alive. And I can hear their mothers outside crying. A man walks past the door, his young boy bandaged but alive, an X-ray in his hand.

I am spent after that; nothing more in me for the rest of the day. I take up smoking for the first time in my life, and for the rest of my time inside Syria.

PART 2

I went into Syria with a concept of war as something that happens far away, in deserts, in jungles, between two opposing military forces. Images of Total War à la *Saving Private Ryan* ran through my head as I approached the border from Turkey. Would there be just a storm of bullets and bombs? Would I need to run and duck for cover? Would I need the body armor I wore?

Instead of finding a chaotic wasteland, I found that we needed to get gas. We stopped and bought gas from a guy in a garage alongside the road. A cigarette pinched tightly between his lips, he filled us up with gas from dirty two-liter bottles as he joked with my driver. We stopped and changed money; we needed cash to go to the crowded restaurant next door and buy sandwiches and cold sodas for the drive to Aleppo.

My goal in being there was not to be a "combat photographer" by any means. My vision was to make portraits of the people affected by and living with this conflict on a daily basis. It was not hard to find people who could share stories of dead relatives, or to find destroyed environments to shoot in. Every street in Aleppo has at least one bombed-out apartment building or walls riddled with bullet holes. And while the war was never out of sight or mind, I was struck more by how normal everyday life seemed in the midst of the carnage. Amid the events that cause this damage, life goes on, and people continue about their business. They can't do anything else.

I spend a night at the house of my interpreter, Abu Ahmad, in the country. His family owns a small farm just outside of town. They grow olives and pistachios, and make olive oil. We sat up that night eating and talking. I met his family. I walked through their pistachio orchards and felt like I was taking a walk in the Pennsylvania countryside. Until the jet came. I could hear it prowling in circles above us. You see them during the day, people gathering around, pointing them out, wondering where they'll strike. If you're in a car, you pull over and watch until it drops its payload and you can move on. One day, I sat with a farmer and drank fresh cow's milk as a helicopter fired flaring rockets at a target a few miles away. We seemed so removed.

So when we heard the jet circling, I wasn't particularly startled or afraid...until the sky ripped open with the extended *braaap* of a heavy cannon. Abu Ahmad's family farm is less than three miles from the Aleppo International Airport, where Opposition forces besieged Government forces. The jet fired several times from directly above us toward the airport. It was the most terrifying sound I've ever heard. And then it was gone, and we went back to our meal of fresh olives, hummus, and makdous.

We sat on the back porch enjoying the night air, when the missiles started to fly, piercing the cloudy night sky with long jets of fire. Abu Ahmad told me that the regime forces launch them from an air force base in central Aleppo. I lost count after fifty, arcing soundlessly to the north, toward Azaz, Marea, Minnagh, and elsewhere. With a photographer's eye, I can see the beauty, how the light threads through the clouds as I frame my shot. But then I realize, guiltily, what those missiles are going to do.

You do not even hear the shelling after a while, unless it is close enough to affect you. I had dinner at an activist's house one evening. Eating family style and chatting, we gathered around a football match on satellite TV. A whistle/whoosh sound started to drill down, distinguishing itself from all the other shelling in the background. We all paused, eyes wide, looking at each other, wondering, is this the one that will hit us? When we heard the explosion a few blocks down we all smiled in relief, but again, I felt guilty, because the explosion may have ended someone else's casual evening.

This contrast between everyday life and instant death and violence is never far from sight. A new clothing store opens next to a building destroyed by shelling. A street strewn with rubble holds a squeaky clean, bright white pharmacy with an immaculate green sign and stacks of medications, all too expensive for most people. The pharmacist keeps a good stock, but must risk his life to cross over to government territory to buy more. And even then he cannot get some common medications.

Before I went, a more seasoned conflict photographer had told me you can edge up to the line and keep as much distance as you want (as long as the line does not move), so you can be in relative safety. And that turned out to be true. Most of Aleppo that I was able to visit is Opposition-held territory they call the "Free Areas." Areas still held by the Government are called "Occupied Territory" on this side of the line. Within these free areas I live and move while I am here. And the people of Aleppo live there too. Just like people live in your hometown. They shop for food or go to a restaurant. Every day I buy coffee, and my crew buys cigarettes. When the car breaks down, we need to get it fixed.

This is not the anarchy that I thought it would be. FSA guys direct traffic. Vendors line up along the streets selling vegetables; butcher stores are full of fresh meat. I even see a cotton candy vendor and an ice cream parlor. In the middle of the destroyed Bustan al Pasha area, not 500 meters from the front line, a group of boys play football in the cleared yard of their bombed-out school. Down the street a widow rummages through the rubble of a building that seems to be spilling its guts onto the street to try to find something of value to sell so she can feed her kids.

I walk down the street and start to recognize people. People are very friendly, and they want you to have coffee with them, or come back to eat at their restaurant. I realize that this can backfire on me, but there is a sense of community here, and in some way I am part of it despite being a foreigner. Though I try to vary my routine to avoid attracting attention, and I try to stay in different homes each night, I still crave some sort of routine and stability. Even with the constant sound of shellfire or jets overhead, you go about your day and hope it is not interrupted with violence.

People warn you not to walk down this street or that alley, because snipers can see you there.

When I go to the front lines, I crawl through holes in buildings, running behind buses crashed crazily, blocking snipers' views, until I can peek out from the fighting holes and see Government positions only 50 or 100 meters away. And despite the ongoing potshots, the fighters offer you tea, or make you have lunch with them. And as you talk, you again realize that you no longer hear the bullets cracking overhead unless they are close enough to affect you, and you look around and people are laughing, joking, eating, watching TV, all the while carrying weapons. A game show blares as the watch changes and a new group of fighters goes out to relieve the guys on the line.

I was present at the funeral of an Opposition fighter killed not an hour before in a firefight. His brother had opened the shroud and motioned for me to photograph his dead brother's face. His name was Ahmed Ibrahim. It is the last photo that anyone will ever take of him. The gravediggers finish the tomb, pile the dirt on, and go back to their fire to make a new pot of tea, laughing and joking. The graves are already dug, long rows, one for each neighborhood; they just add new tombs in the line and cover them up. I have had enough of death, and I just want to leave. But we have one more visit to the hospital.

This time there is no shelling. It is quiet at the hospital, and they invite me upstairs. I see a man who has had a heart attack. This hospital is equipped to deal with cardiac care. I did not even think about this type of care with the more violent happenings outside. A boy lies in bed, his father next to him. I ask what happened to him, the father says his son has a severe ulcer from stress. I get it.

In another ward, in another building, I find a nursery. Three newborn babies lie peacefully in incubators. The nurses hide their faces; no one wants to be photographed, and I promise not to show pictures that will give away the location of this site. They cannot afford for it to be bombed, because even in the midst of this conflict, people are making babies, and people are still taking care of them.

I meet a man who is preparing his car for his wedding that night. I see people walking with their kids, and when I am invited into people's homes, women show me pictures of their grandkids playing, just as anyone might do. But just to remind me, there is always a picture of the son or grandson they lost. The war is never far from heart or mind.

Most Syrians just want to live their lives. In the end, these are just people who wanted more freedom, freedom to have political discourse or dissent, and ended up having to fight for it. The war has gotten very complex, very sectarian, and very violent. I am no expert on geopolitics. What I see are the people on the ground doing their best to live their lives the way we all do. They may be sandwich makers, mothers, activists, fighters, refugees, shopkeepers, farmers, or imams, but they all have to sleep, eat, feed their kids, go to work—even if that is fighting—and even get married and have babies.

I am relieved when it is time for me to go. I breath a sigh of relief when I can see the well-lit streets of Turkey in the distance. But I feel that familiar tug of guilt because I get to leave, and my friends and colleagues stay and try to live their lives amid the death that hovers around them. I smoke my last cigarette with my driver at the border, say goodbye, give him an extra hundred dollars, and walk back to a world where violent death is a fluke, not a daily expectation.

كل العالم عميان

All the world is blind

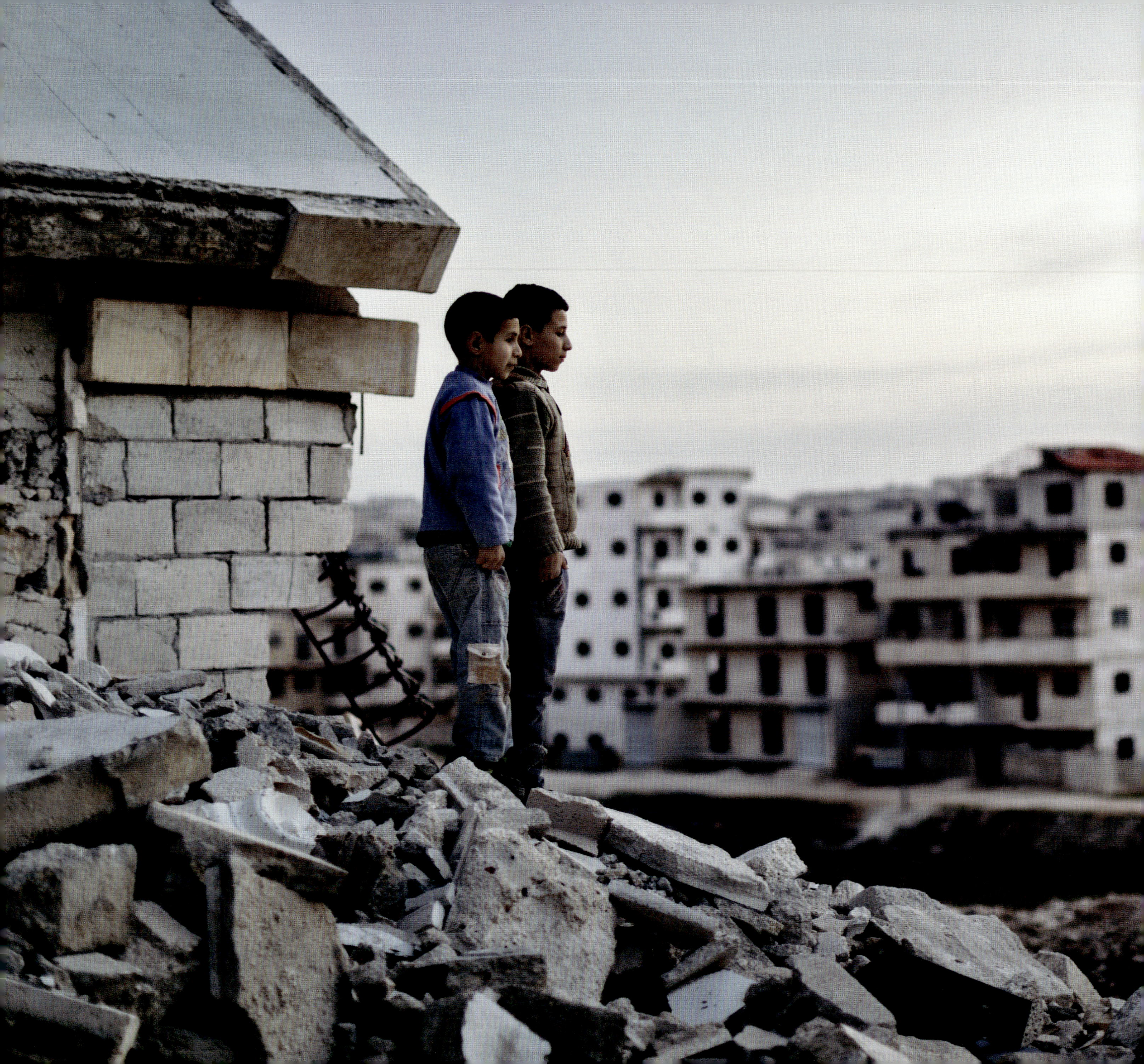

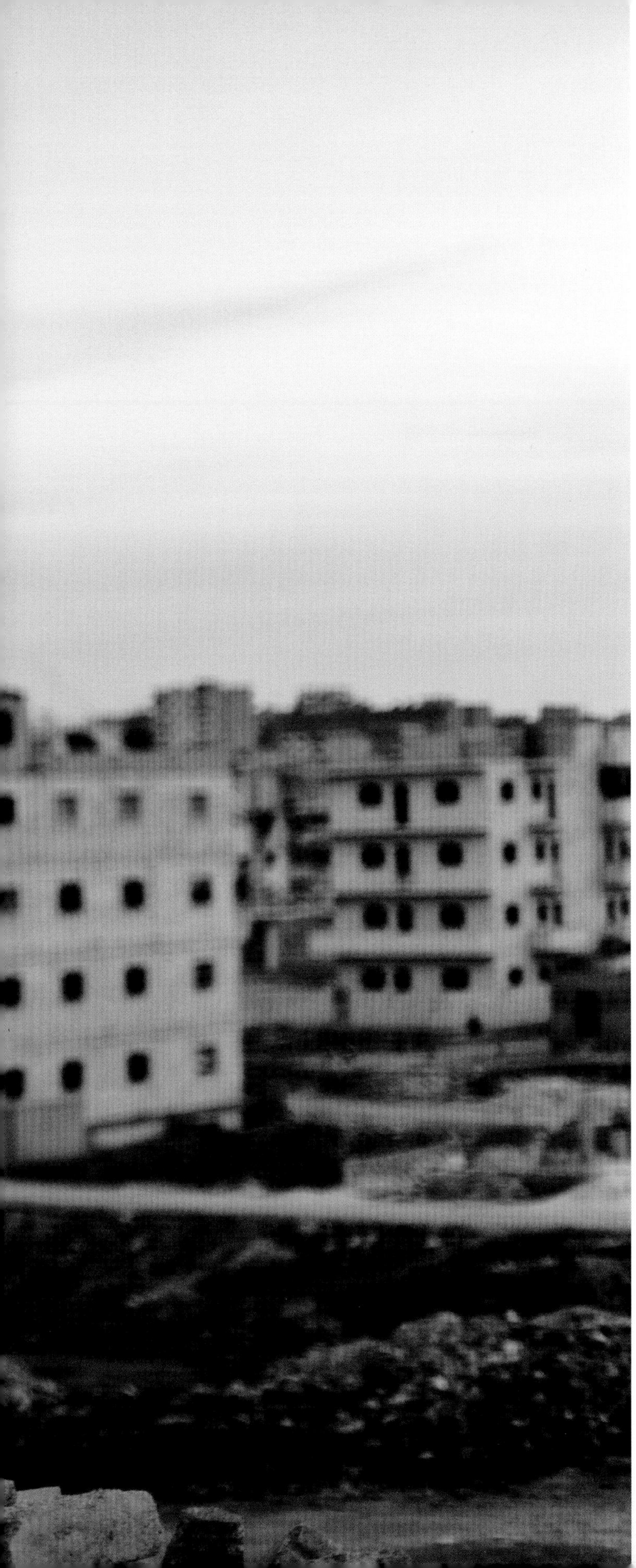

April 5, 2014, Maarat al-Numaan, Idlib.

At the time I made this picture, the area was controlled by Jamal Marouf's Syrian Revolutionaries Front (SRF), but was still contested by Syrian Government forces from their Wadi Deif and Hamadiyah bases about 2K away. SRF, which had recently displaced ISIS from the area, was itself displaced by Al Qaeda Affiliated Jabhat al Nusra (JAN) later in 2014. Wadi Deif and Hamadiyah bases were captured by Islamist rebels including JAN and Ahrar ash-Sham in December of 2014.

February 10, 2013, Shaar District, Aleppo.

Dar al Shifa Hospital was destroyed by Syrian Government bombing on November 22, 2012. Dar al Shifa had been the target of at least six previous attacks and was one of the few remaining hospitals available to residents of Opposition-controlled Aleppo.

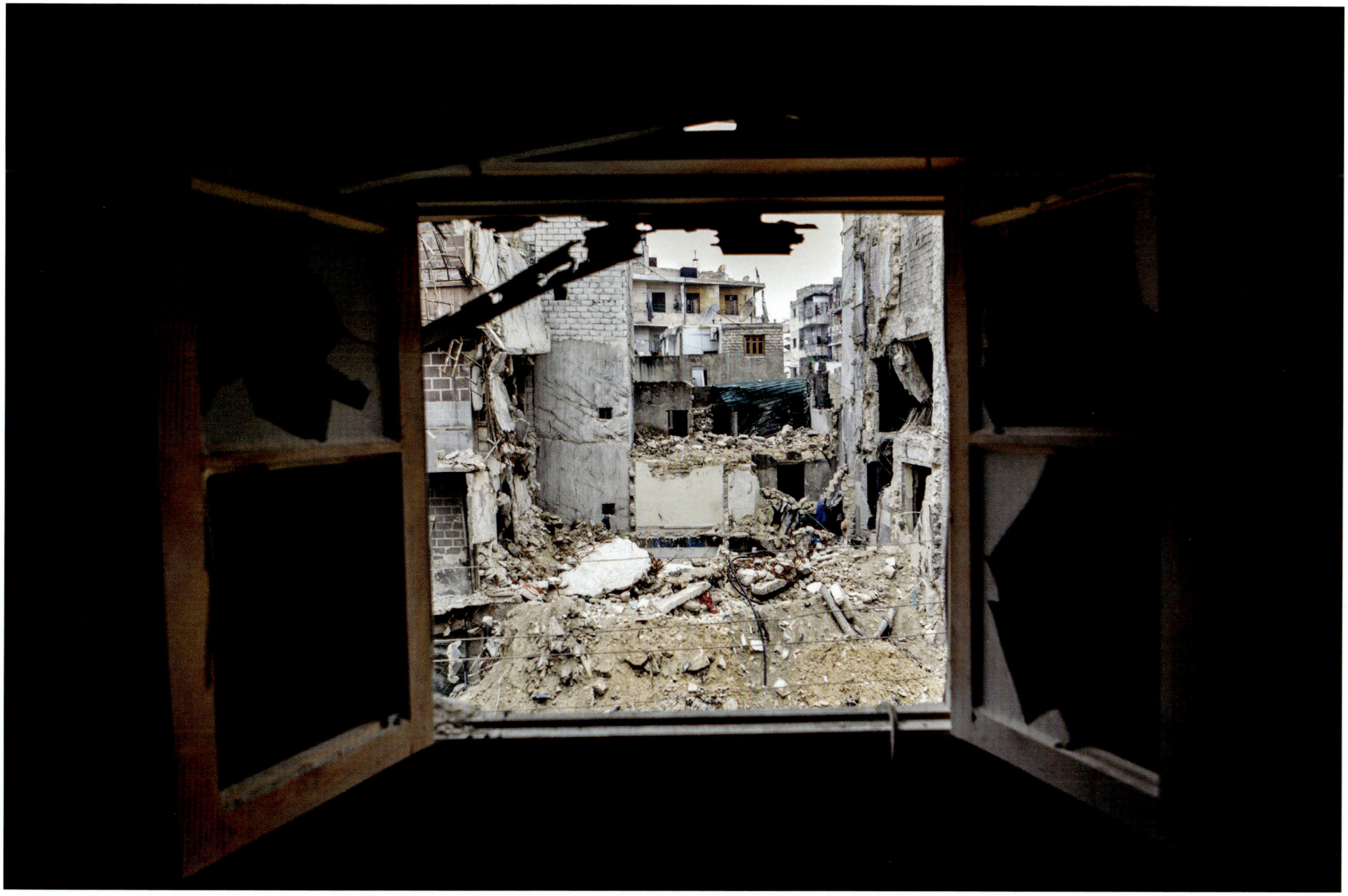

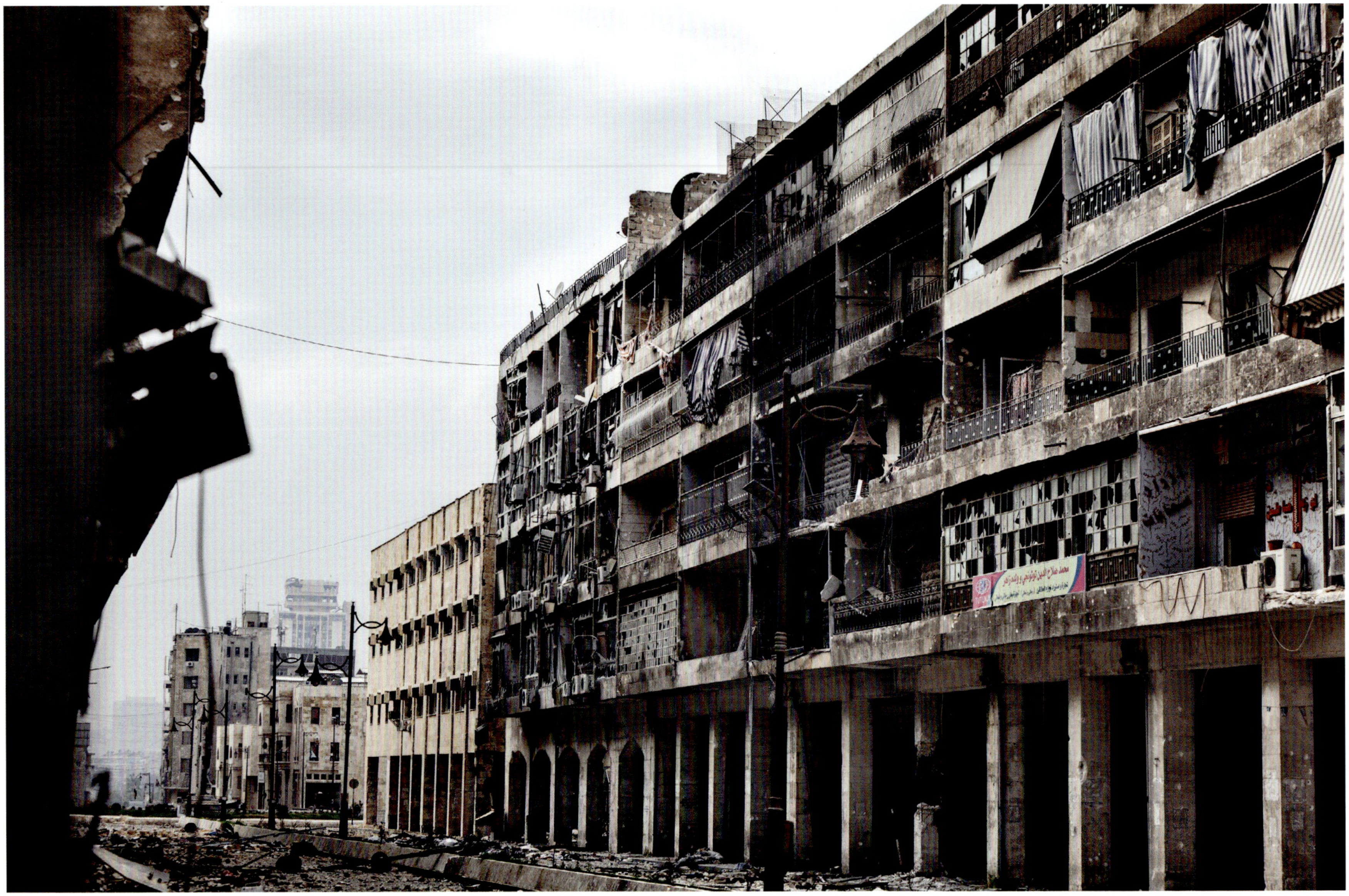

February 10, 2013, Al Farafirah, Aleppo.

Apartment buildings, offices, and stores along Al Mutanabbi Street, damaged by heavy fighting between Syrian Government troops and Opposition forces during clashes in 2012. By 2013 this area had become a perpetual front line. In the background you can see the Aleppo City Hall building, from which Syrian Government snipers controlled the area.

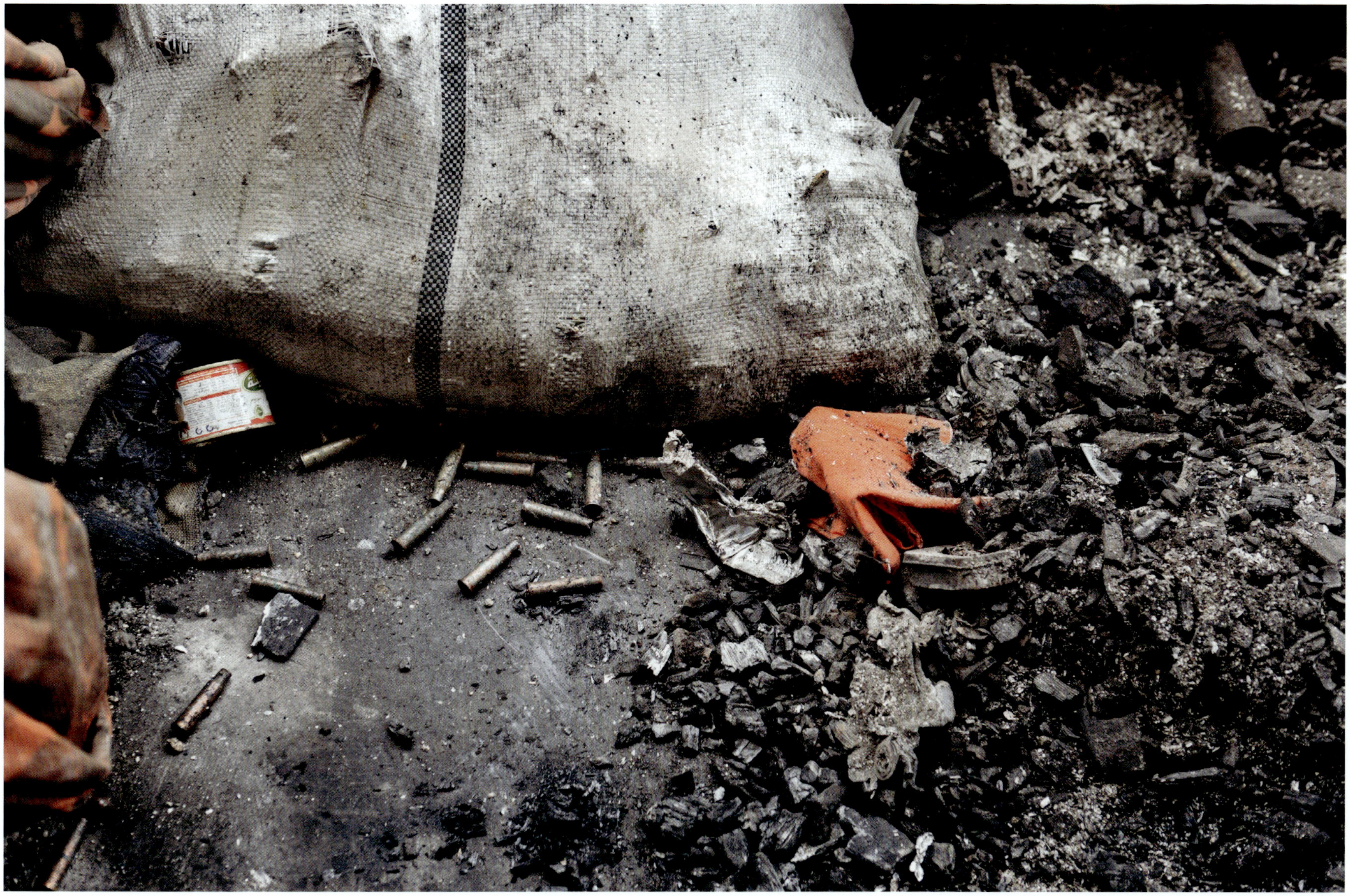

February 9, 2013, Old City, Aleppo.

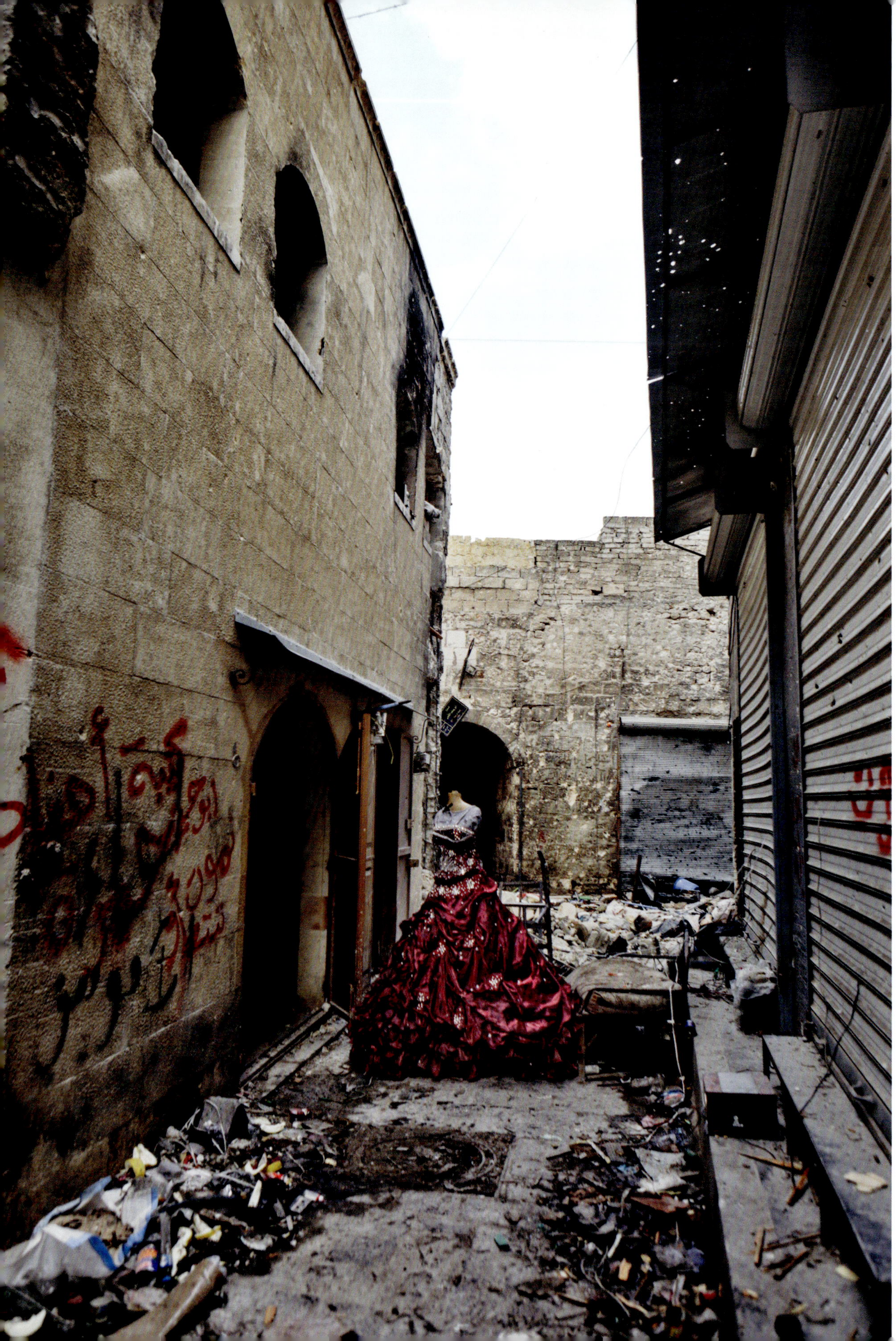

February 9, 2013,
Al Farafirah, Aleppo.

Opposition fighters used this dress to distract Syrian Government snipers.

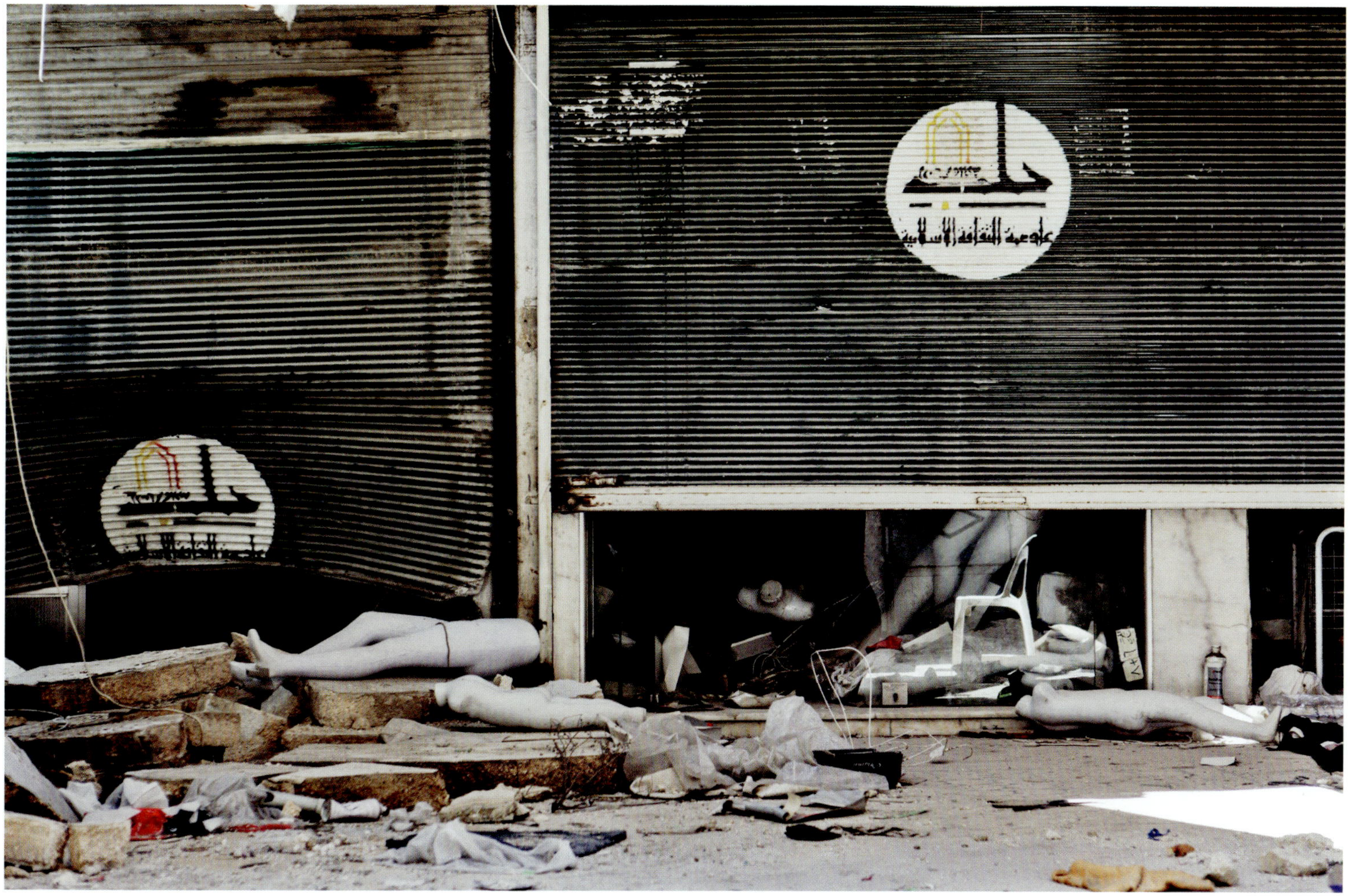

April 25, 2013, Bustan al Basha, Aleppo.

April 18, 2013, Shaar, Aleppo.

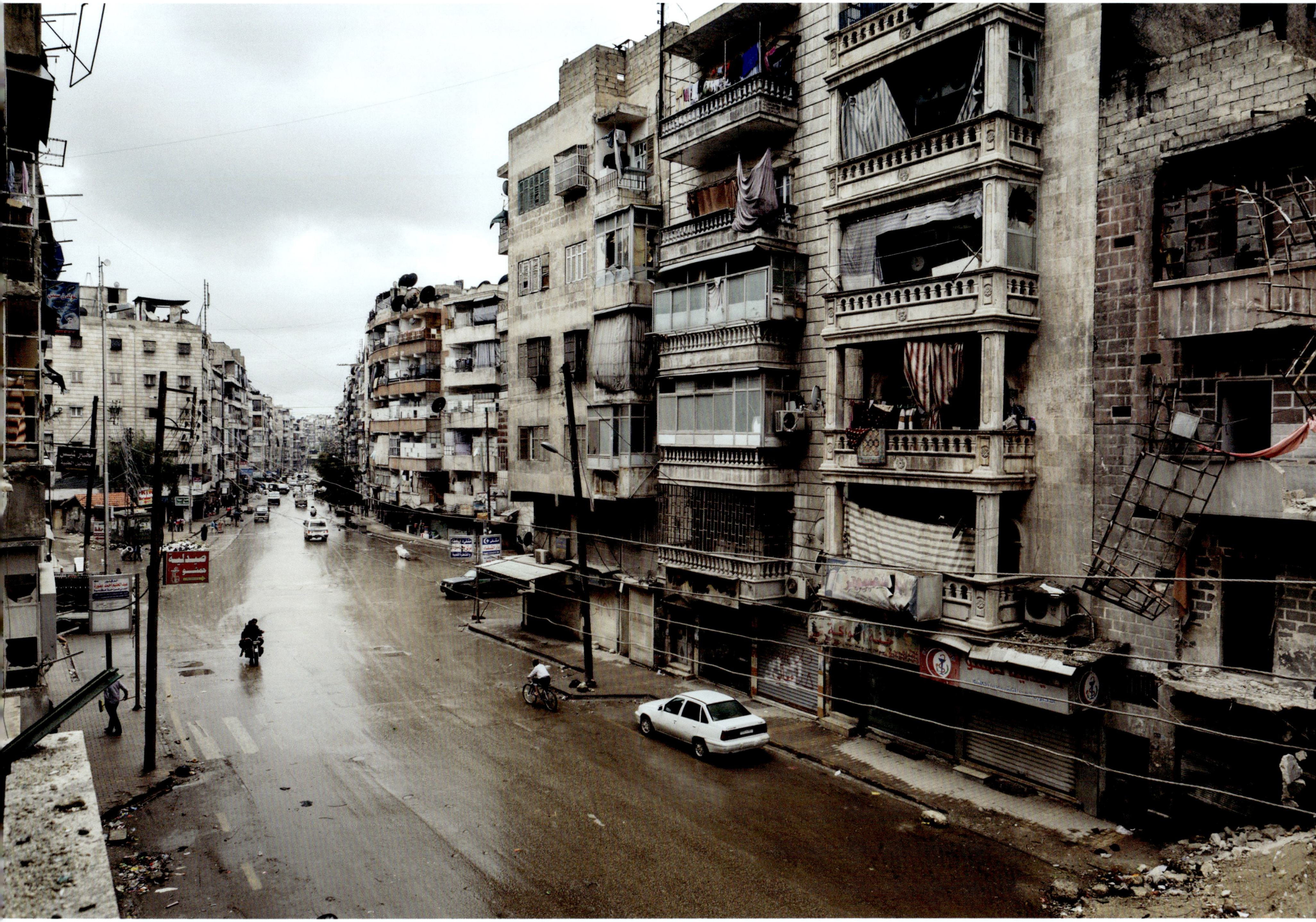

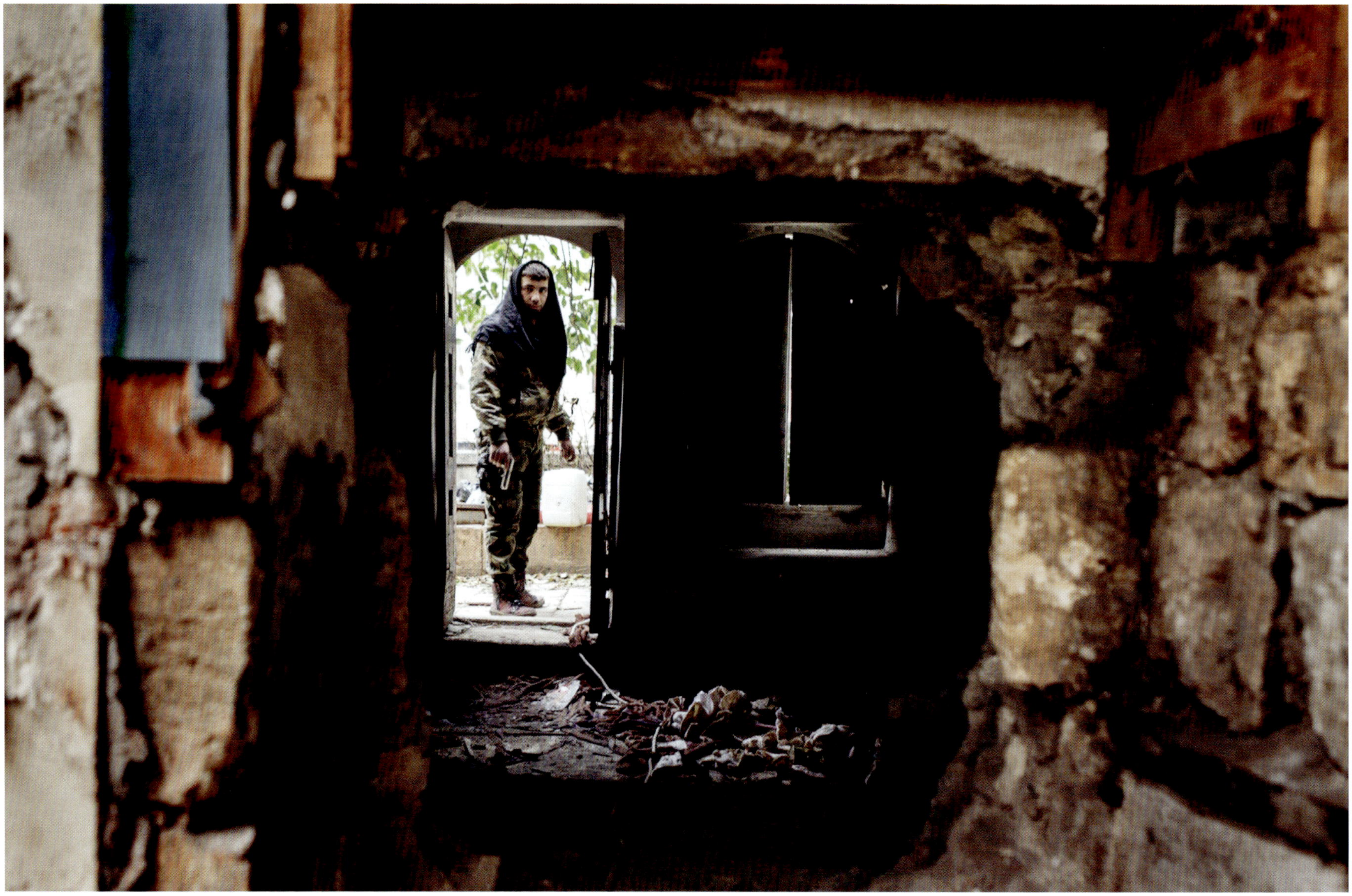

February 9, 2013, Al Farafirah, Aleppo.

Opposition fighters punch holes in structures to enable them to move without being targeted by Government snipers.

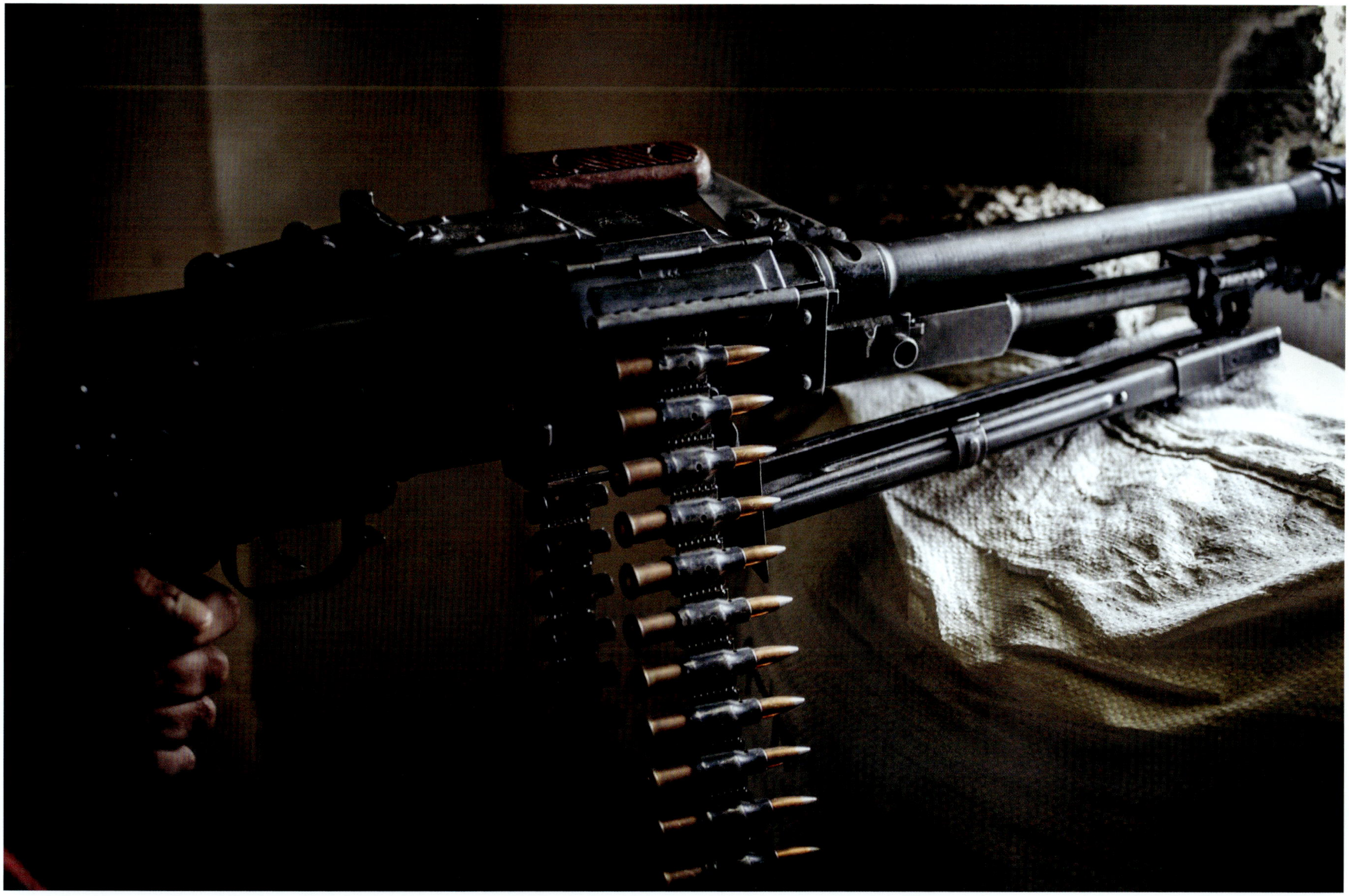

April 21, 2013, Sheikh Maqsood, Aleppo.

A YPG fighter mans a machine gun on the front line. The YPG is the military branch of the Kurdish Democratic Union Party, operating in primarily Kurdish districts of Syria. In April 2013 this militia and the FSA were cooperating in the conflict against the Syrian Government, an arrangement that has not held up.

April 19, 2013, Sheikh Maqsood, Aleppo.

A Kurdish fighter named Garee.

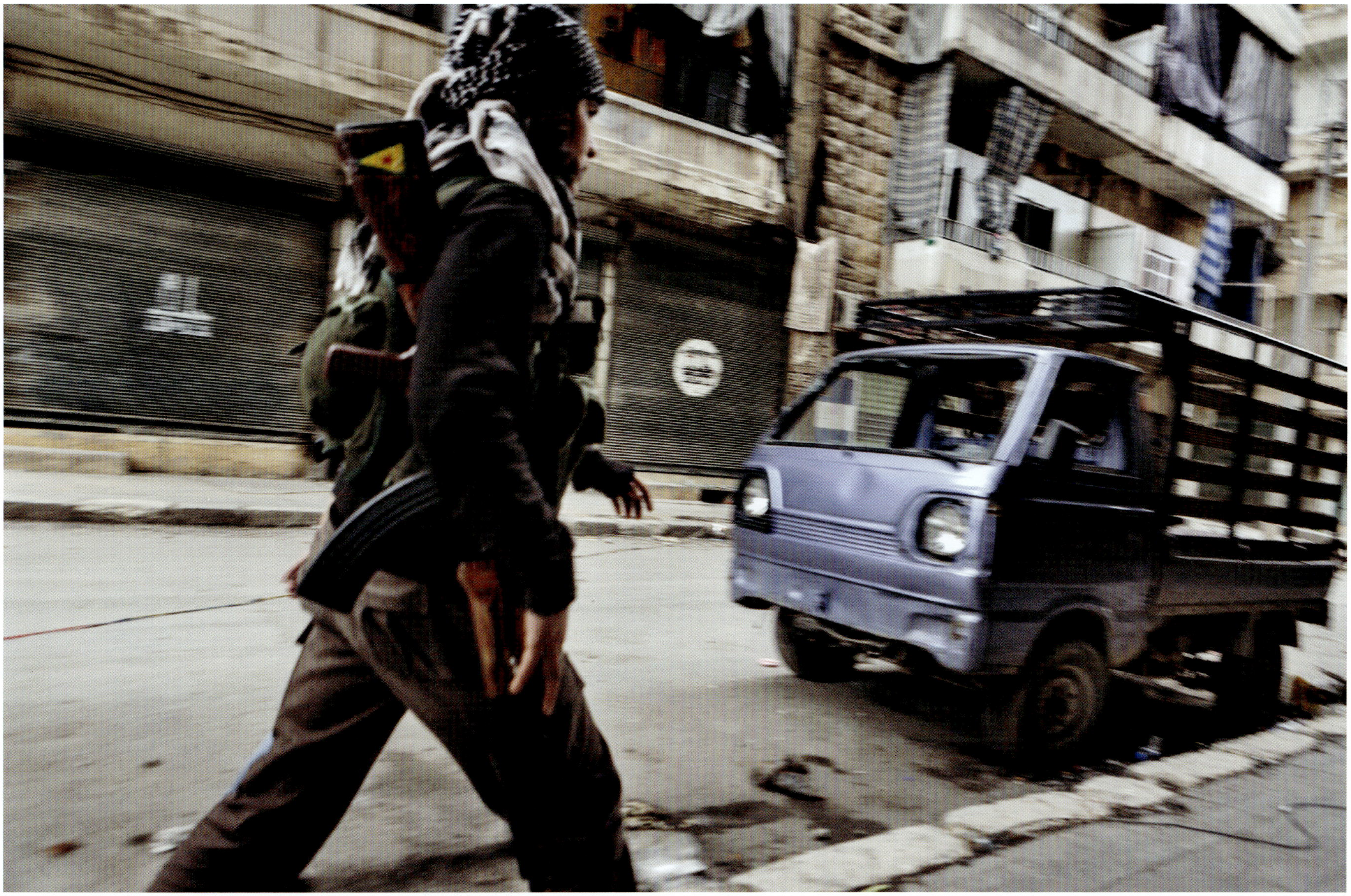

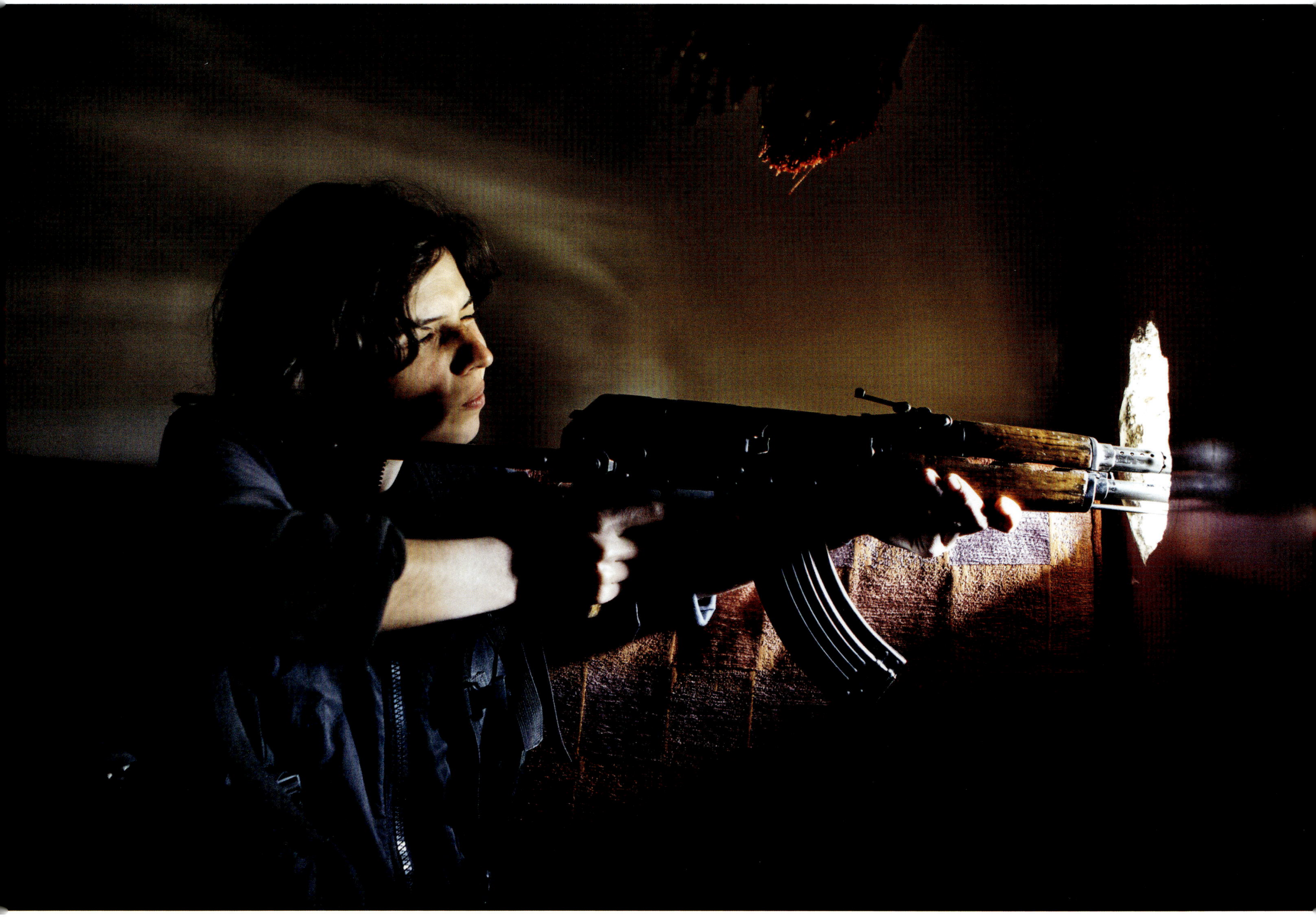

Left: *April 19, 2013, Sheikh Maqsood, Aleppo.*

Rukan, a Kurdish fighter and unit leader, aims her weapon from a fighting position overlooking the front line with Syrian Government forces. Rukan was killed in a Syrian Government air strike in 2014.

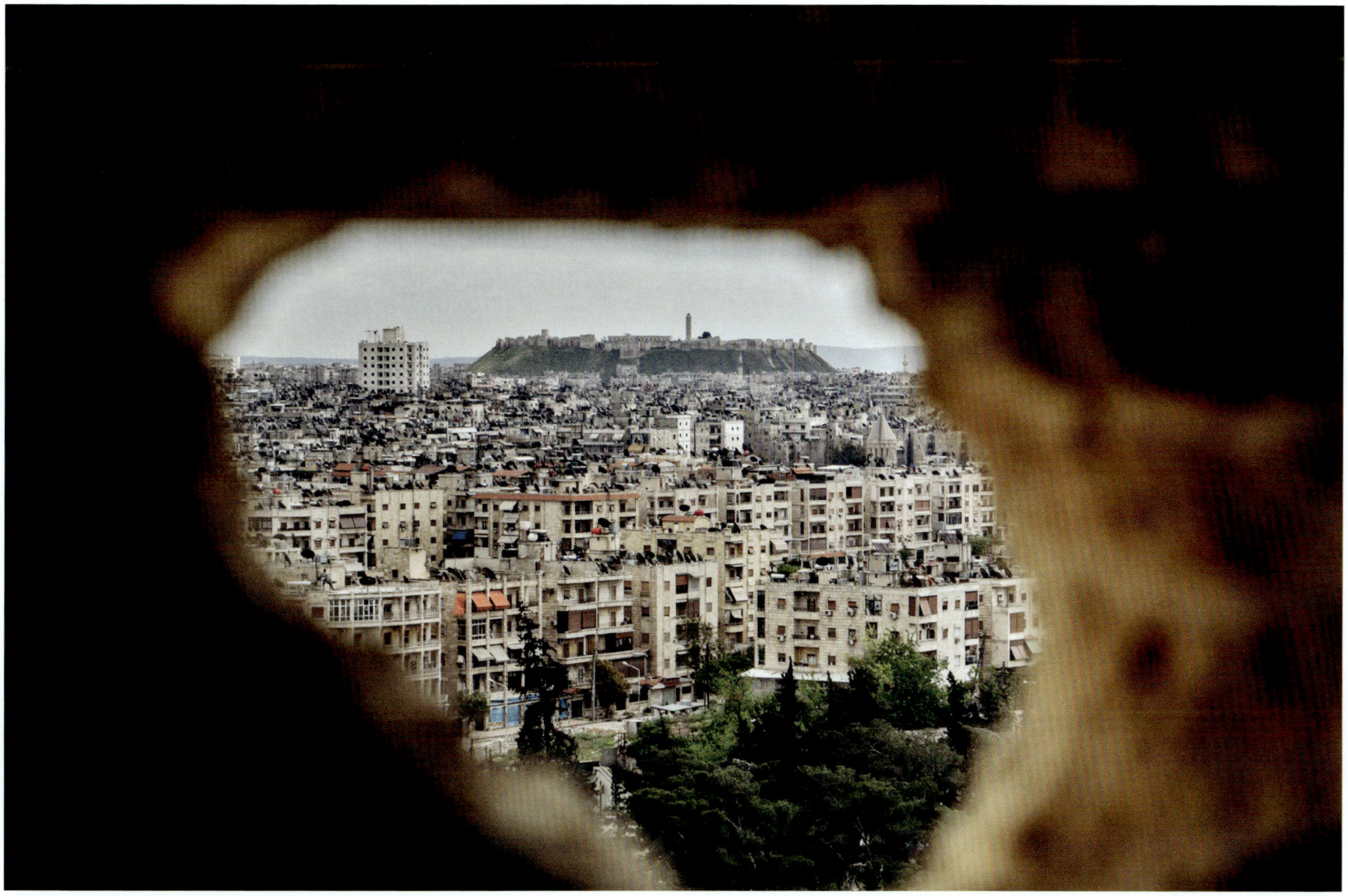

Top: *April 19, 2013, Sheikh Maqsood, Aleppo.*

The Citadel of Aleppo.

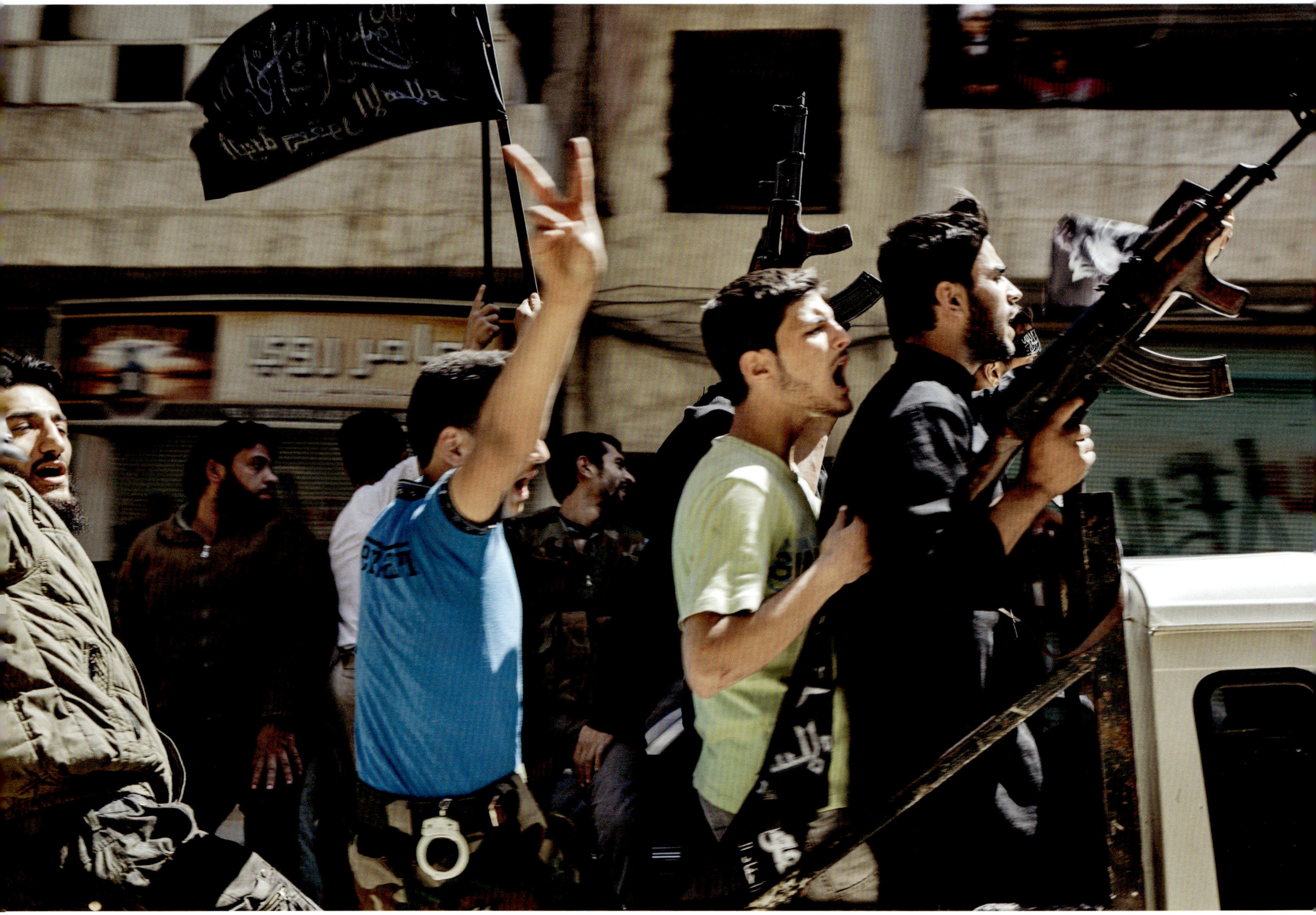

April 26, 2013, Salaheddine, Aleppo.

Opposition fighters take part in a protest against the Syrian Government and its leader, President Bashar al Assad.

April 25, 2013, Old City, Aleppo.

An Opposition fighter prepares to fire a rock with a large makeshift slingshot toward Syrian Government positions.

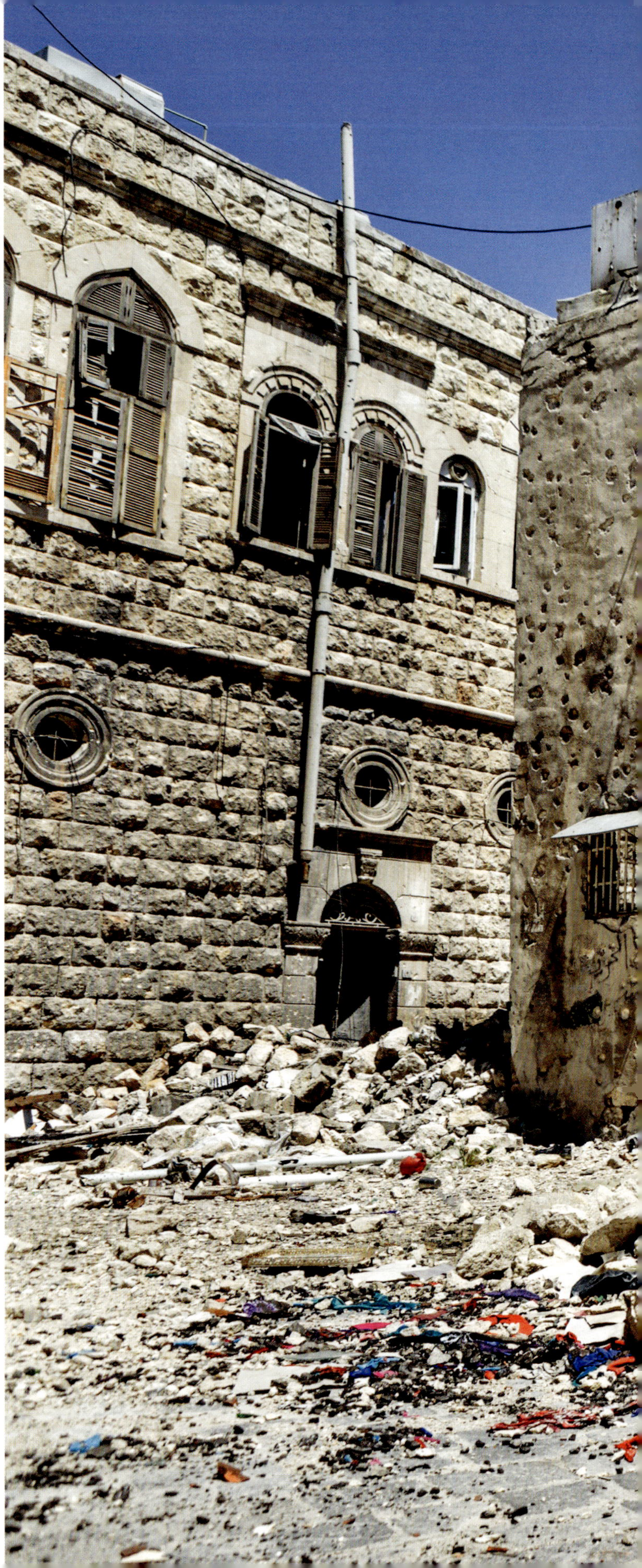

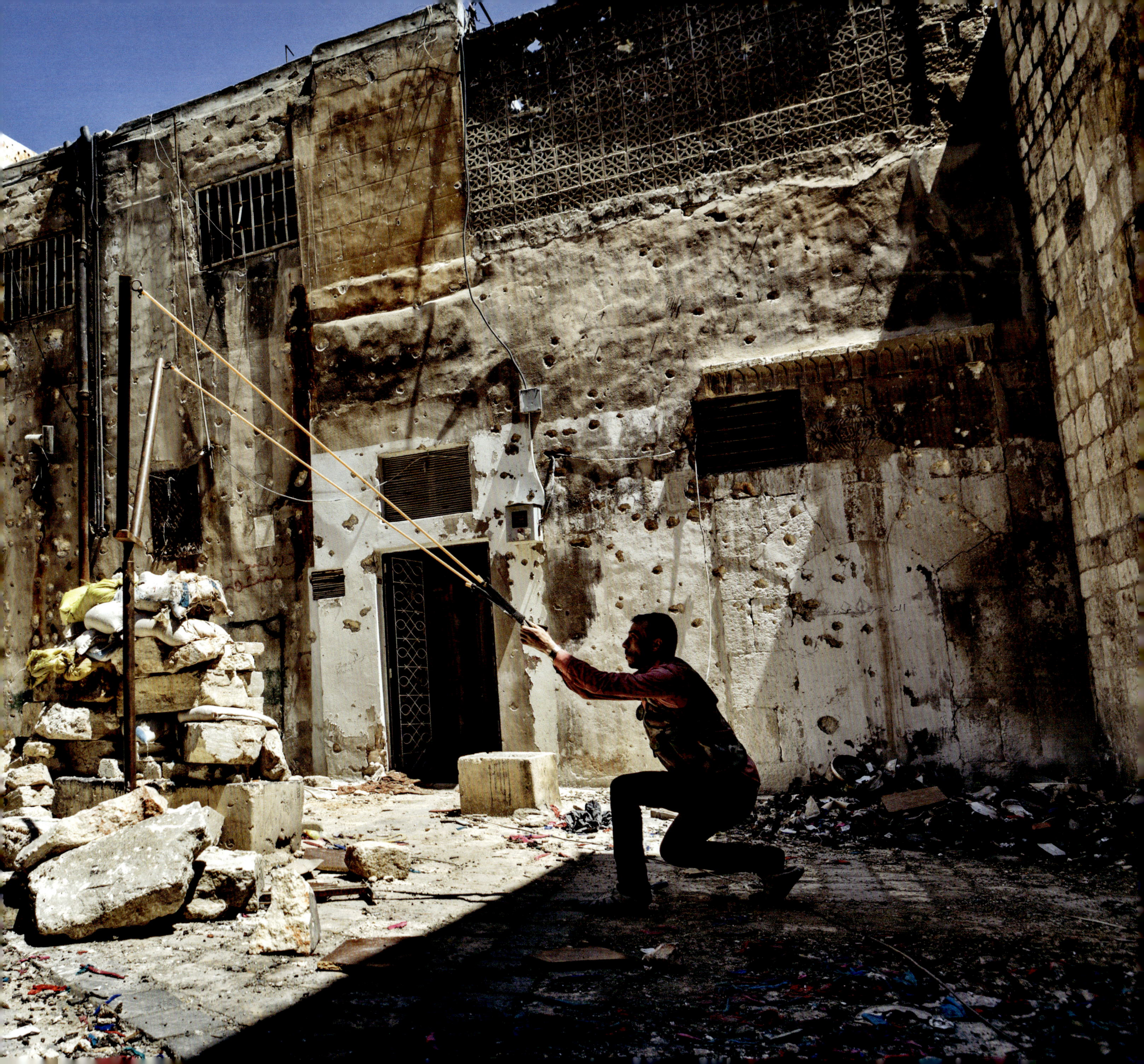

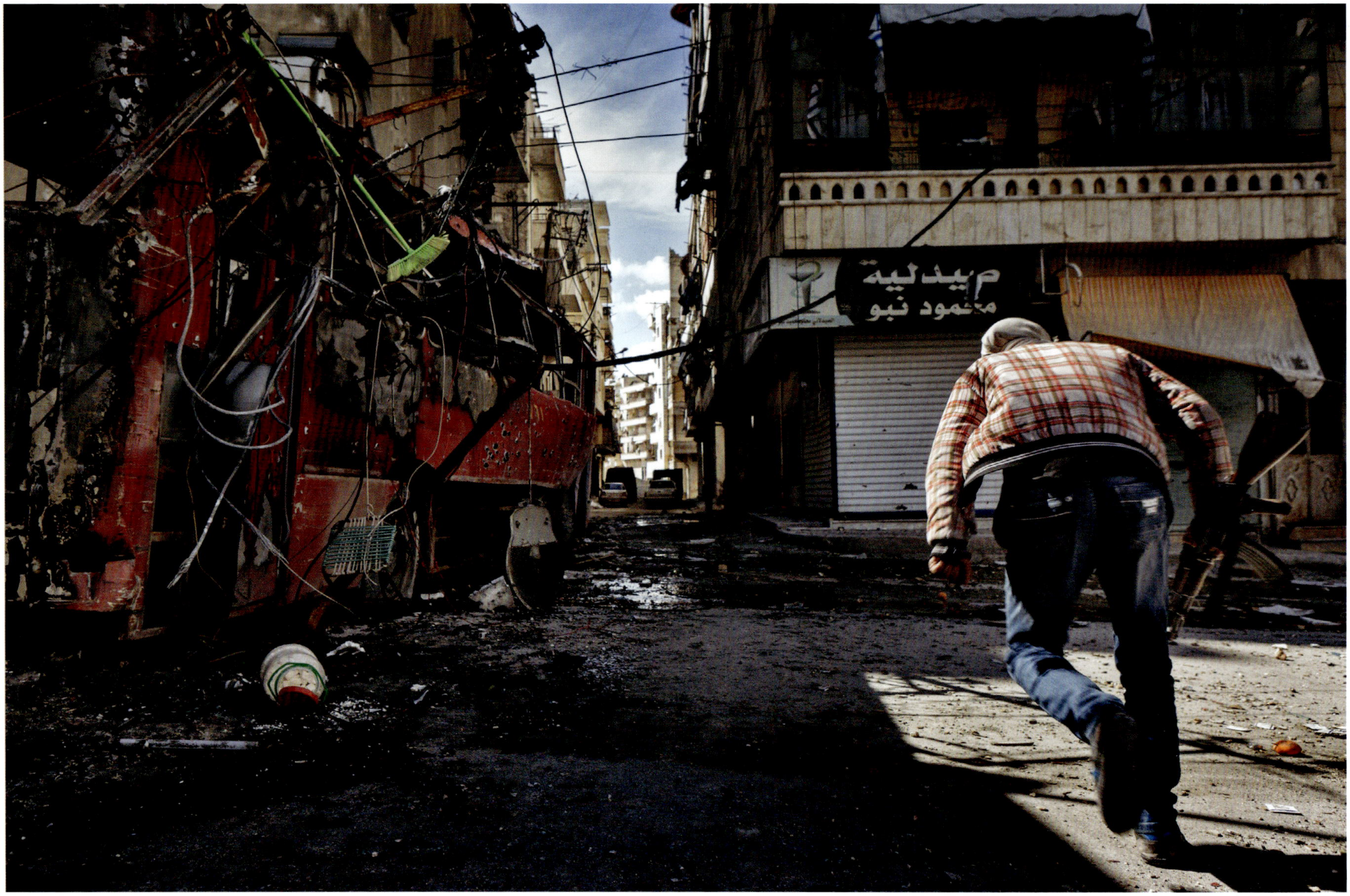

April 20, 2013, Ashrafieh, Aleppo.

A Kurdish fighter sprints across an intersection to avoid Syrian Government sniper fire. Opposition fighters often placed vehicles like this bus to provide cover and concealment from sniper fire.

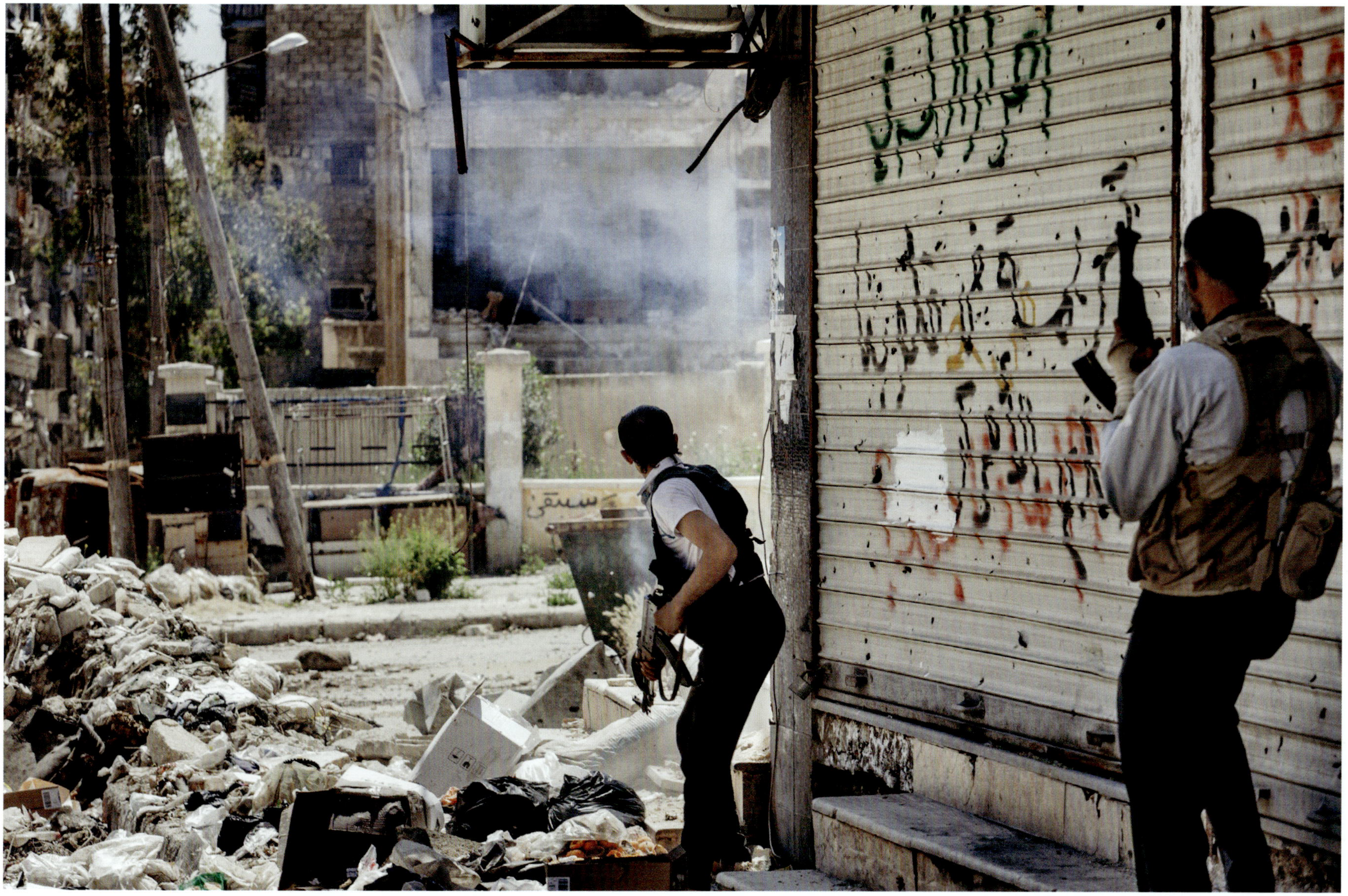

April 26, 2013, Salaheddine, Aleppo.

Opposition fighters engage Syrian Government positions in a brief firefight.

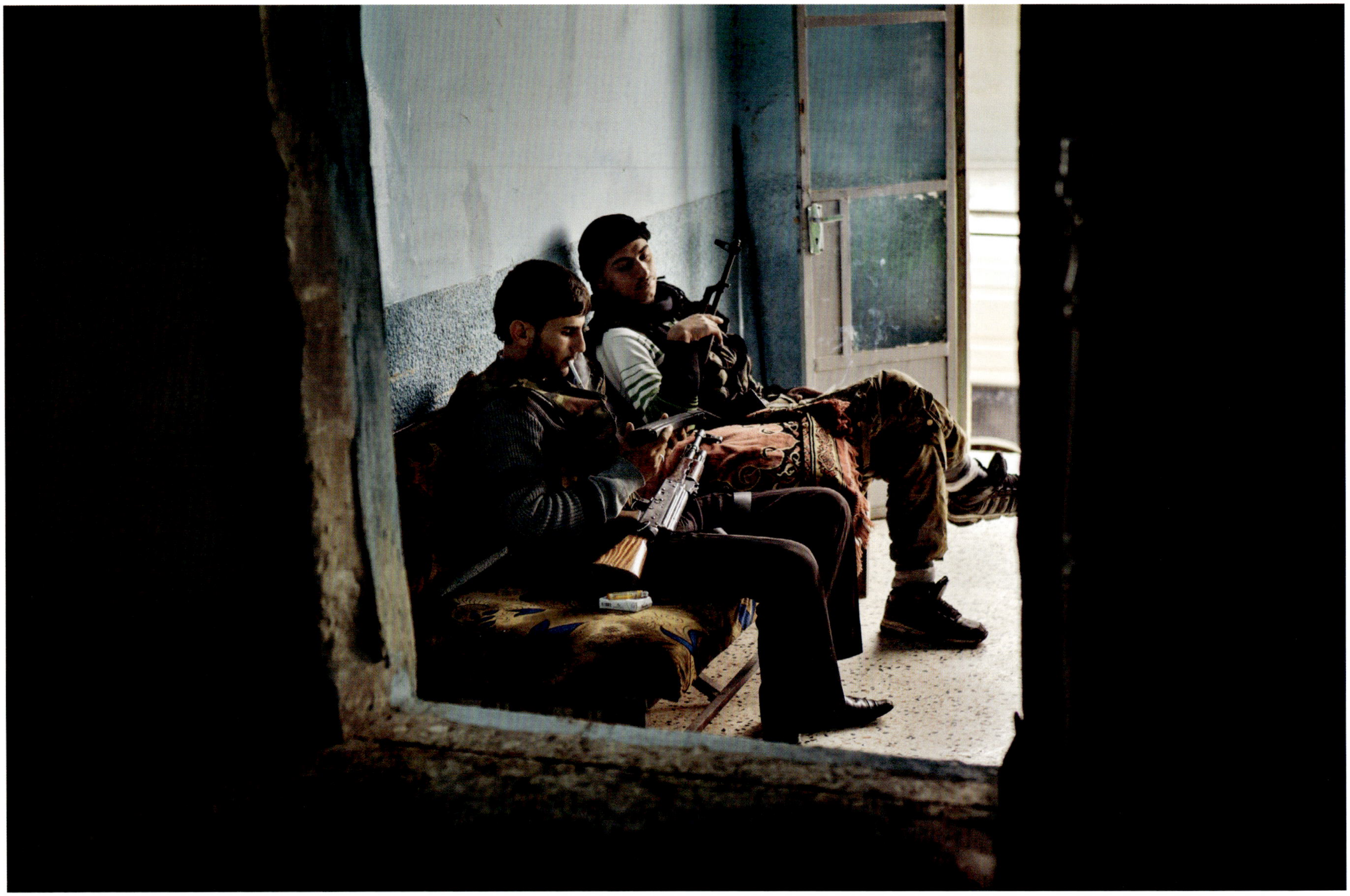

April 18, 2013, Sakhour, Aleppo.

Members of a local FSA Khatiba [Free Syrian Army battalion] clean their weapons at their unit headquarters.

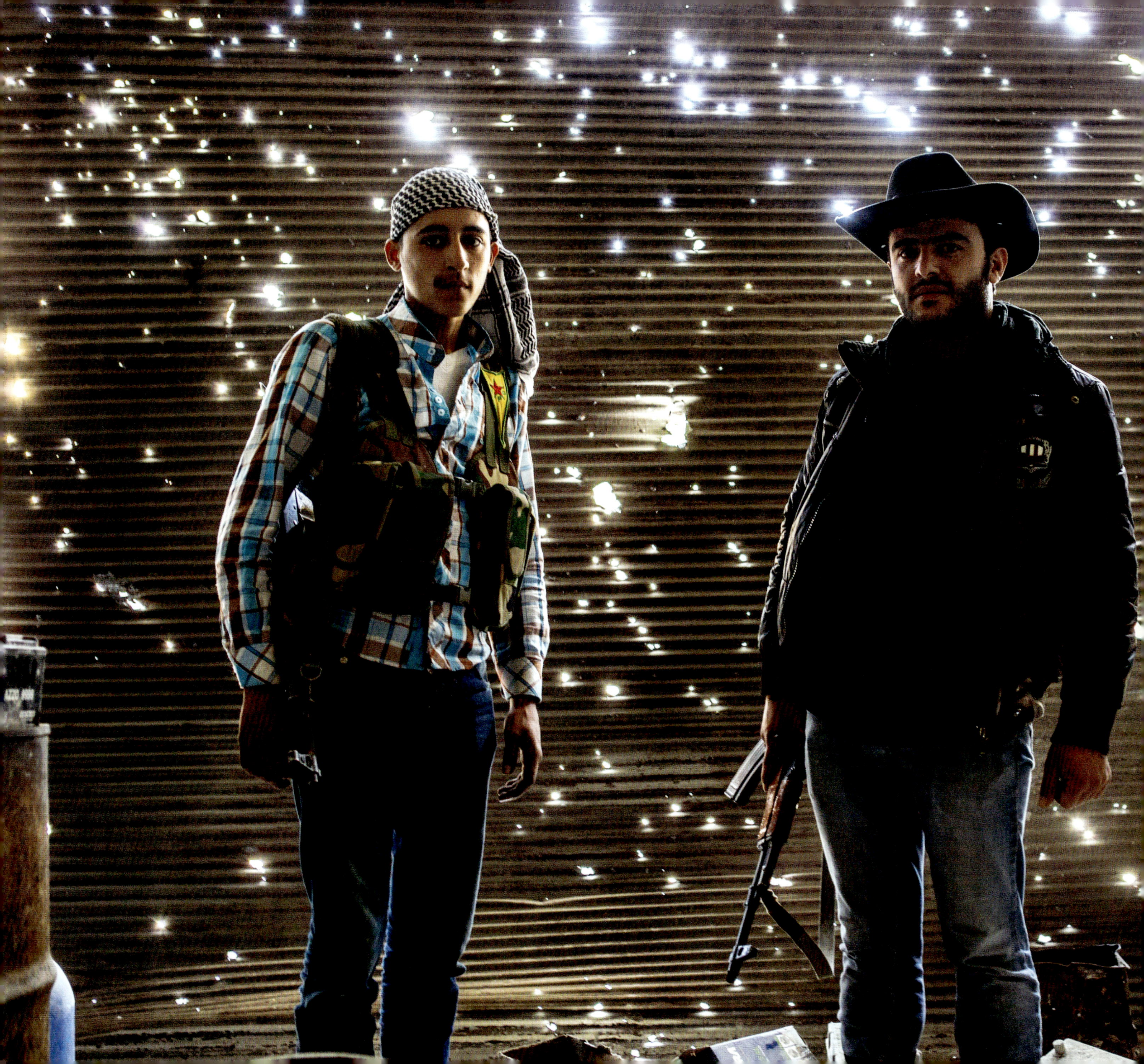

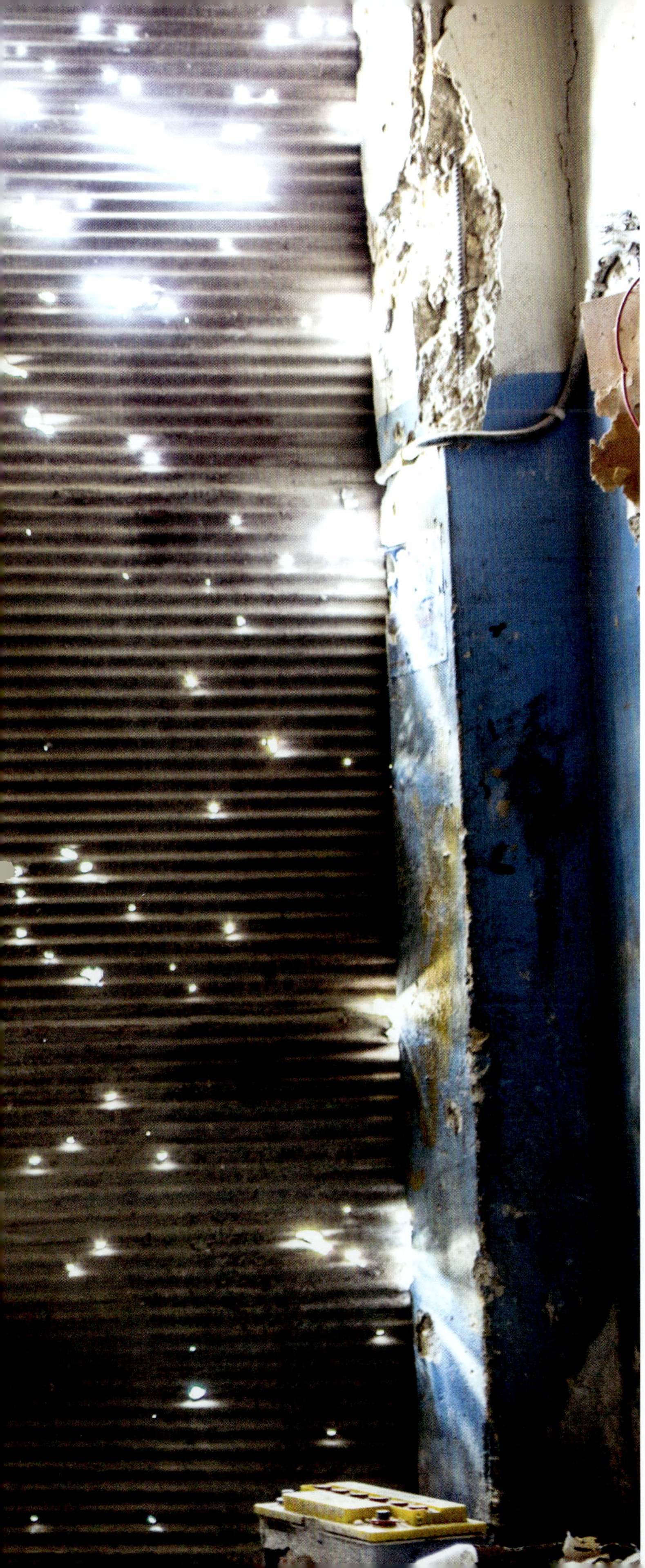

April 20, 2013, Sheikh Maqsood, Aleppo.

Two Kurdish fighters stand in a damaged garage on the front line with Syrian Government forces.

One of the hardest problems to overcome in a war zone is figuring out what on earth is going on at any given time. It truly is organized chaos. Adding to this fog is not being able to speak the local language. Even with a fully bilingual translator you can only understand the literal meaning, but not the nuance of what is said. You have to rely on body language as much as the spoken word. Given this lack of a common language, you can easily find yourself in a situation you wouldn't have gone into had you known, or you would have preferred to have been aware of earlier.

There are situations that can only happen in war, like sitting in no-man's land drinking sweet tea, your shoes lined up neatly by the door while the TV shows footage from Homs of heavy bombing, yet you could be watching it with the sound off and allow the shelling outside the building to fill in the audio.

—Will Wintercross

April 20, 2013, Ashrafieh, Aleppo.

Outside the headquarters of the mixed Kurdish militia Jabhat al Akkrad.

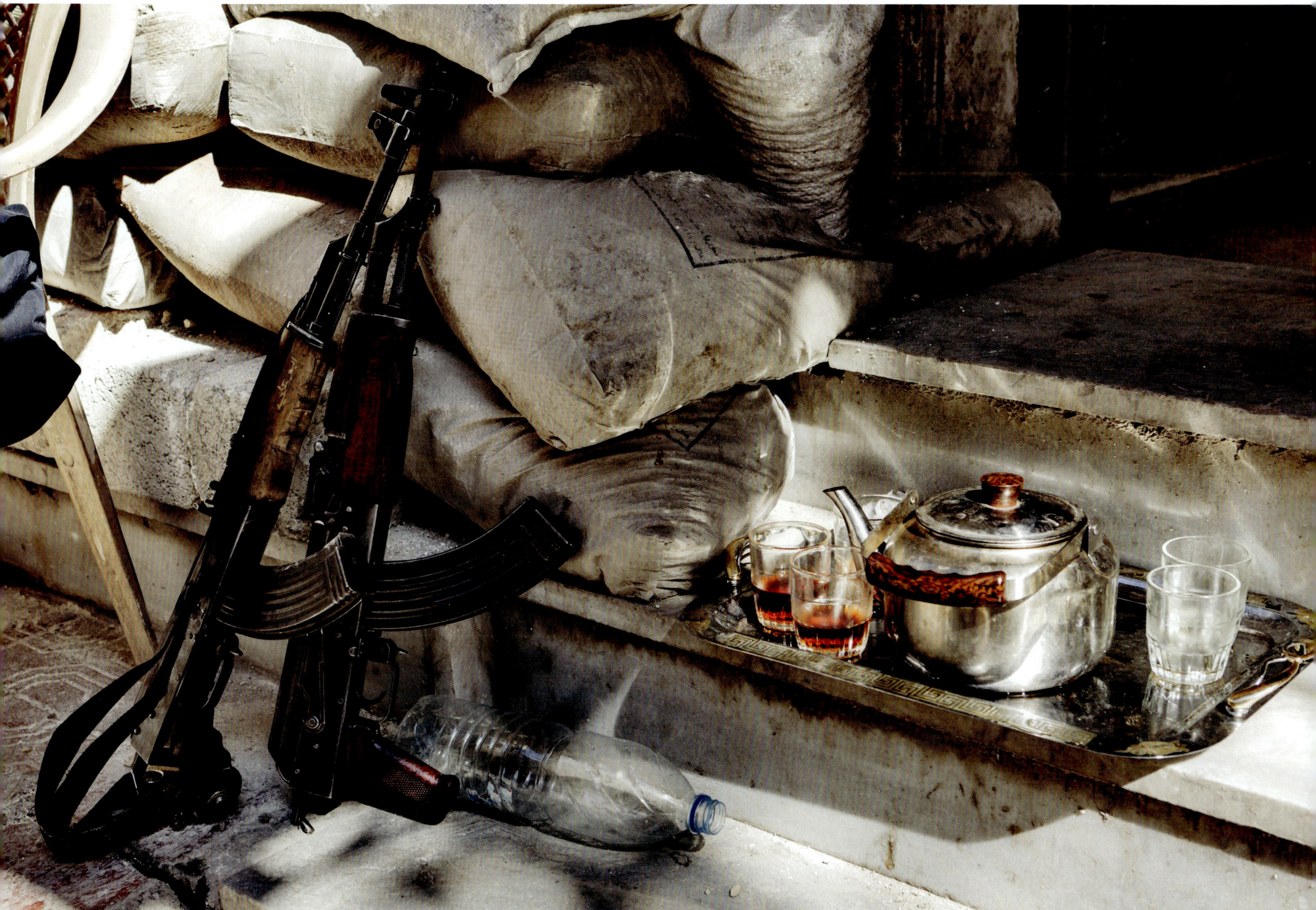

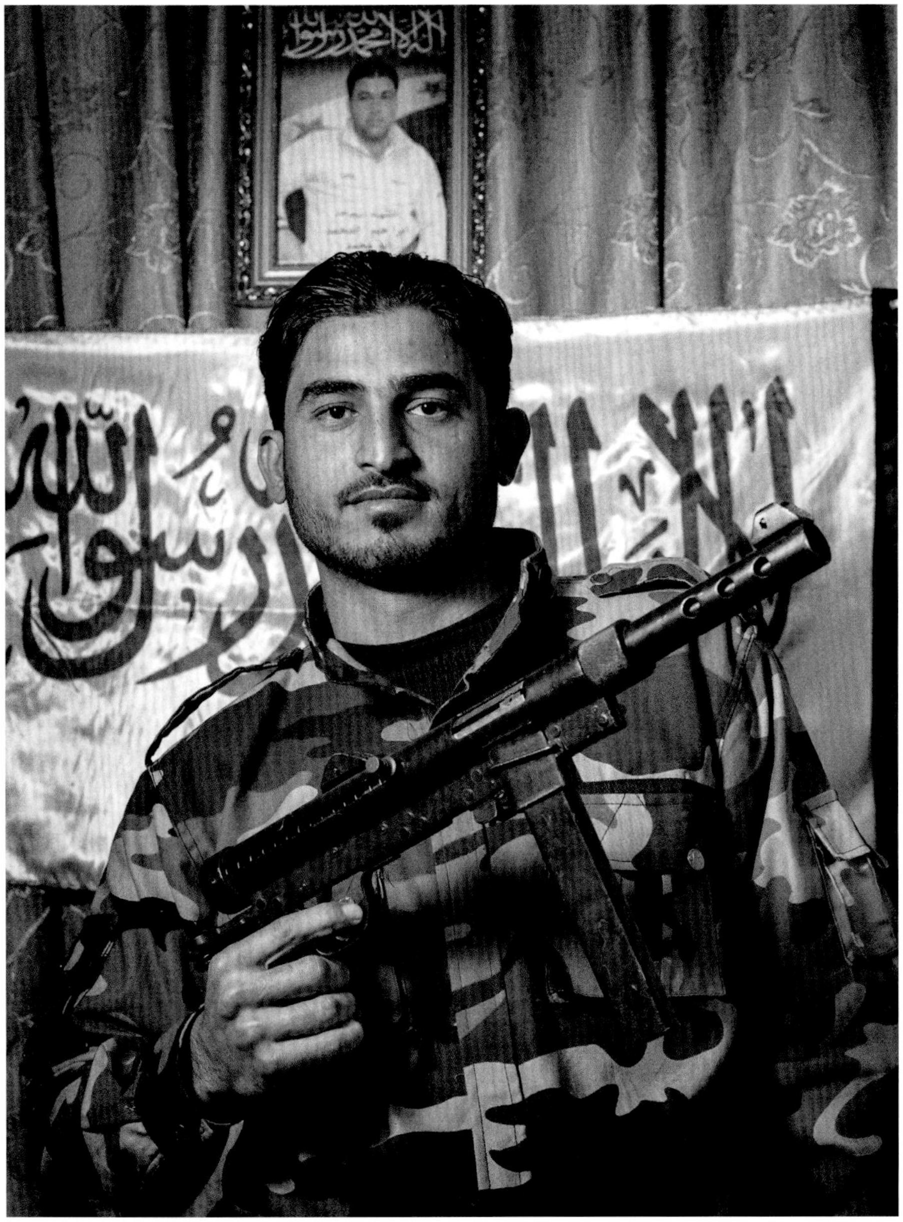

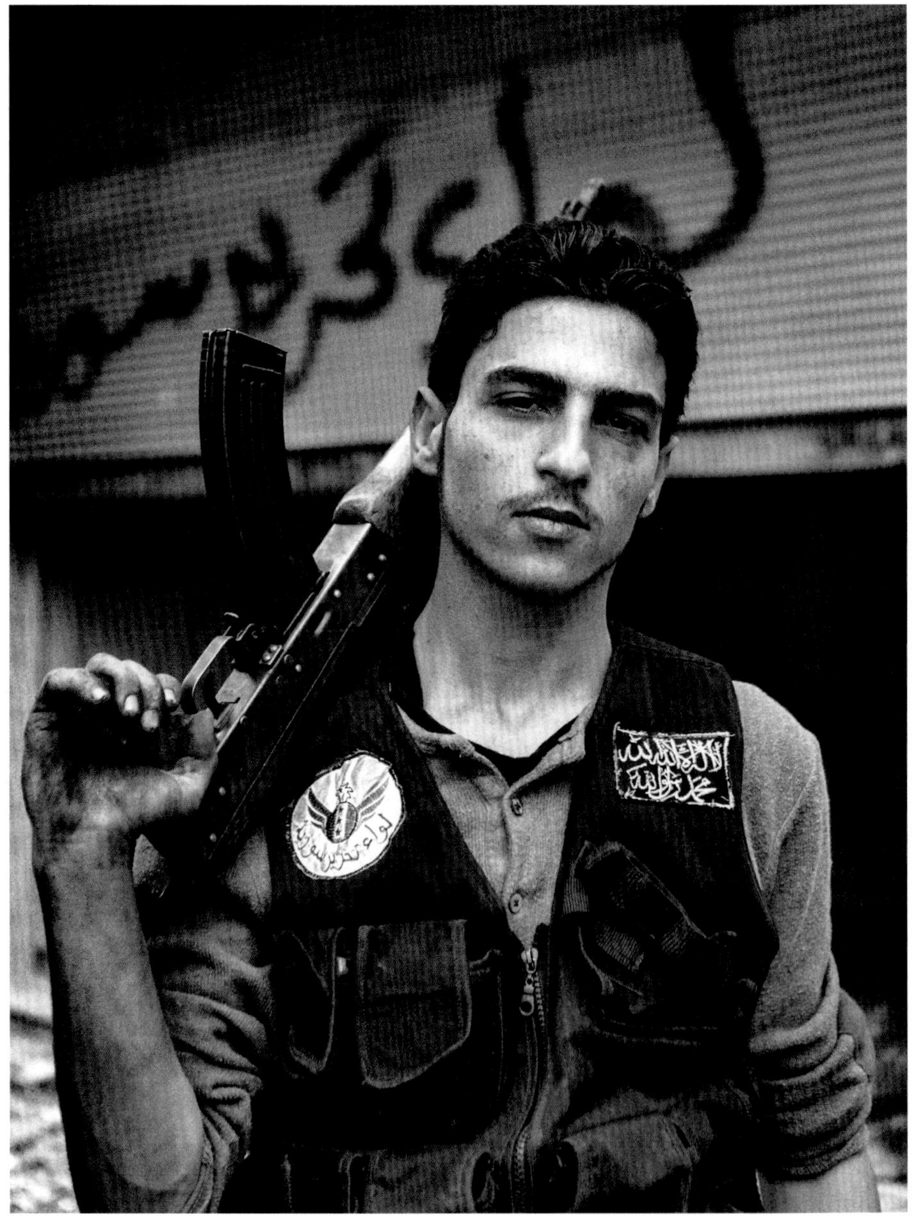

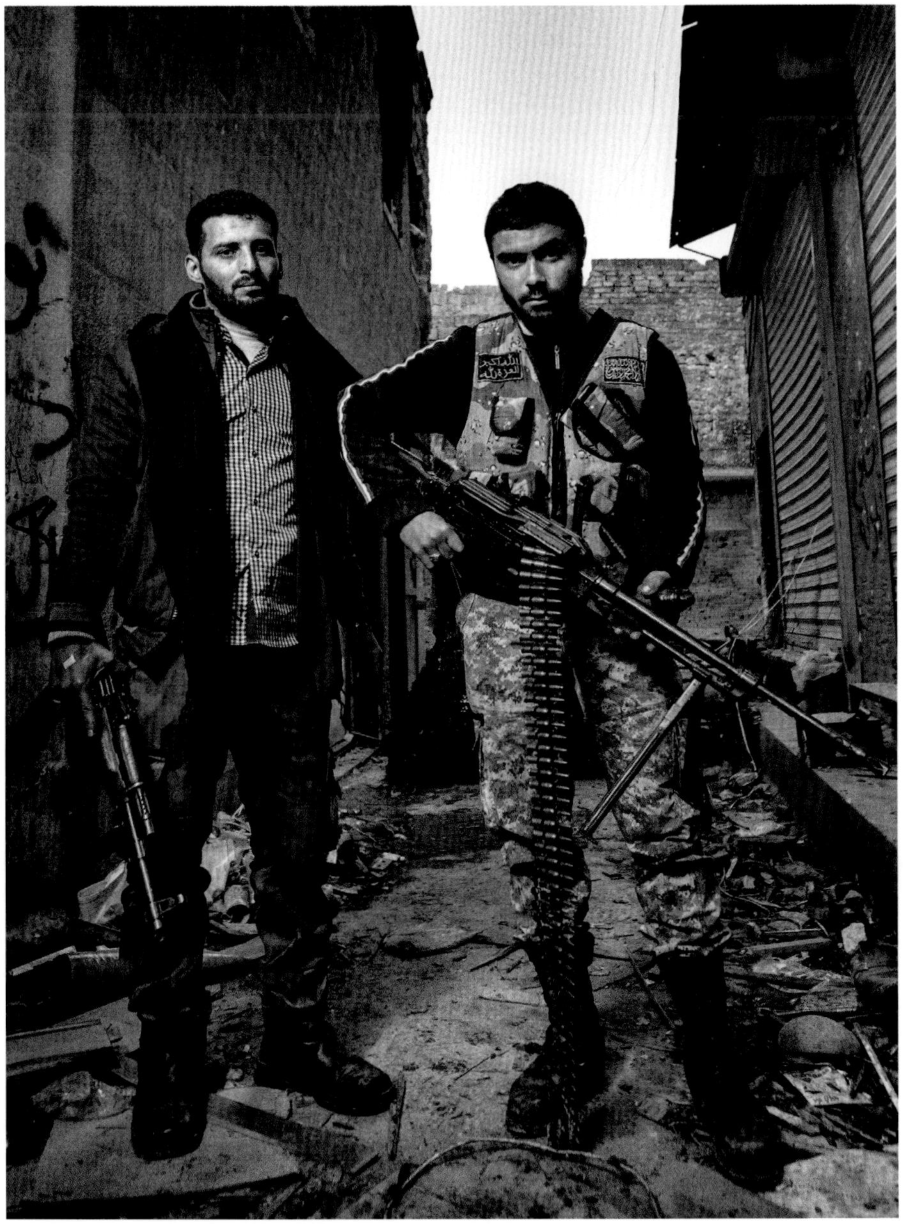

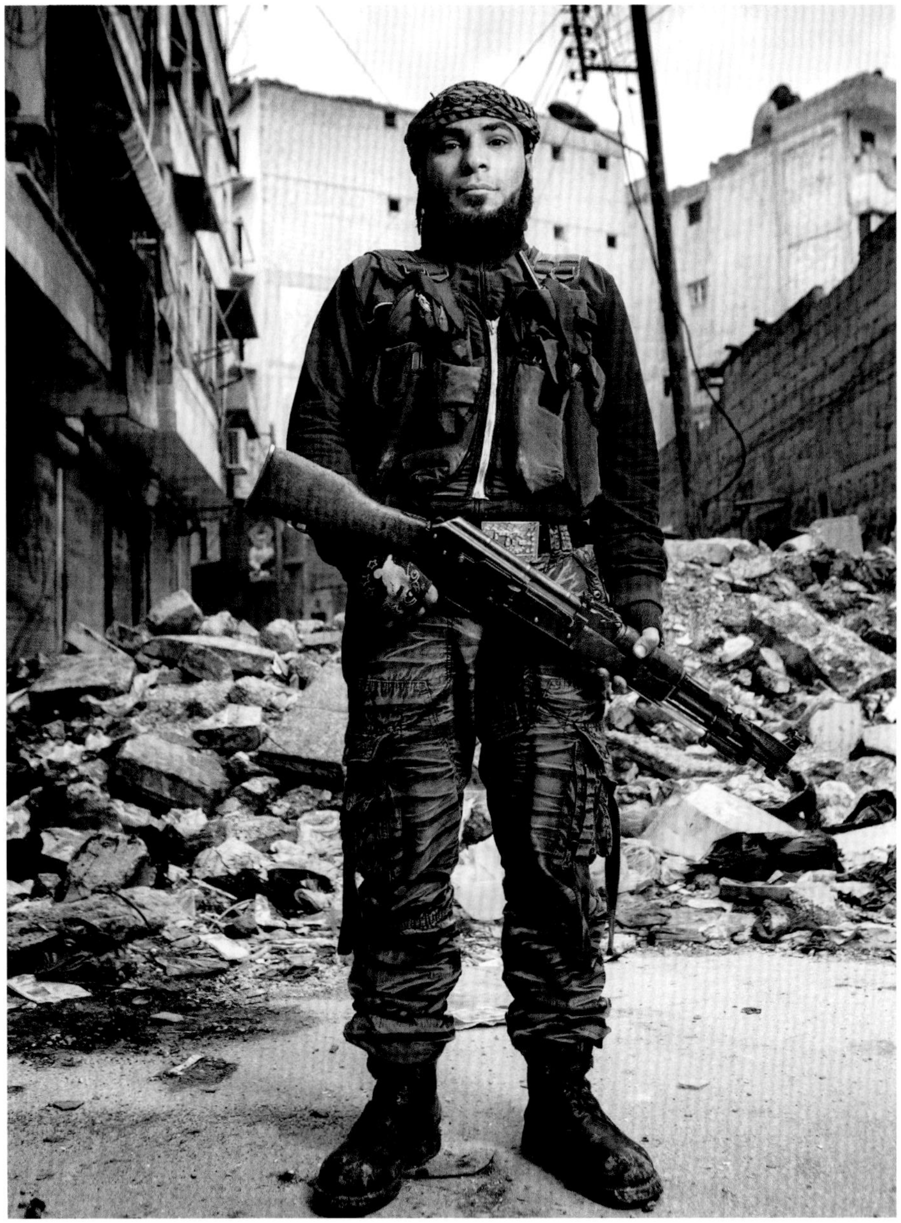

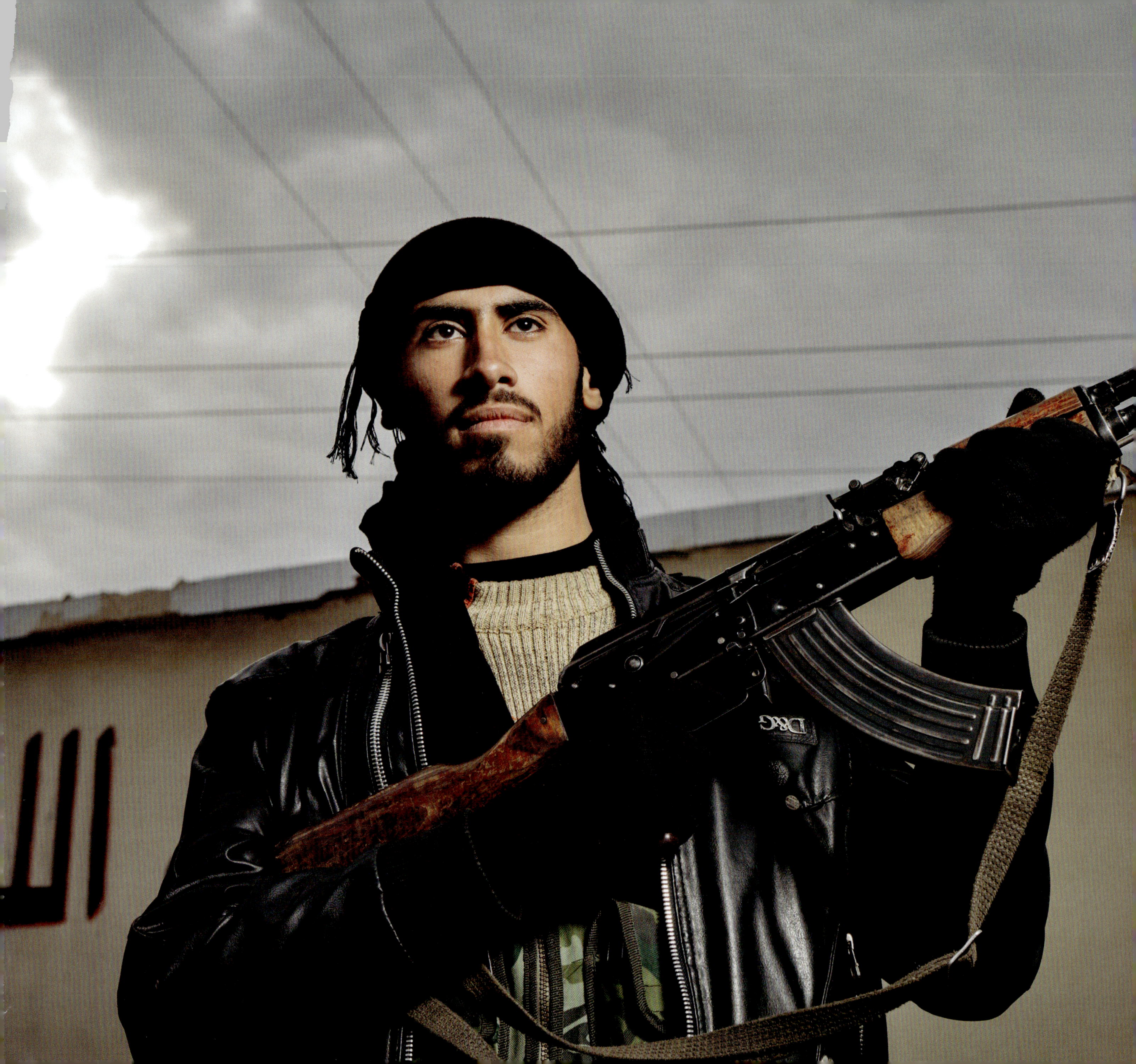
D&G

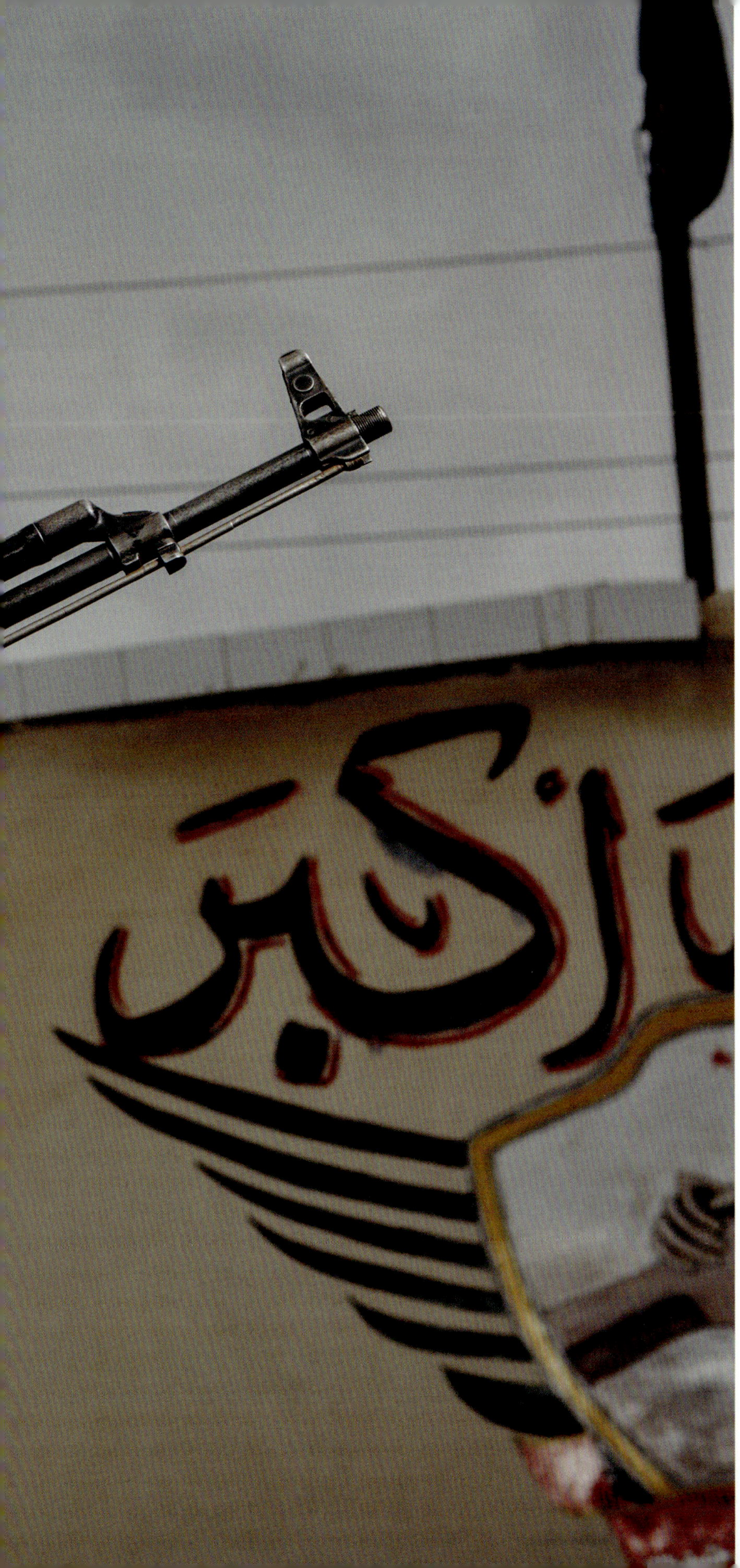

"PEACE IS PREFERABLE TO WAR. BUT IT'S NOT AN ABSOLUTE VALUE, AND SO WE ALWAYS ASK, 'WHAT KIND OF PEACE?'"

— *Noam Chomsky*

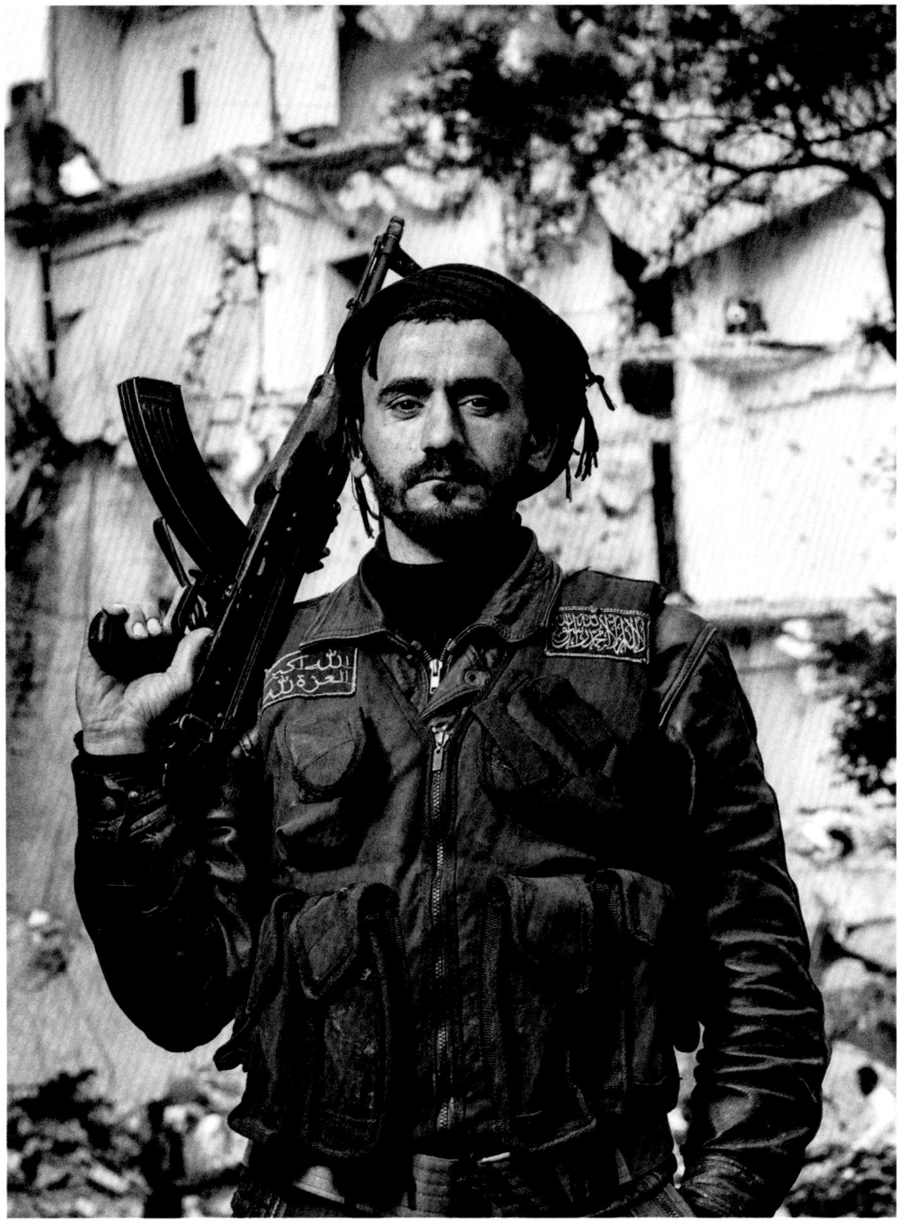

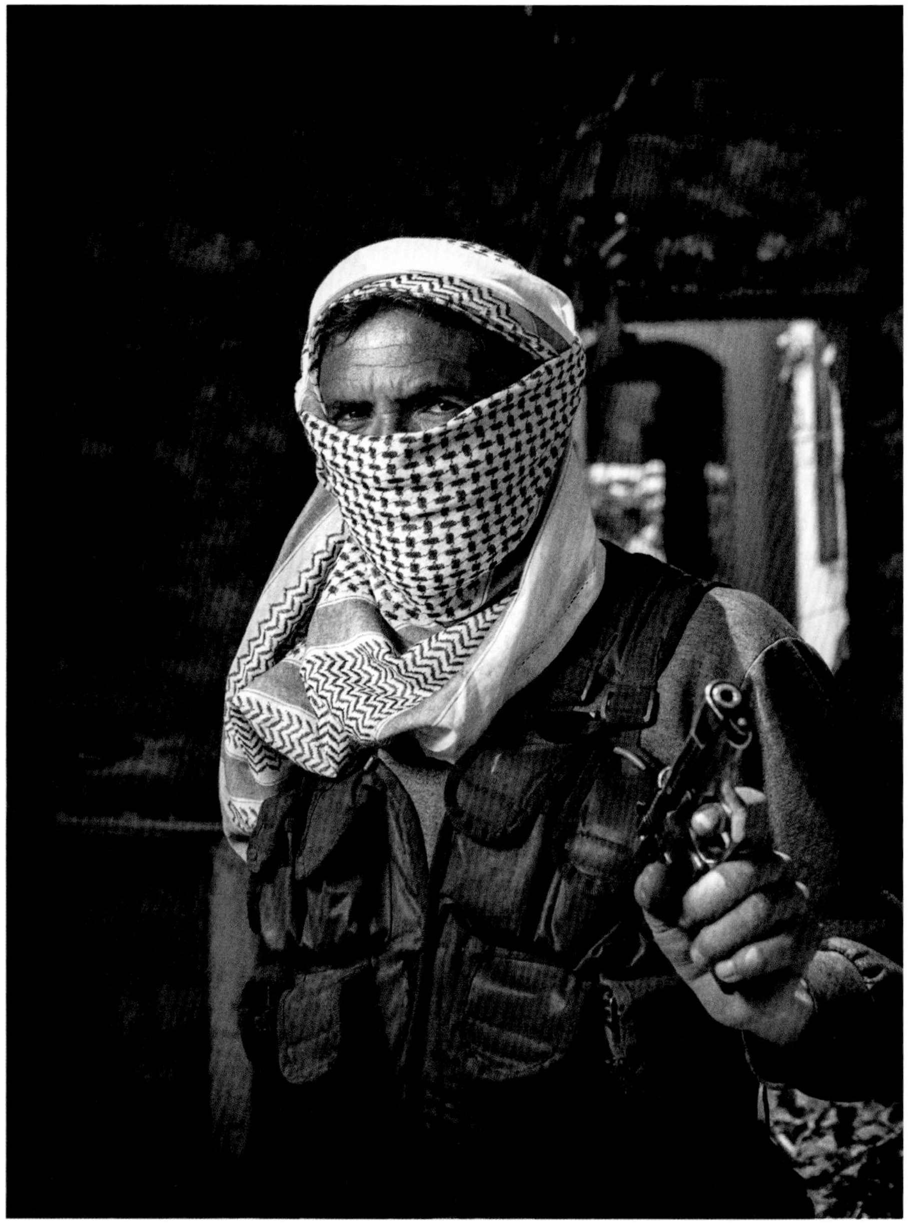

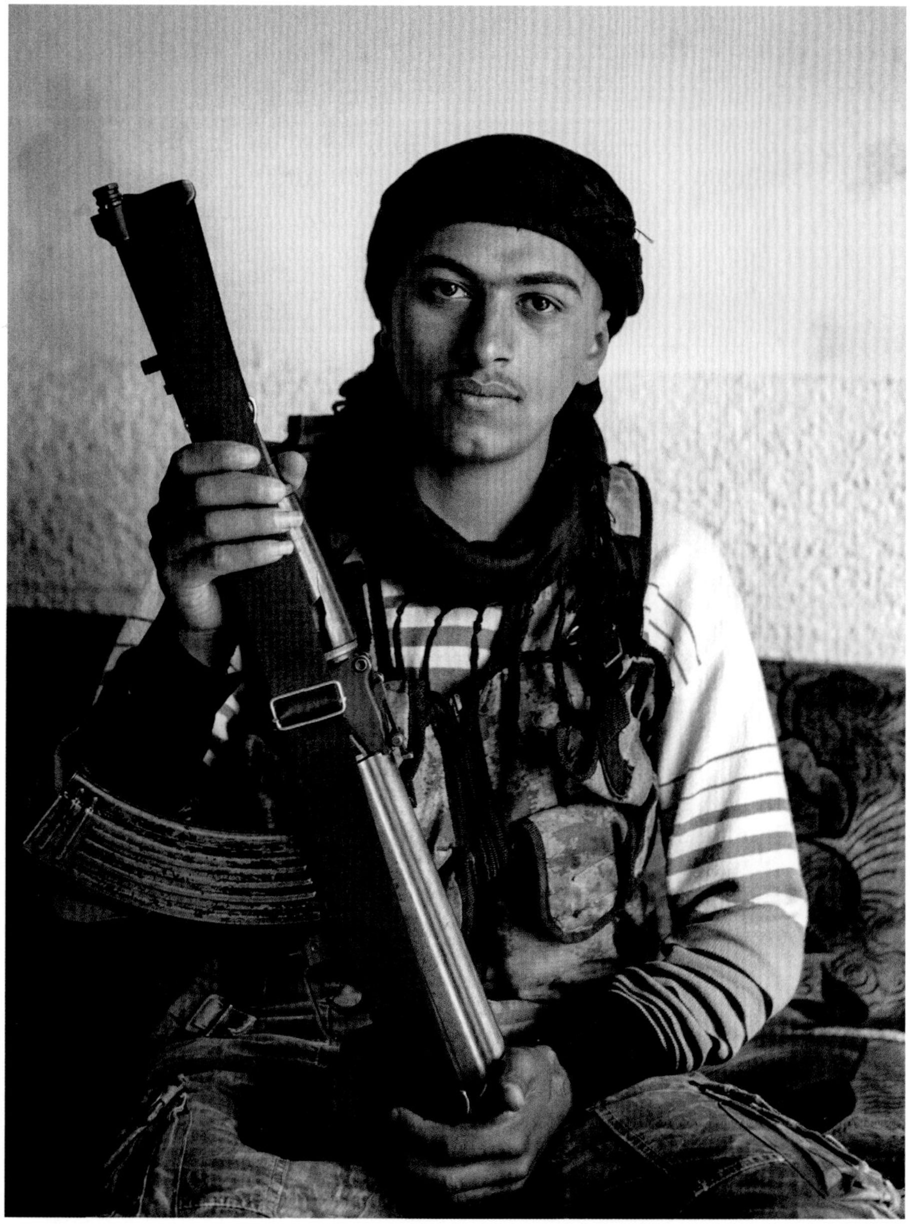

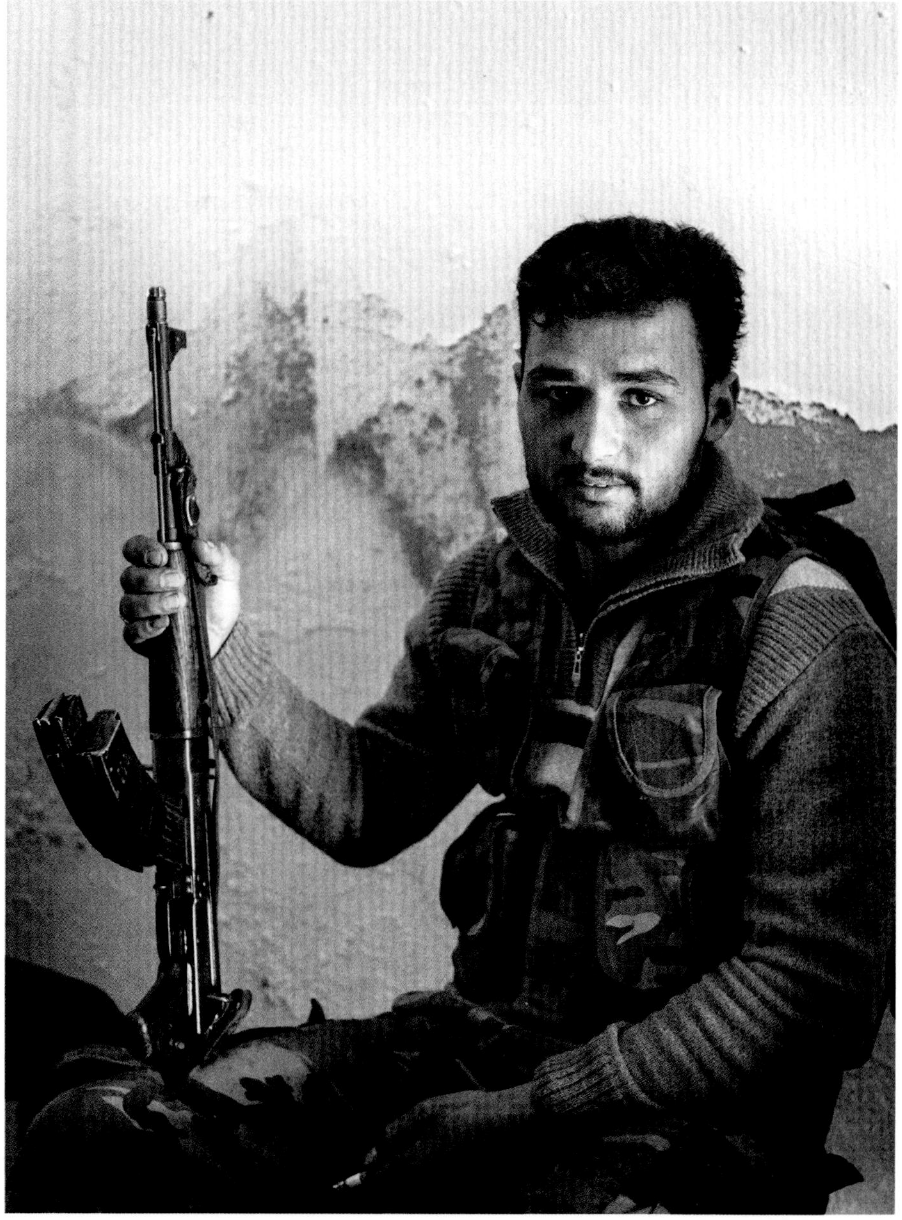

April 18, 2013, Naqqarin, Aleppo.

I counted more than fifty rockets fired by Syrian Government forces that night. They arced silently up through the clouds toward the northern countryside of Aleppo.

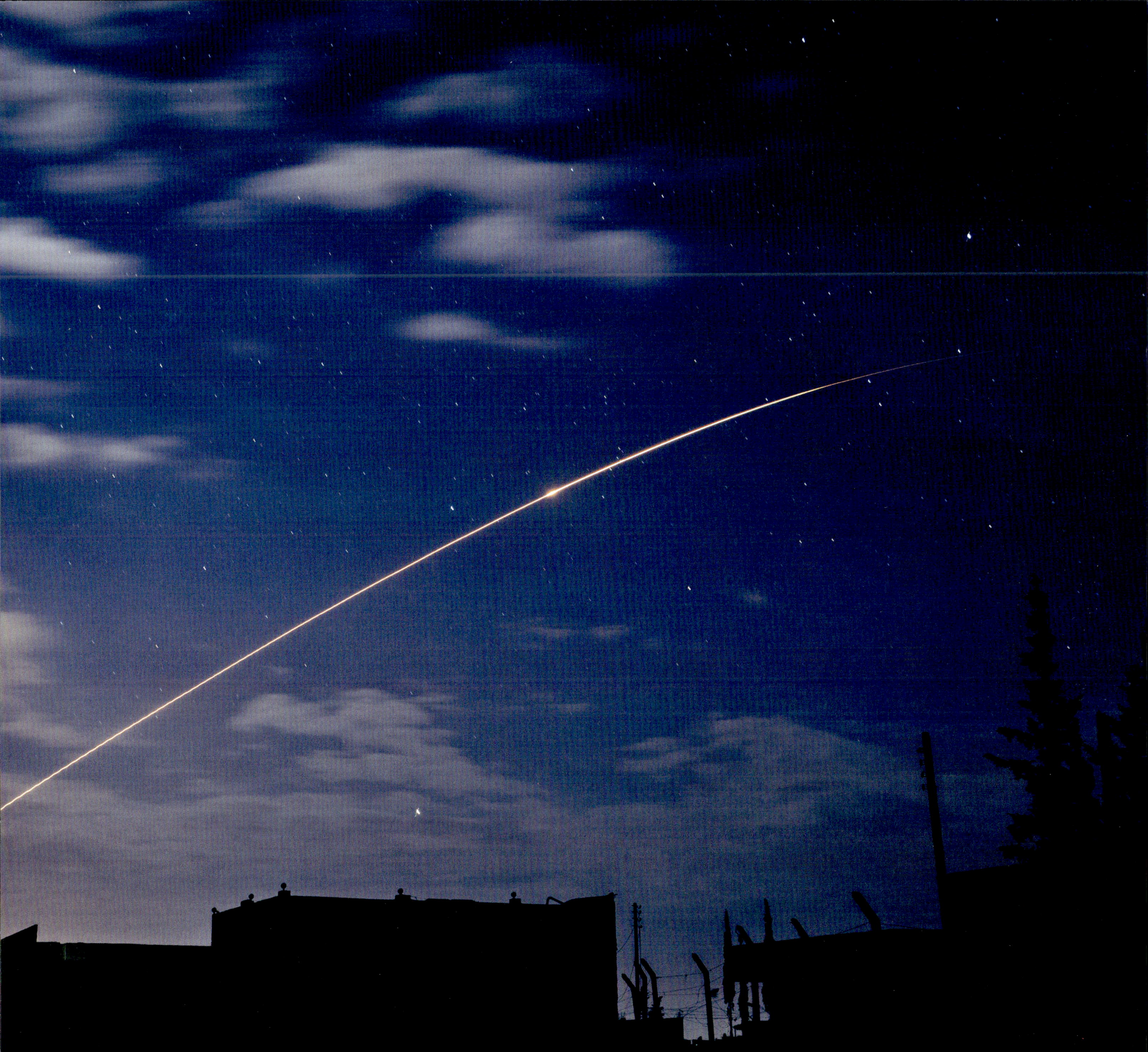

April 19, 2013, Sakhour, Aleppo.

A huge array of television satellite dishes sit on every building. People continue to stay abreast of the latest satellite news and local and international programming despite the ongoing civil war.

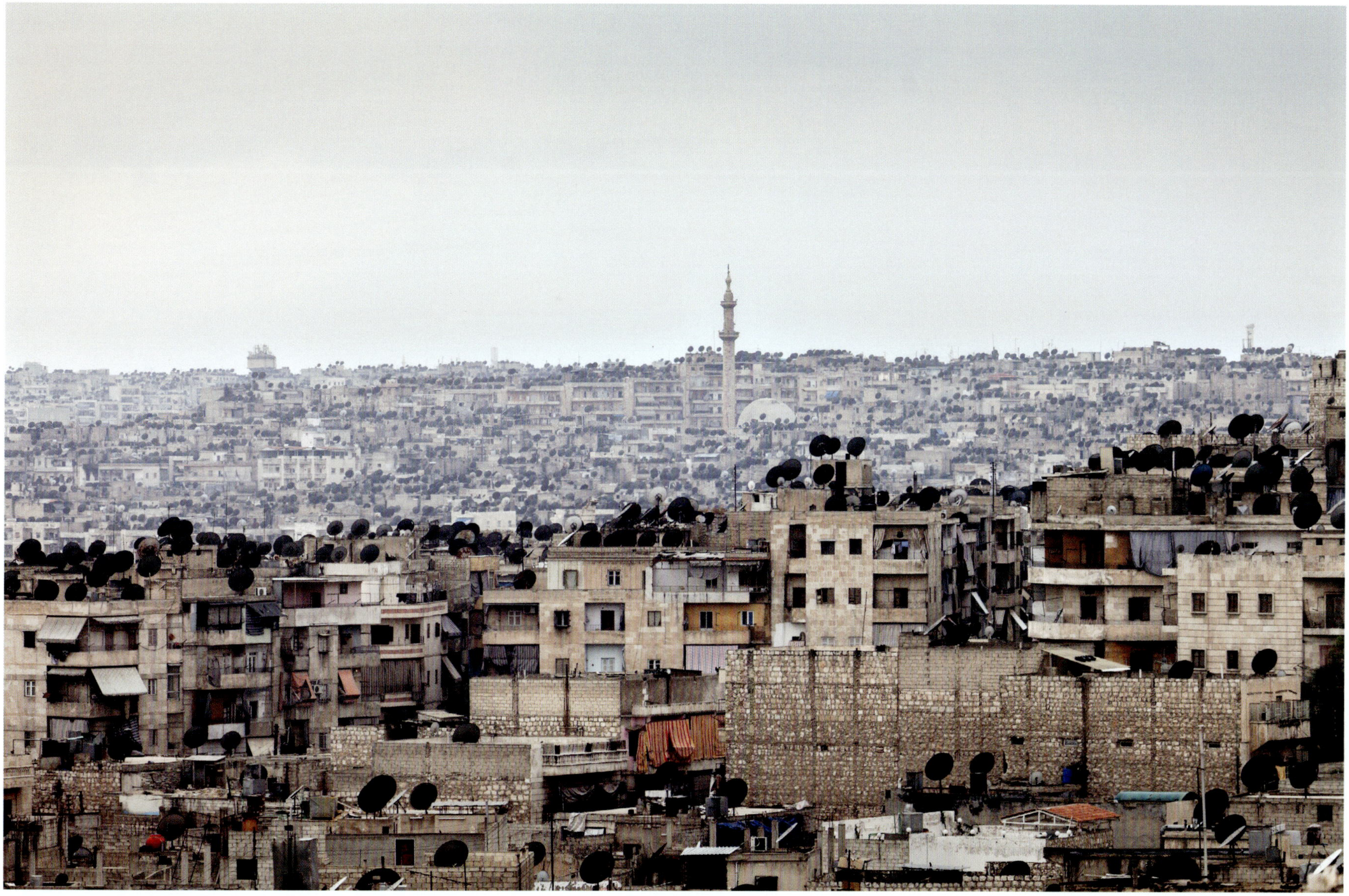

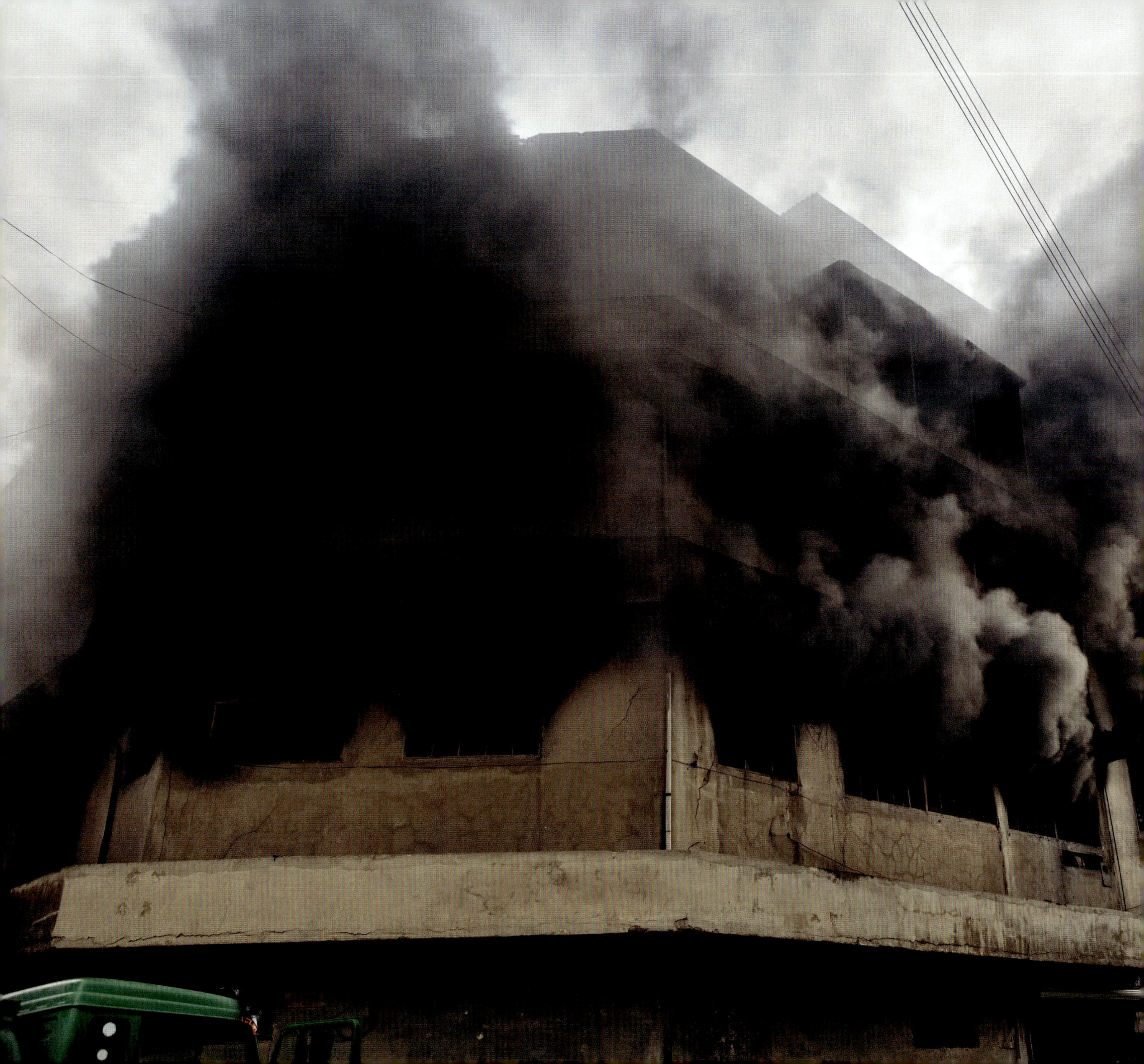

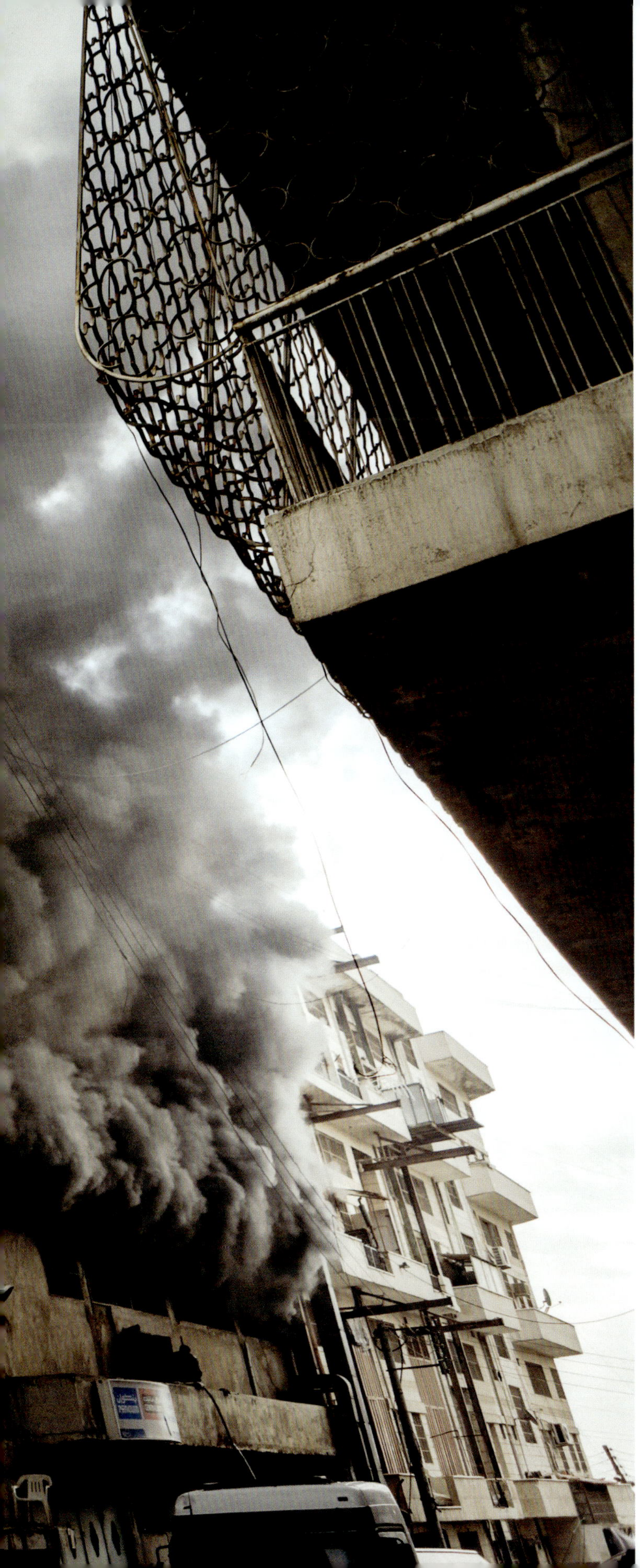

February 7, 2013, Sakhour, Aleppo.

A building burns after being struck by Syrian Government artillery fire.

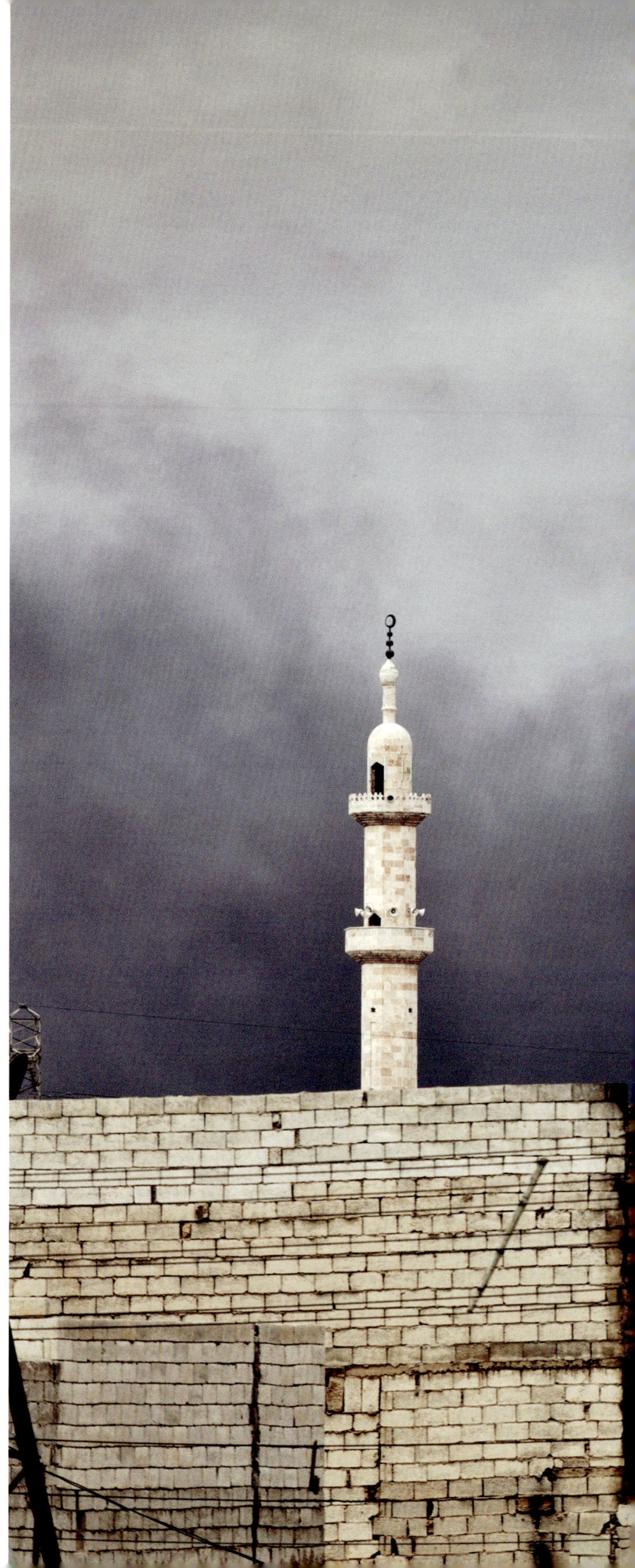

February 7, 2013, Sakhour, Aleppo.

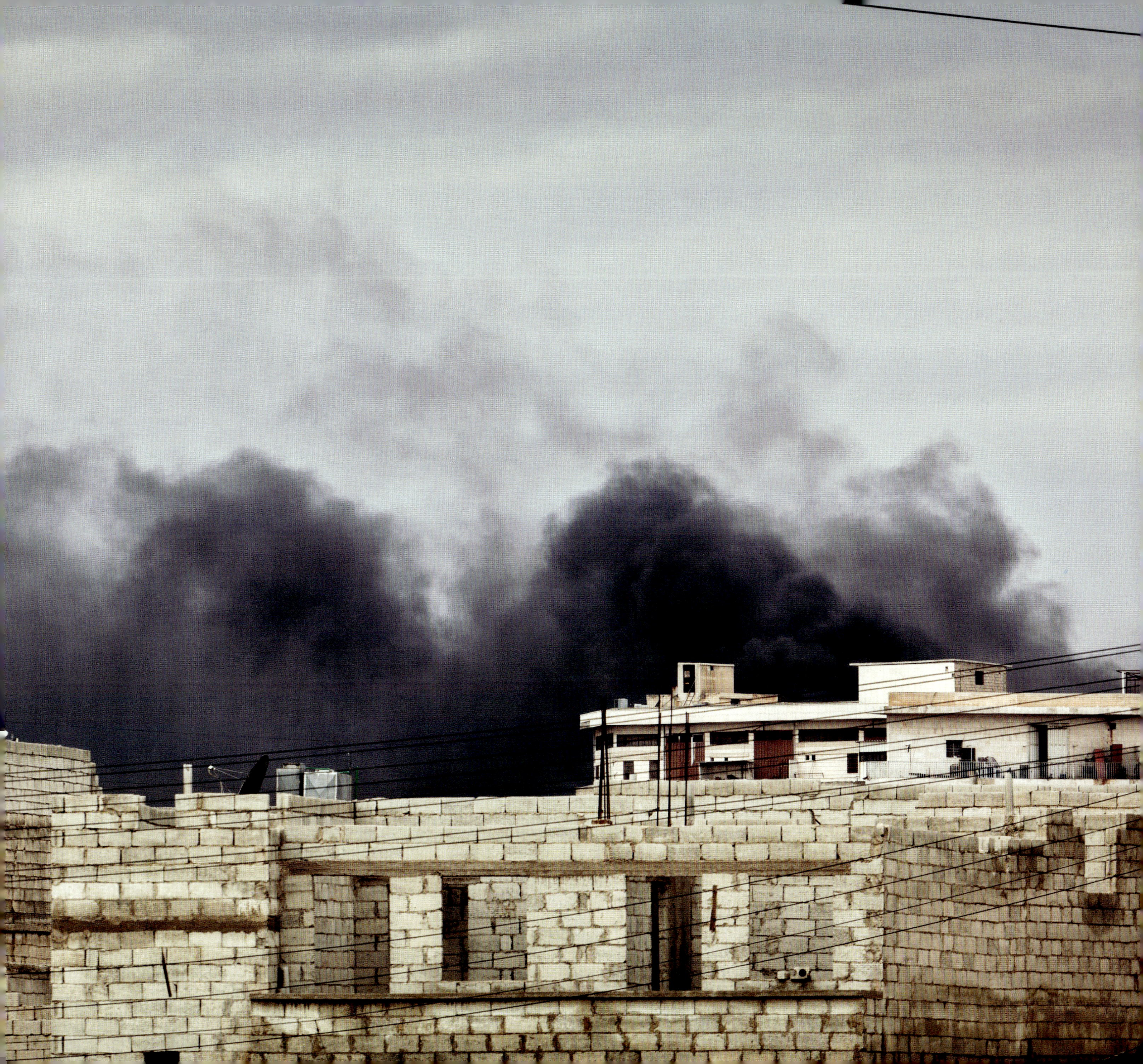

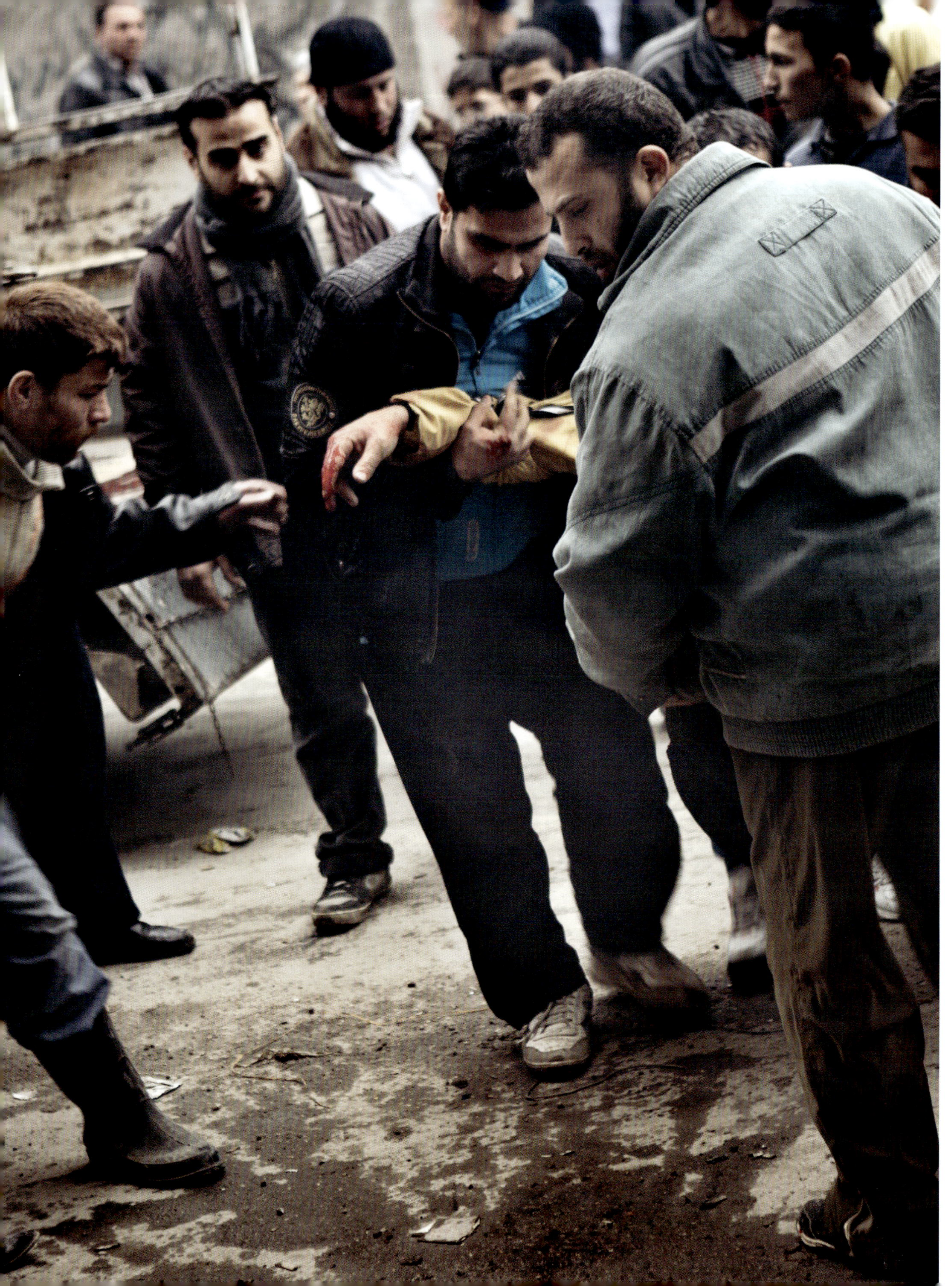

February 7, 2013, Shaar, Aleppo.

A man wounded by Syrian Government shelling is carried into a field hospital.

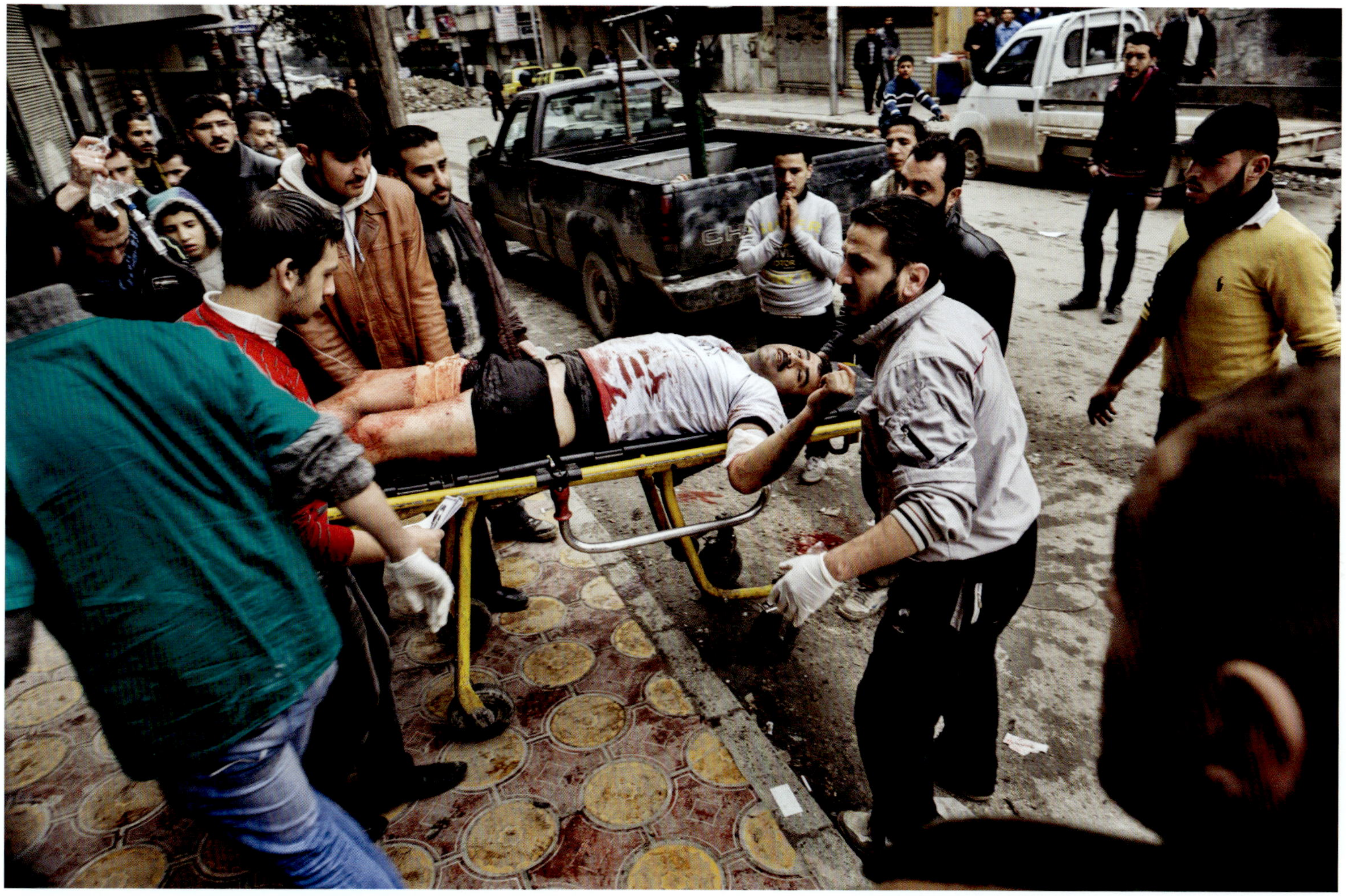

February 7, 2013, Shaar, Aleppo.

People gather to watch as a man wounded by Syrian Government shelling is wheeled into a field hospital on a stretcher.

February 7, 2013, Shaar, Aleppo.

A hospital worker rushes a boy wounded by Syrian Government shelling into a field hospital.

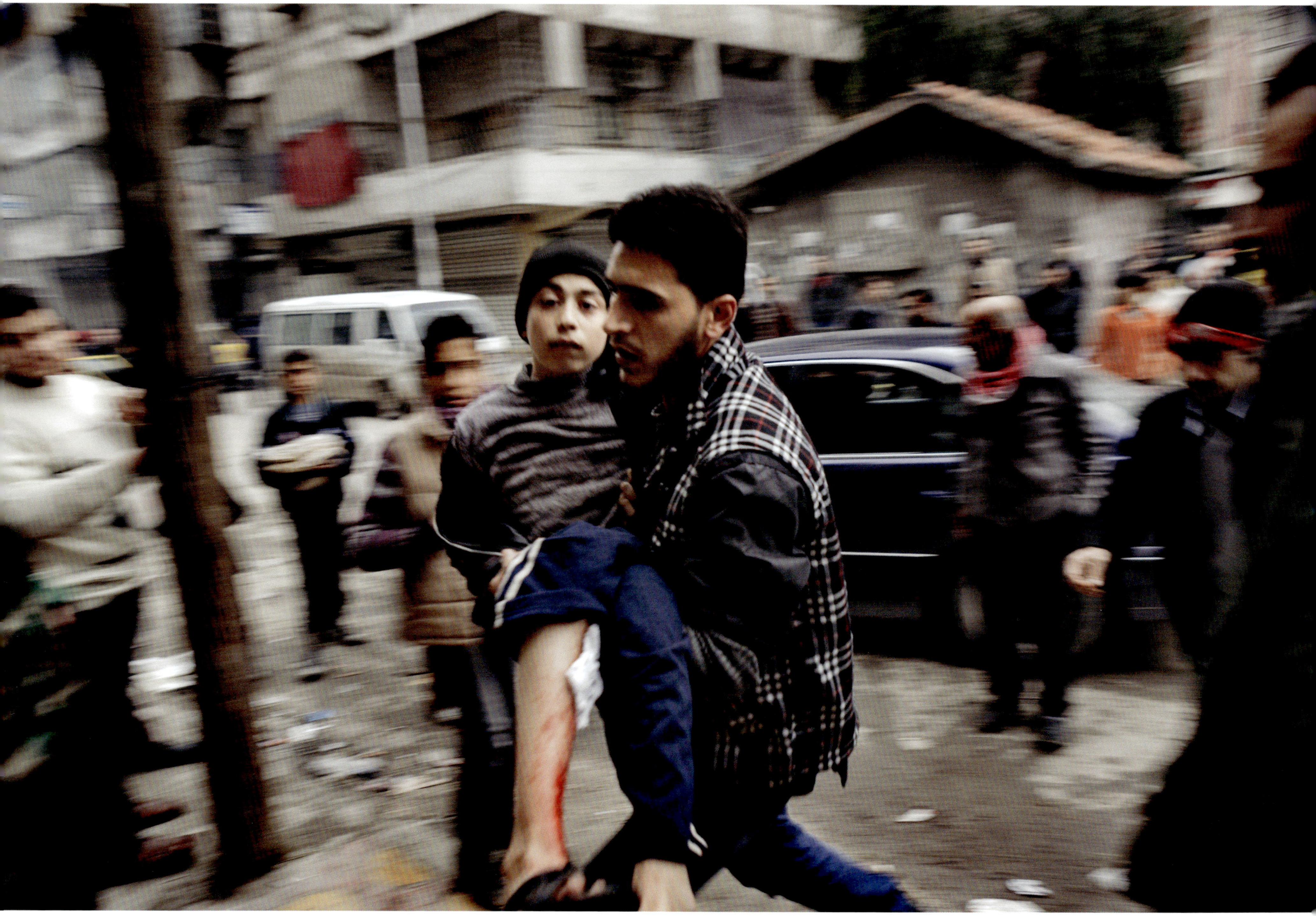

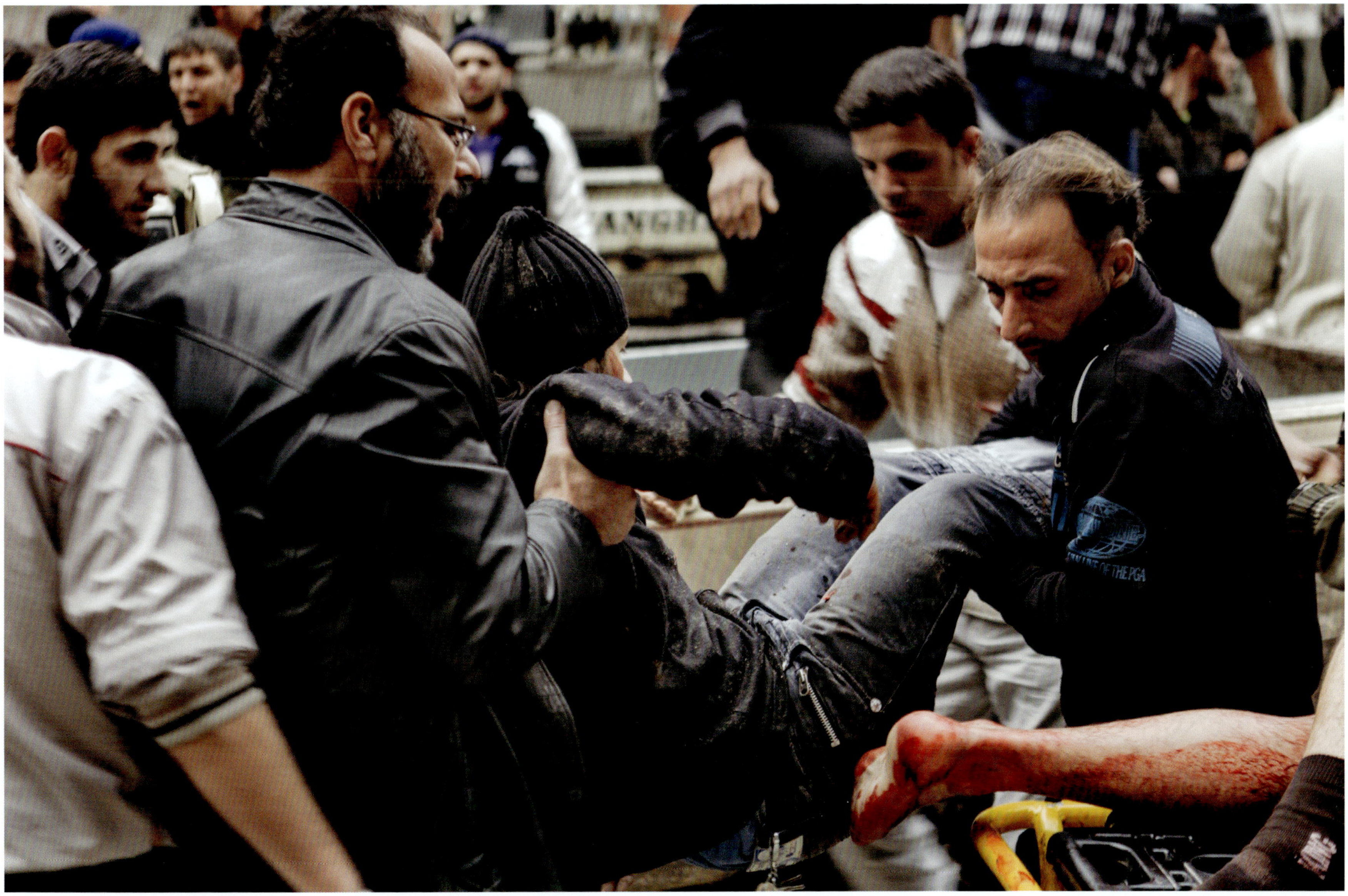

February 7, 2013, Shaar, Aleppo.

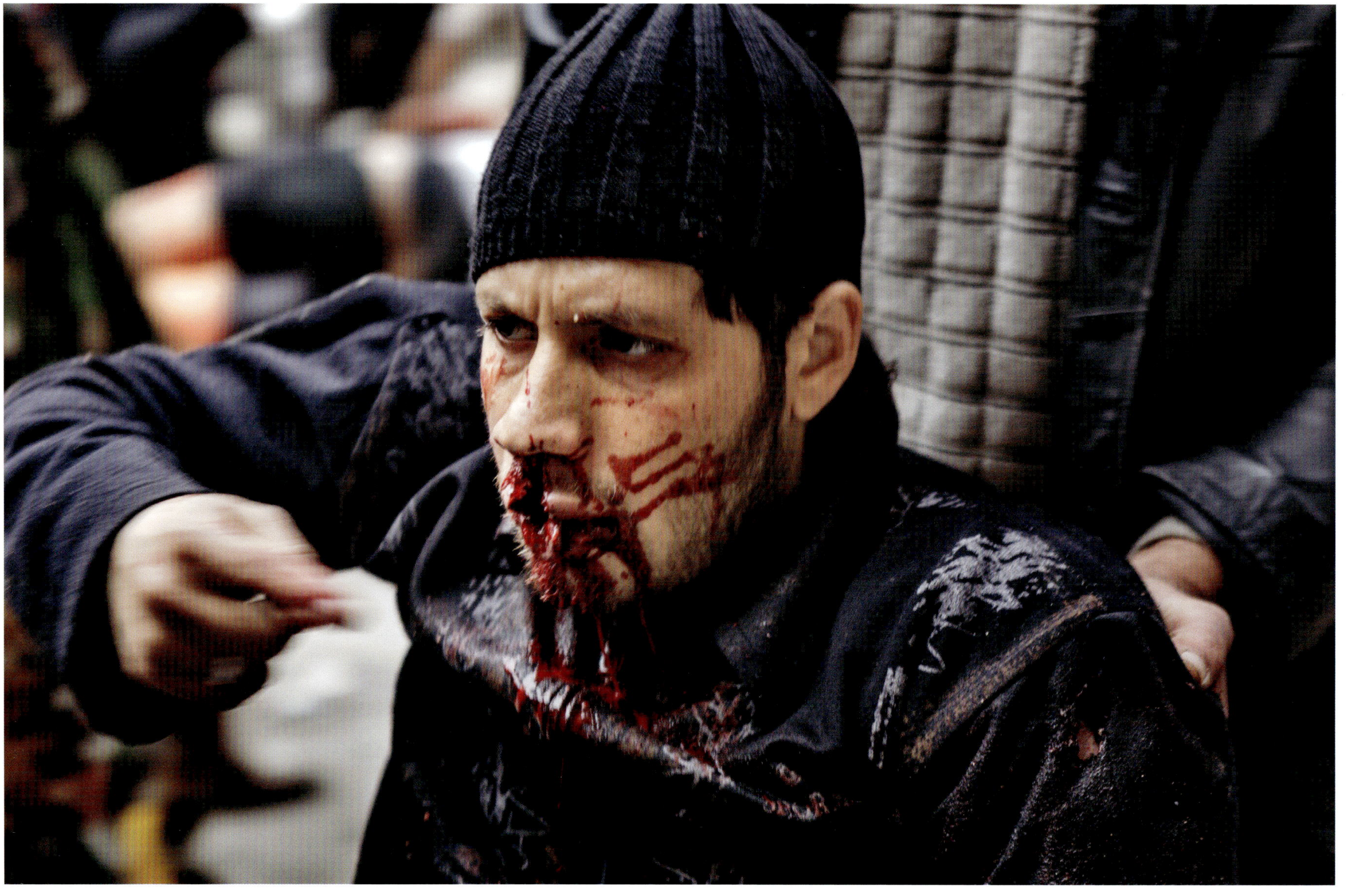

February 7, 2013, Shaar, Aleppo.

Right: *February 10, Shaar, Aleppo.*

A girl lies dead amongst others in a makeshift morgue.

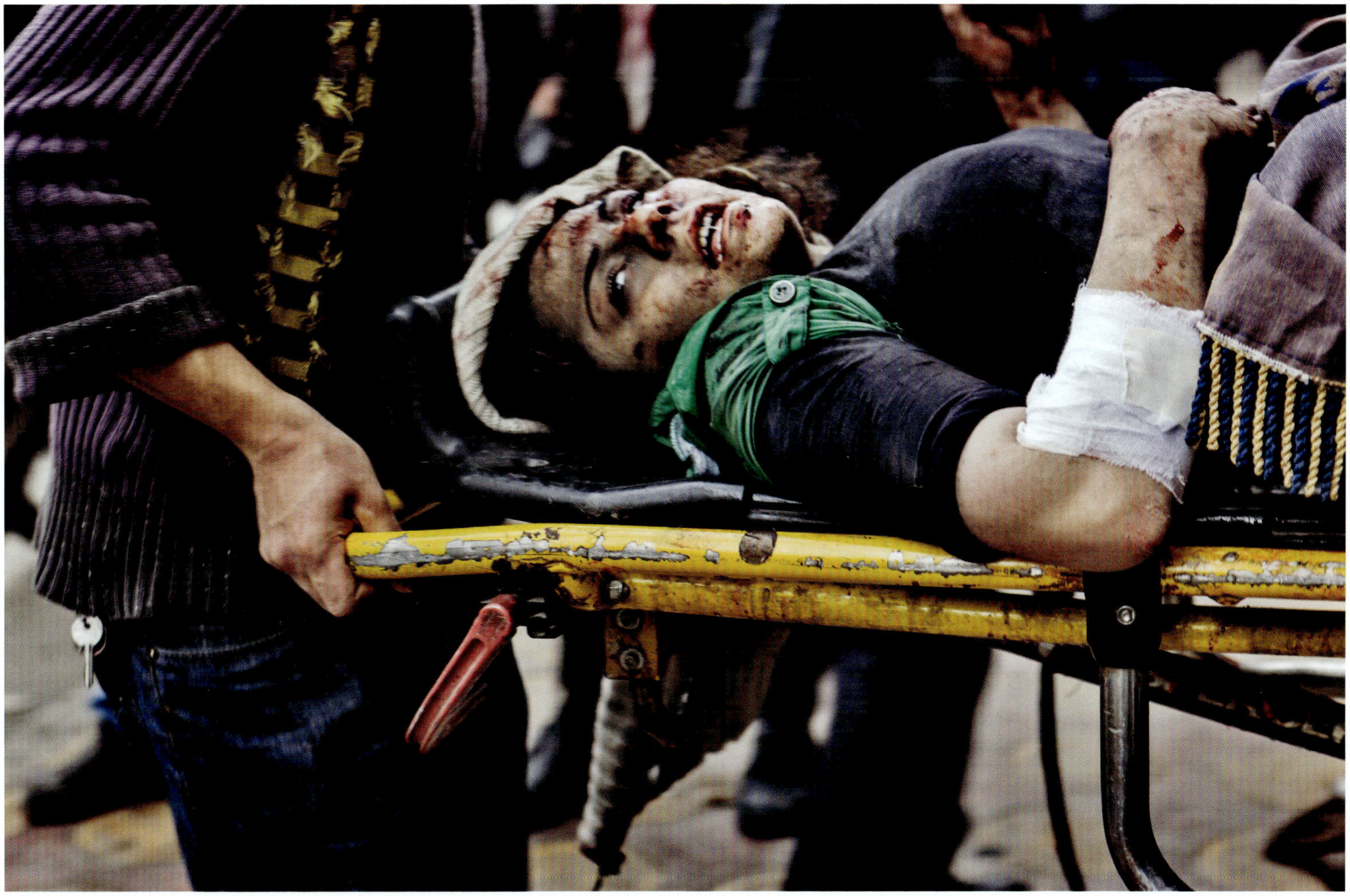

Top: *February 10, Shaar, Aleppo.*

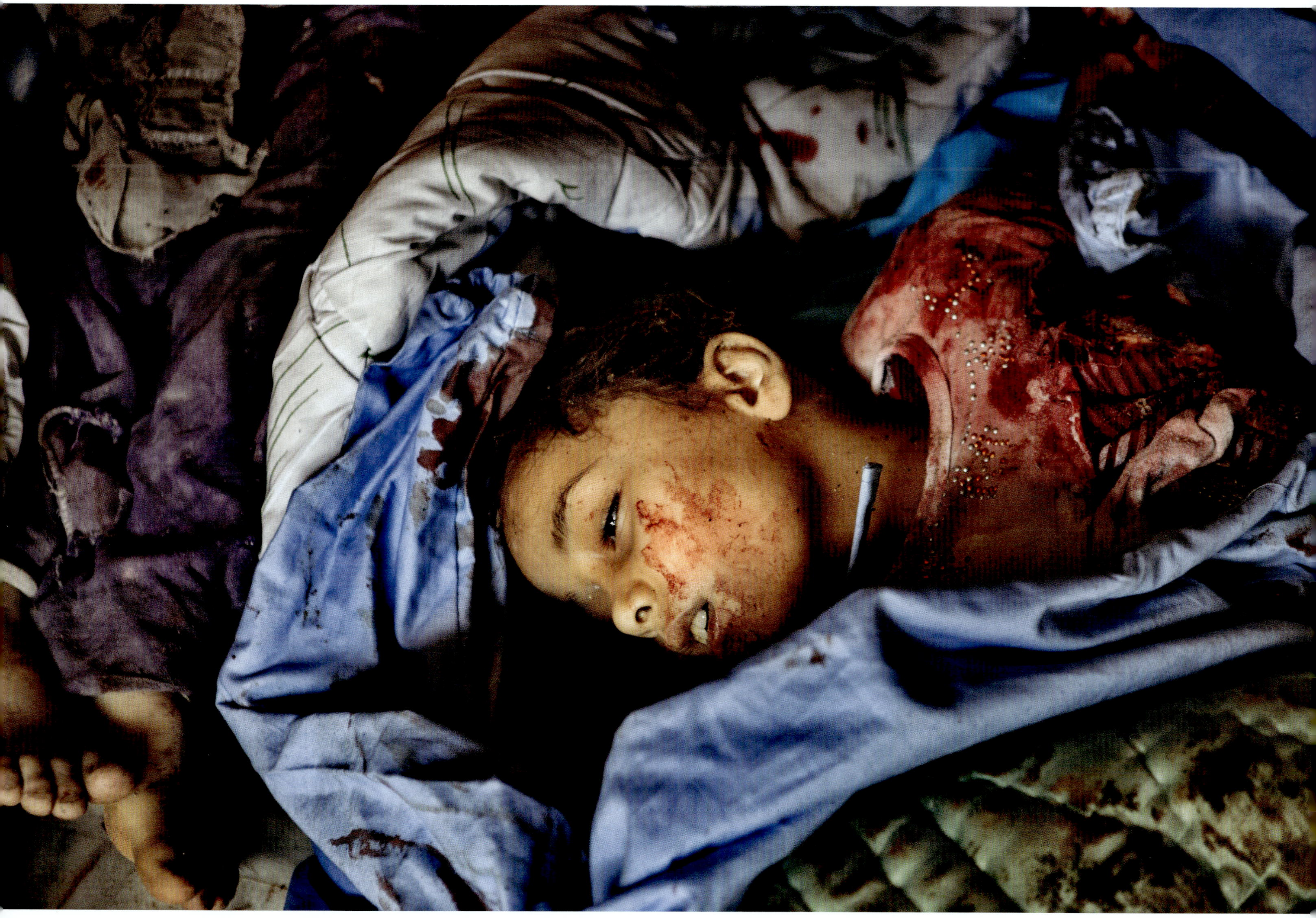

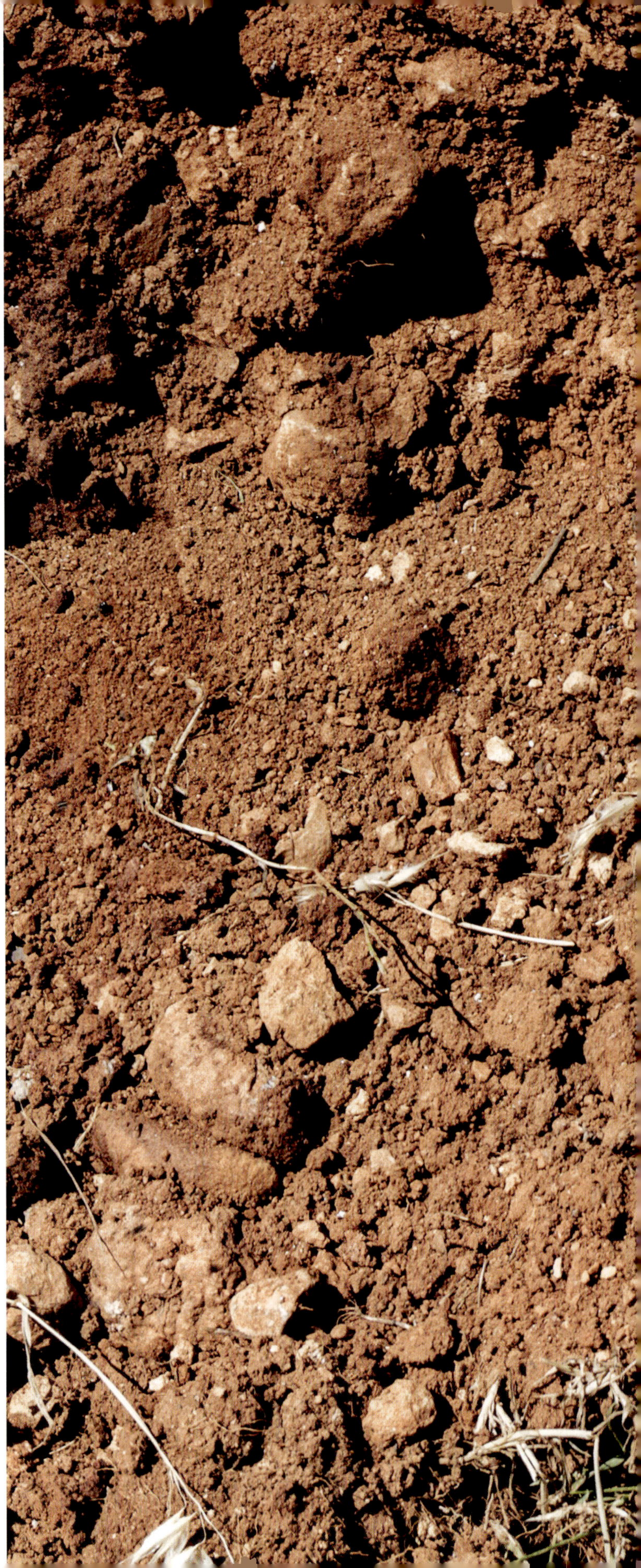

April 23, 2013, Martyr's Cemetery, Aleppo.

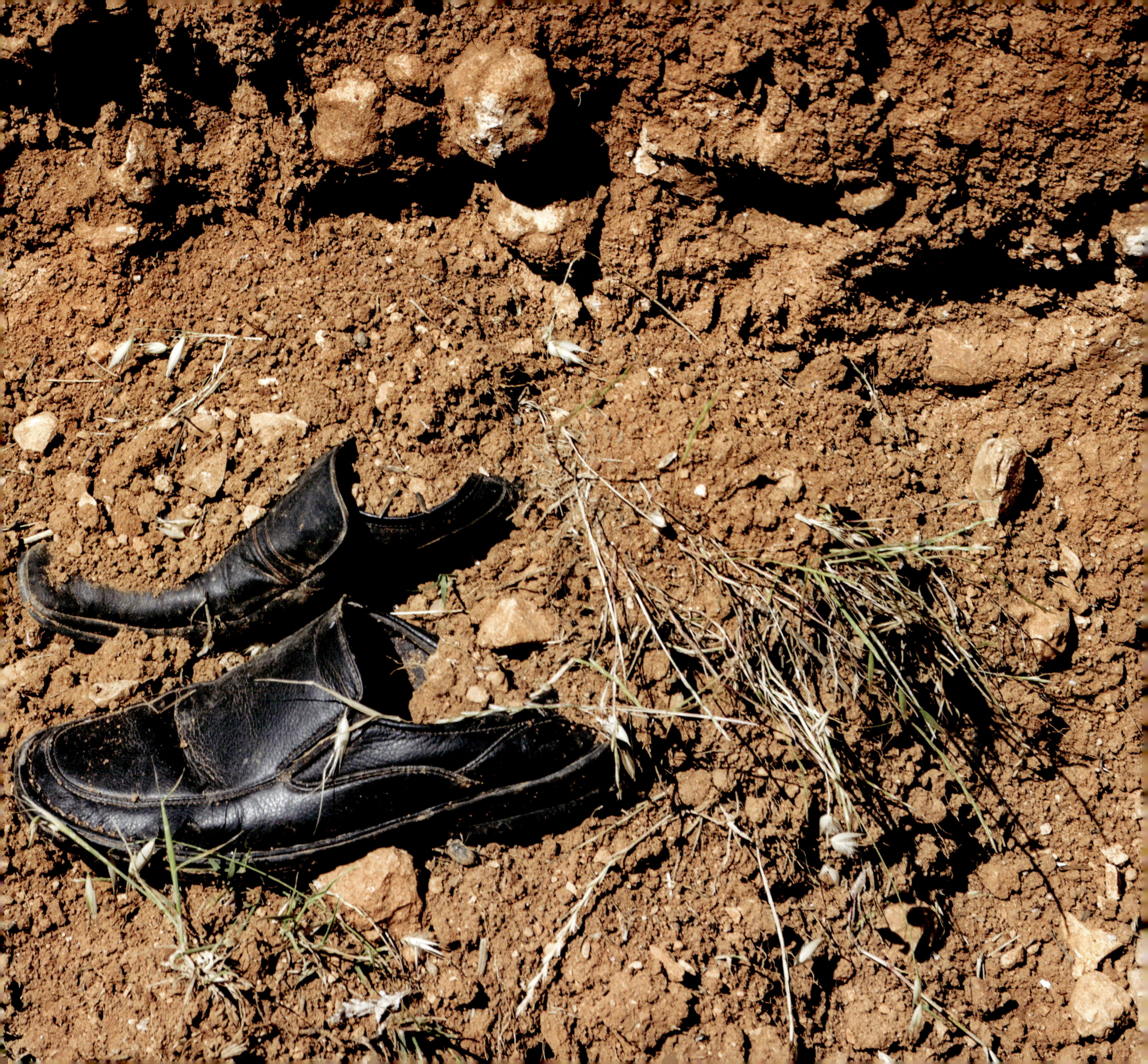

Right: *April 23, 2013, Martyr's Cemetery, Aleppo.*

Long trenches are dug to serve as graves for residents of the city who have been killed. Each row is for the dead from a particular neighborhood.

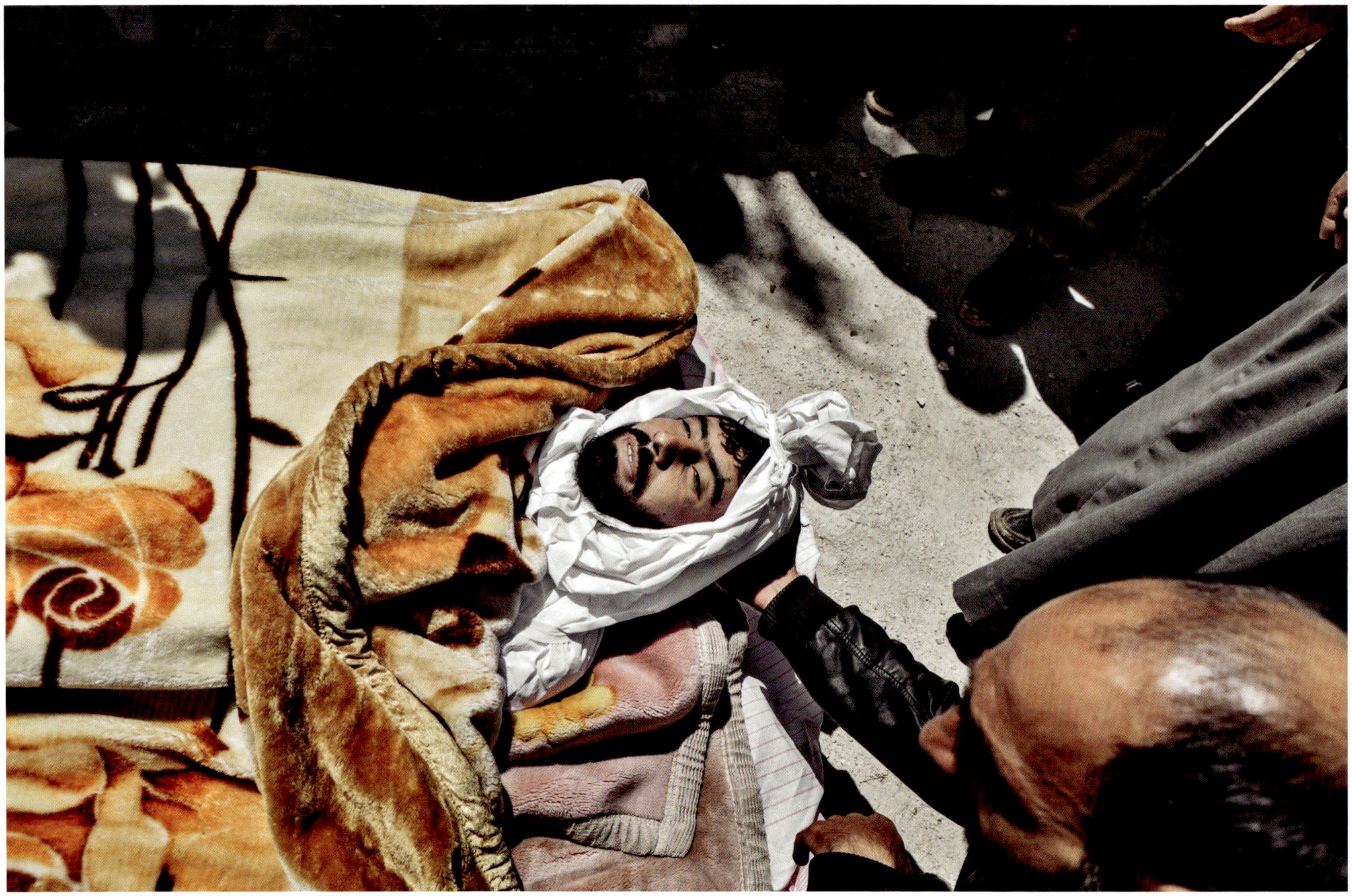

Top: *April 23, 2013, Martyr's Cemetery, Aleppo.*

Ahmed Ibrahim's brother opened his shroud to allow me to photograph him before his burial. Ibrahim, 25 years old, was killed fighting in clashes with Syrian Government forces hours earlier.

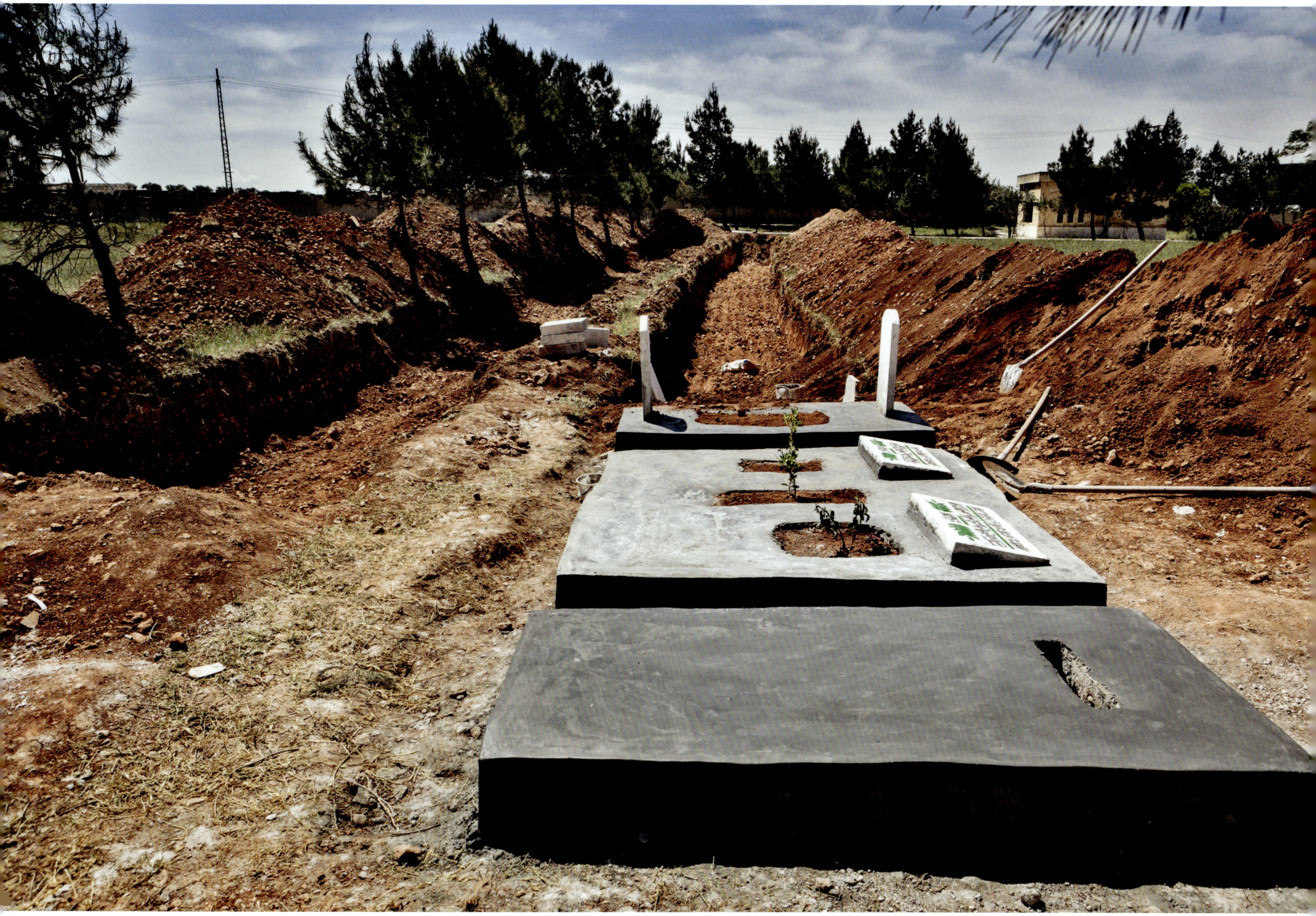

April 23, 2013, Martyr's Cemetery, Aleppo.

Family members and comrades bury Ahmed Ibrahim.

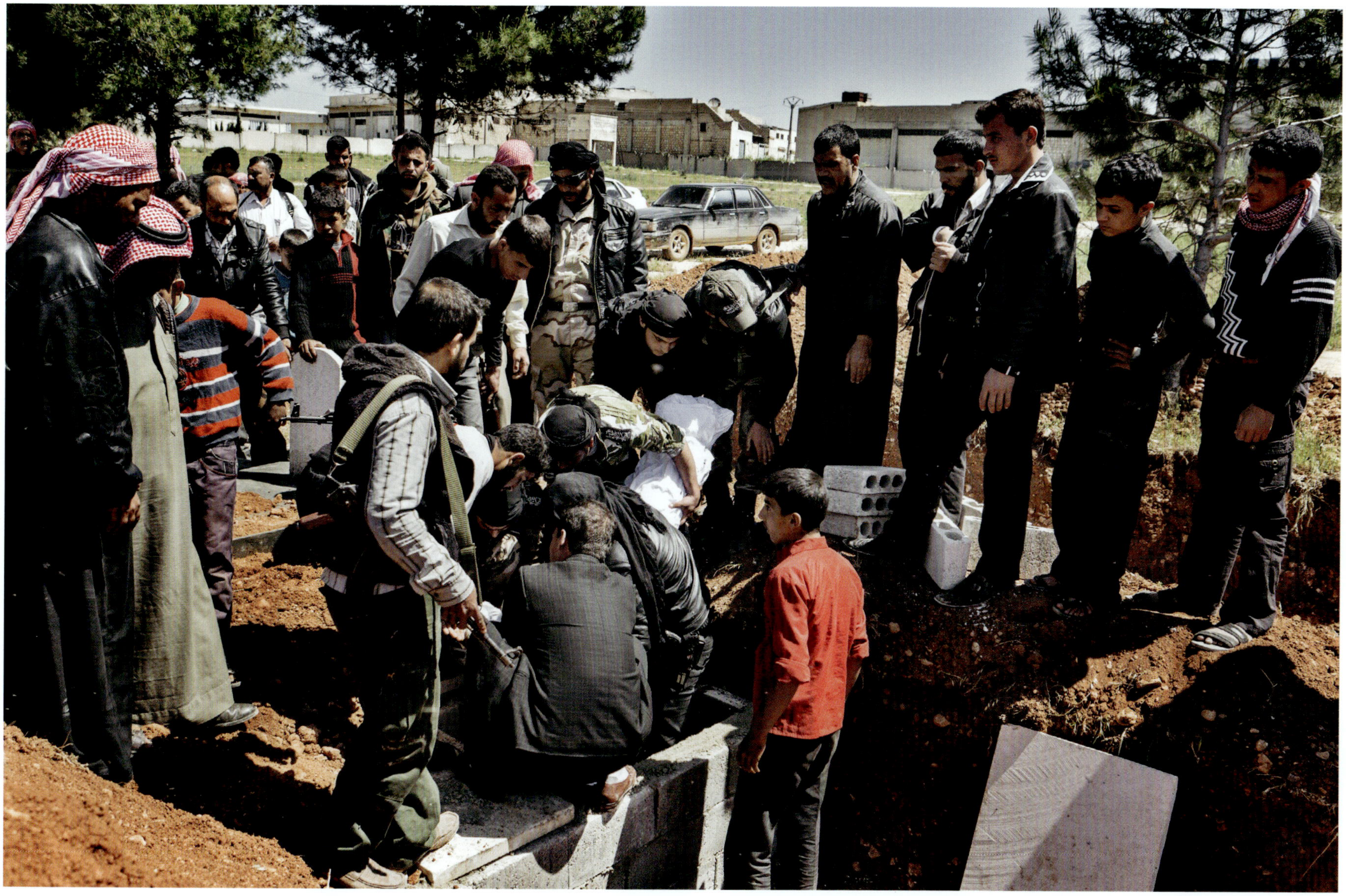

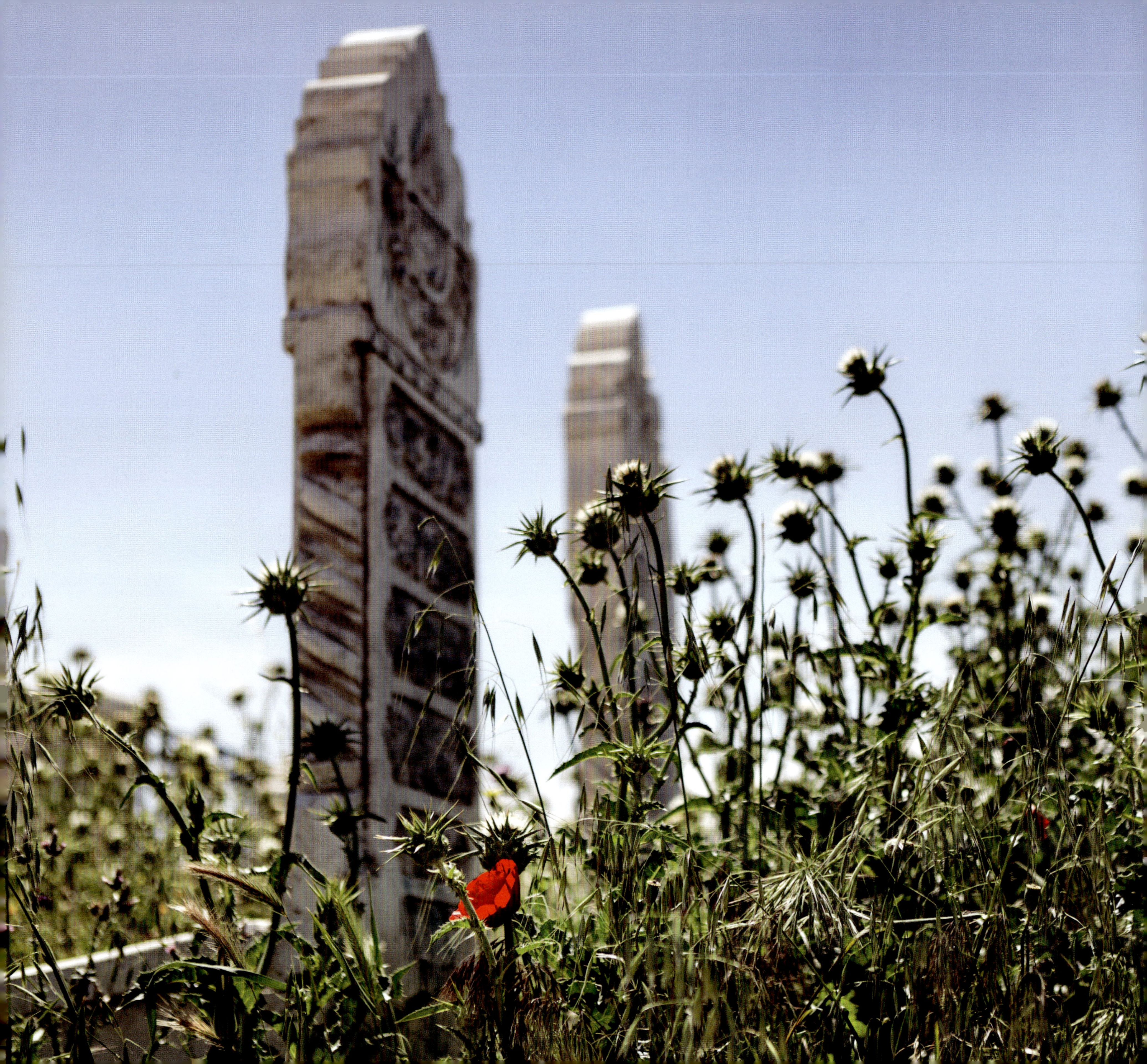

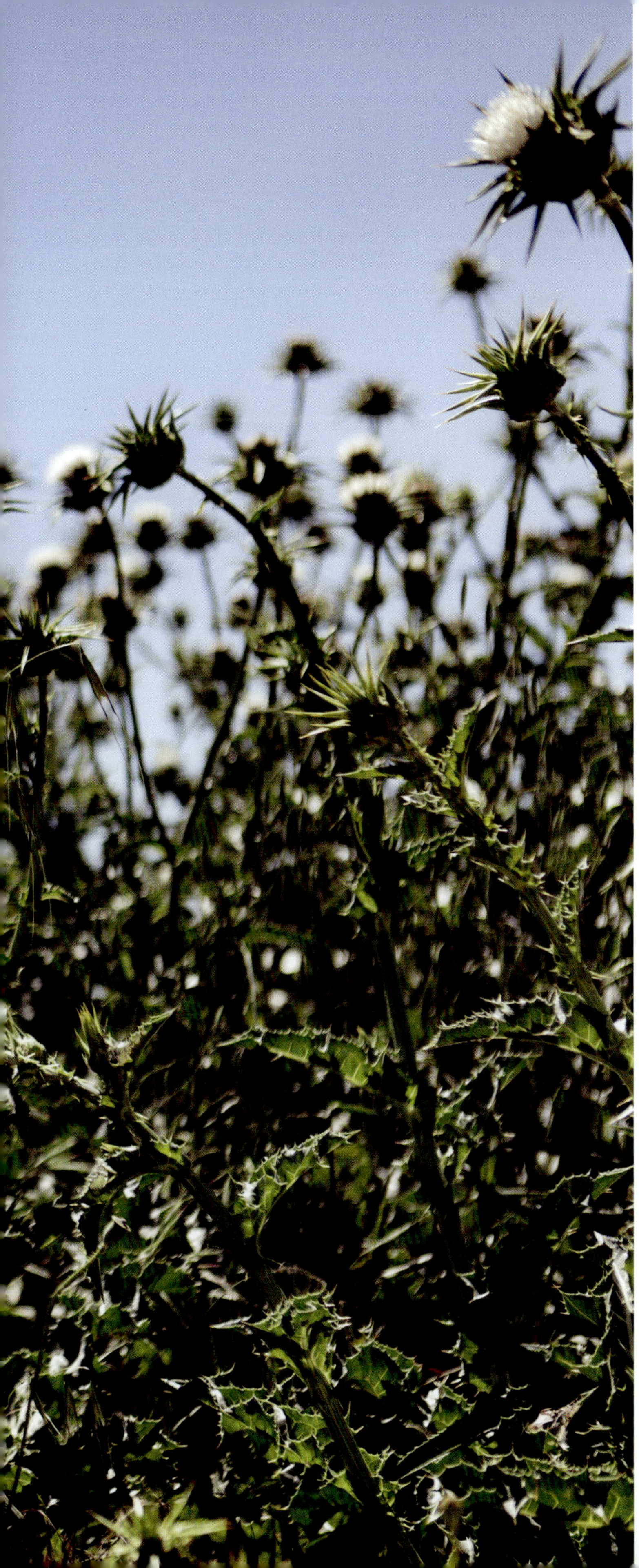

April 23, 2013, Islamic cemetery, Aleppo.

February 8, 2013, Azaz, Aleppo Province.

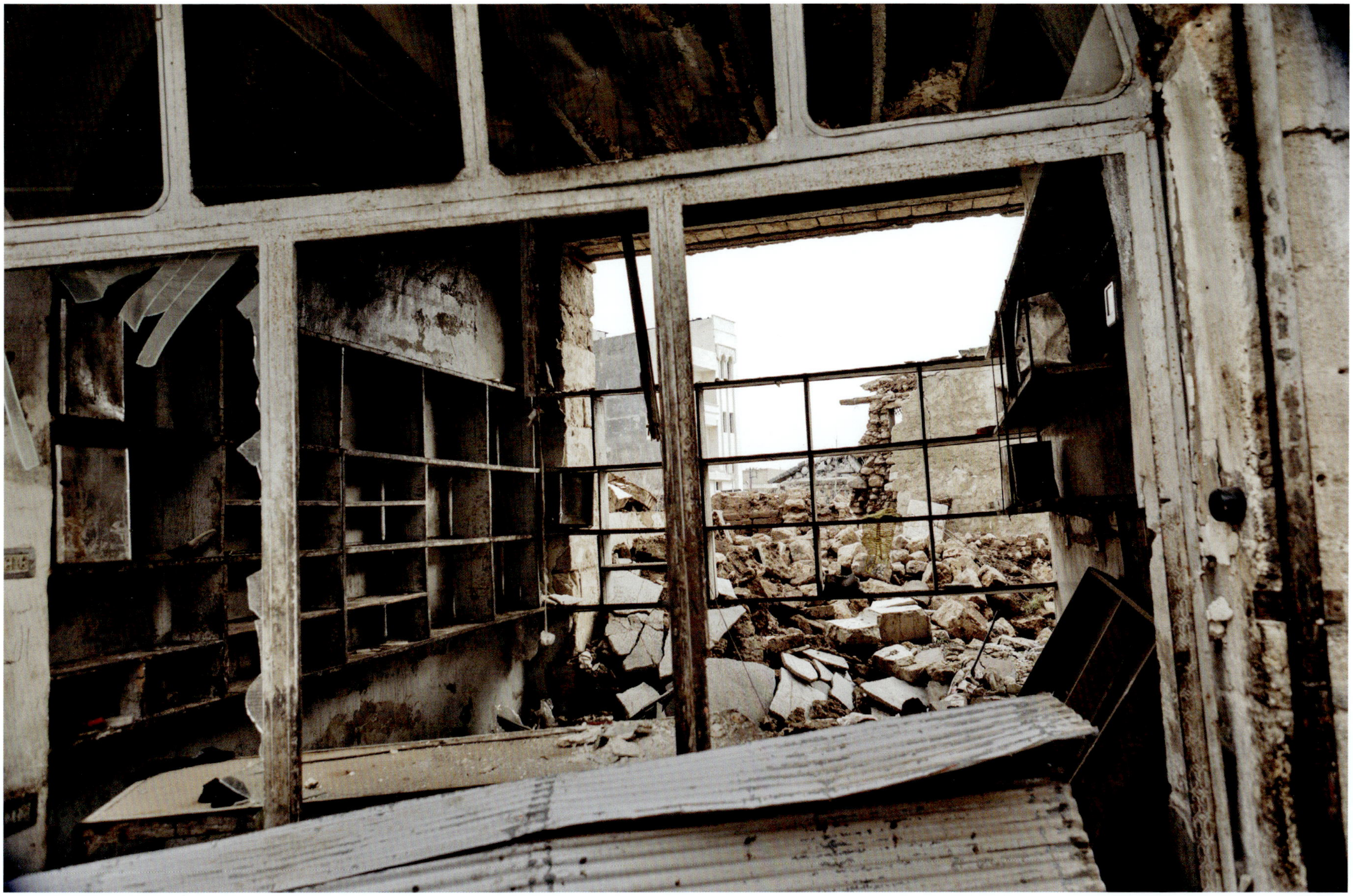

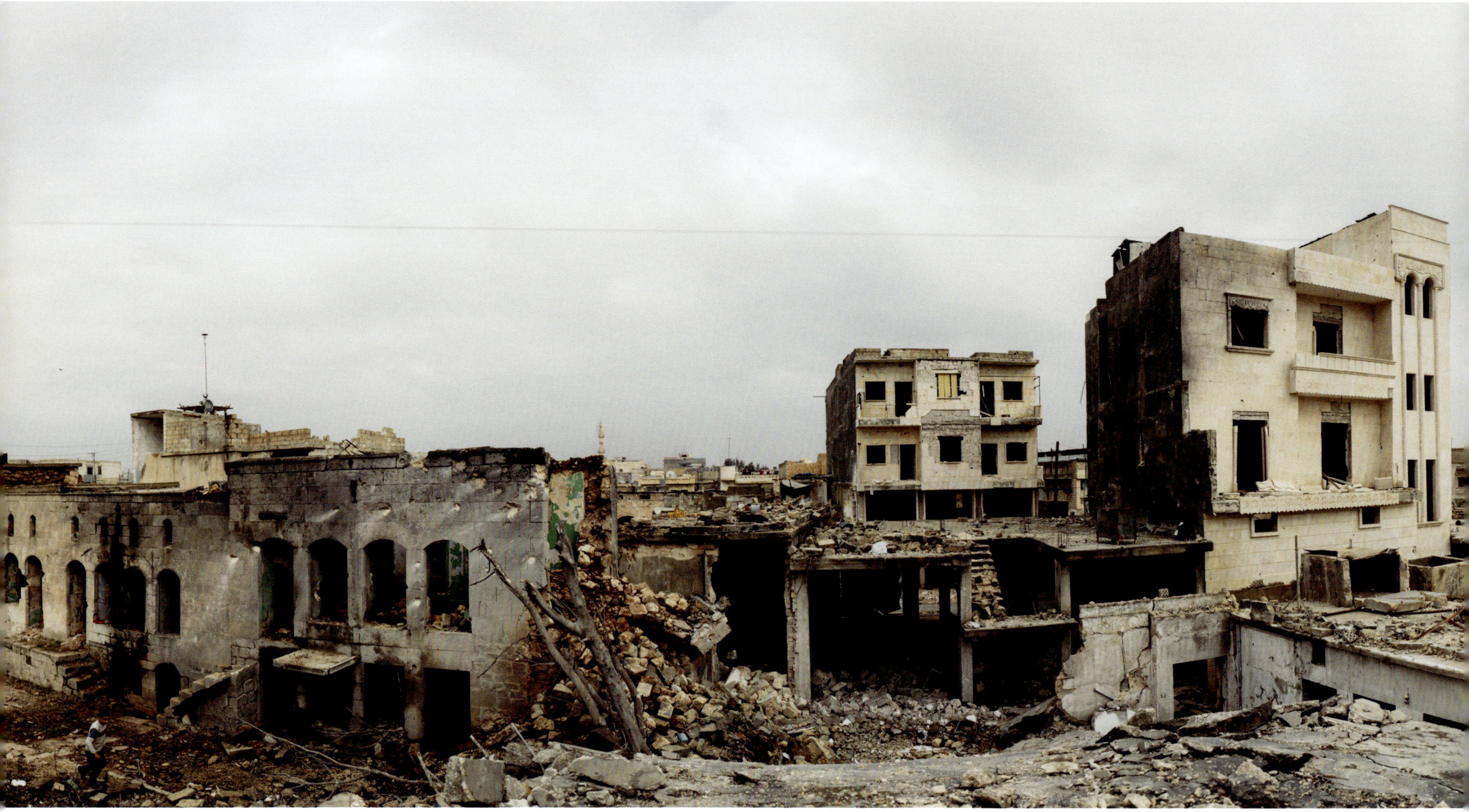

February 8, 2013, Azaz.

Neighborhood destroyed by Syrian Government bombing in 2012. Image is a composite panorama.

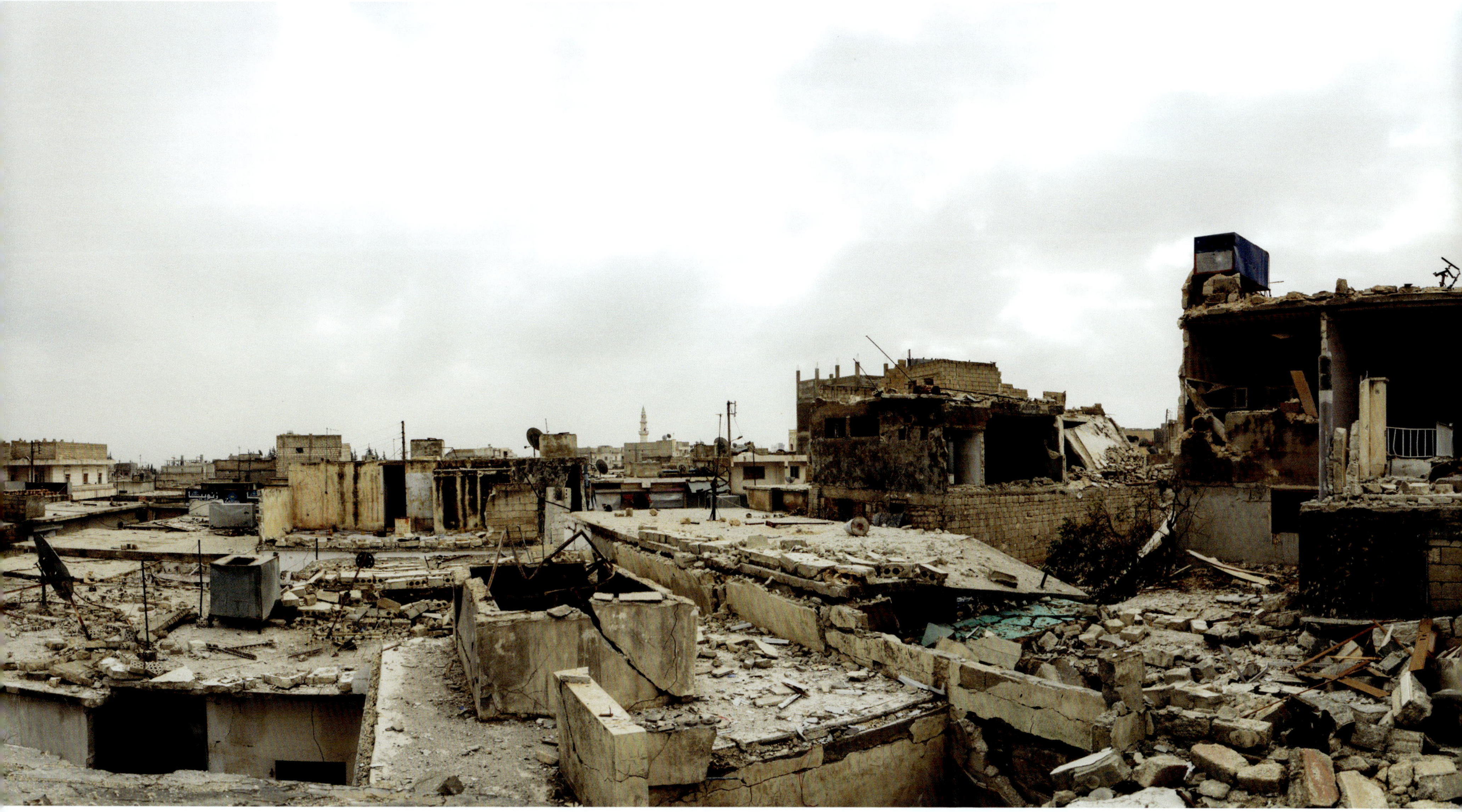

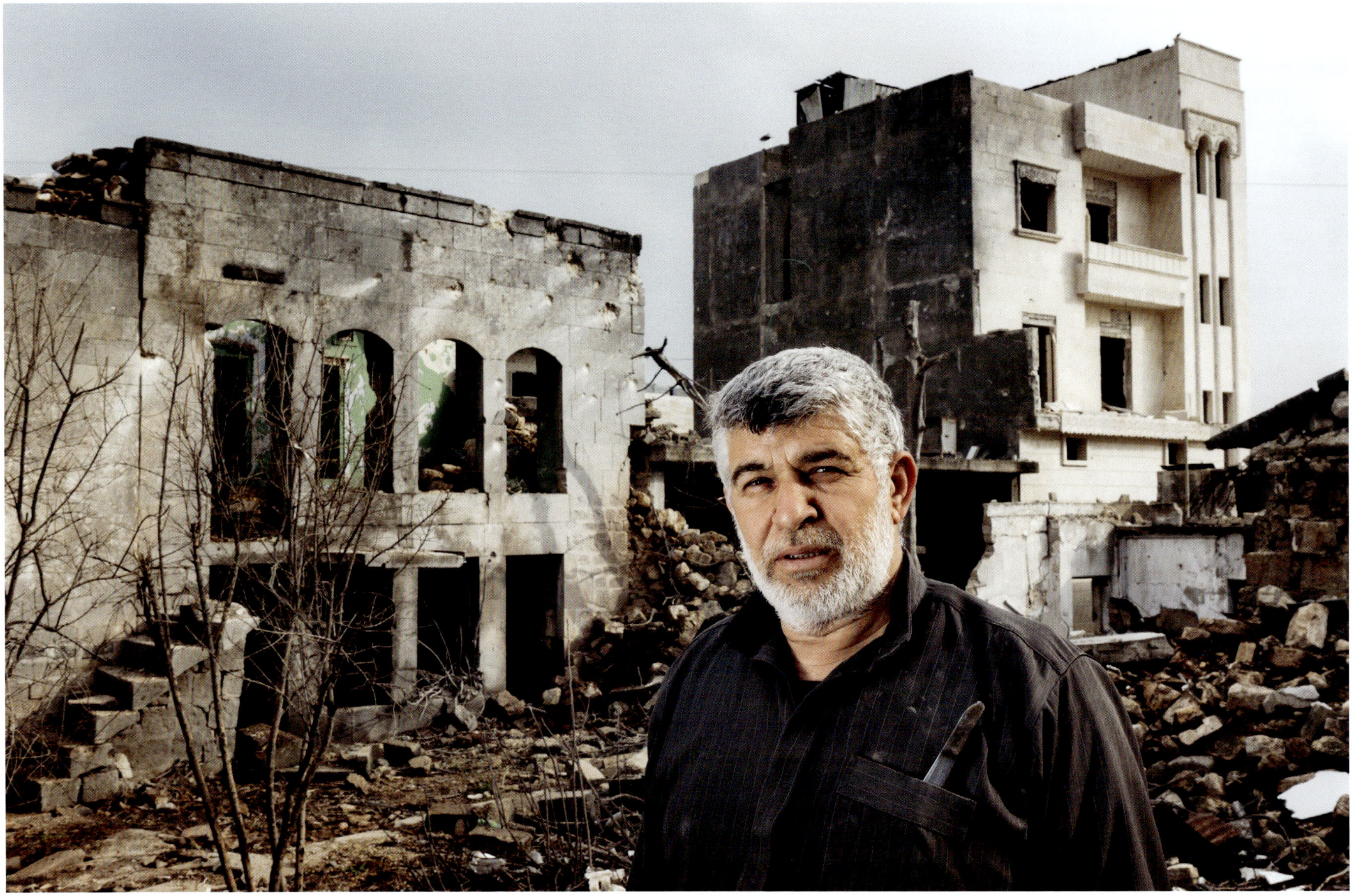

February 8, 2013, Azaz.

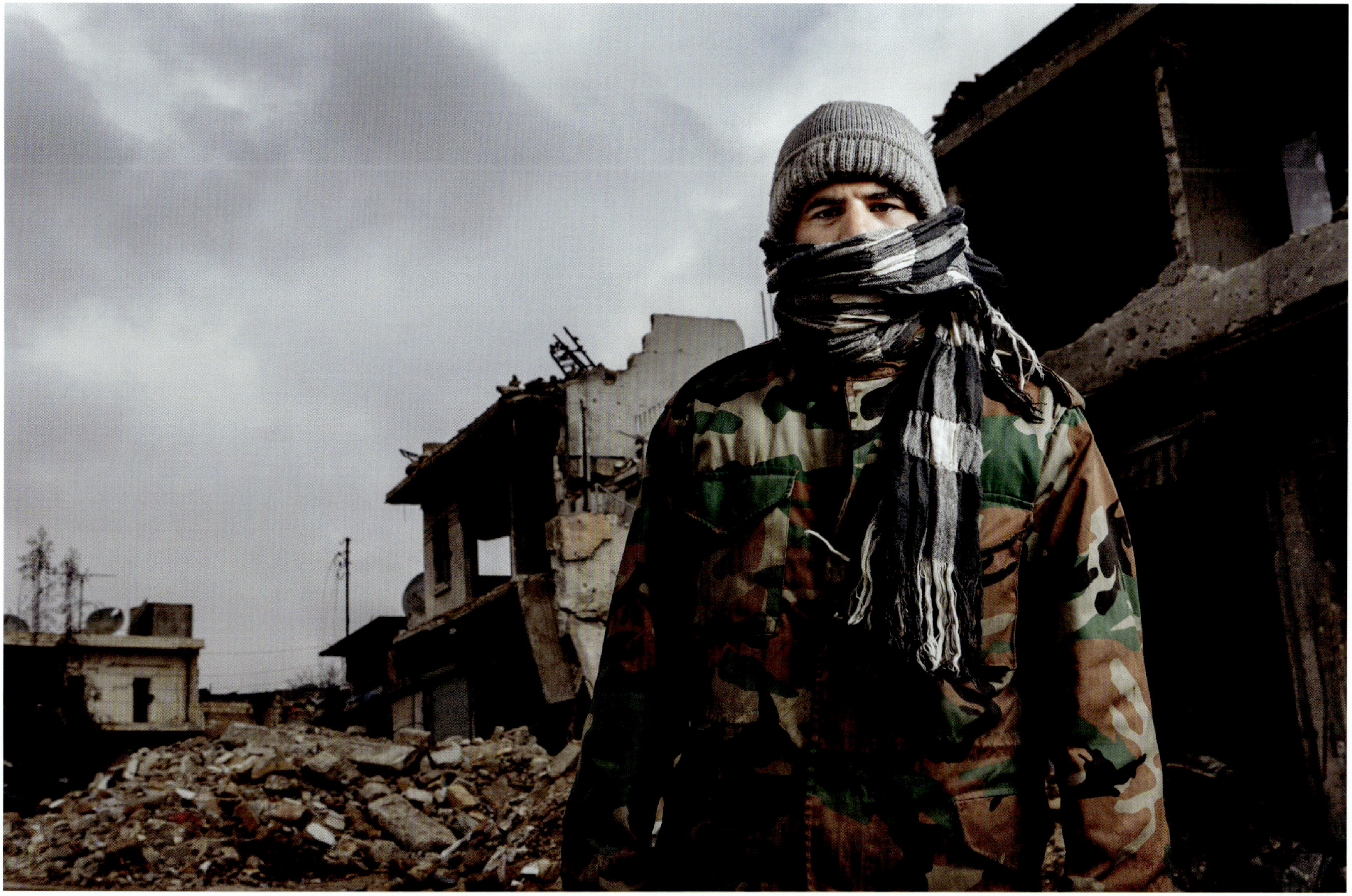

February 8, 2013, Azaz.

February 8, 2013, Azaz. Image is a composite panorama.

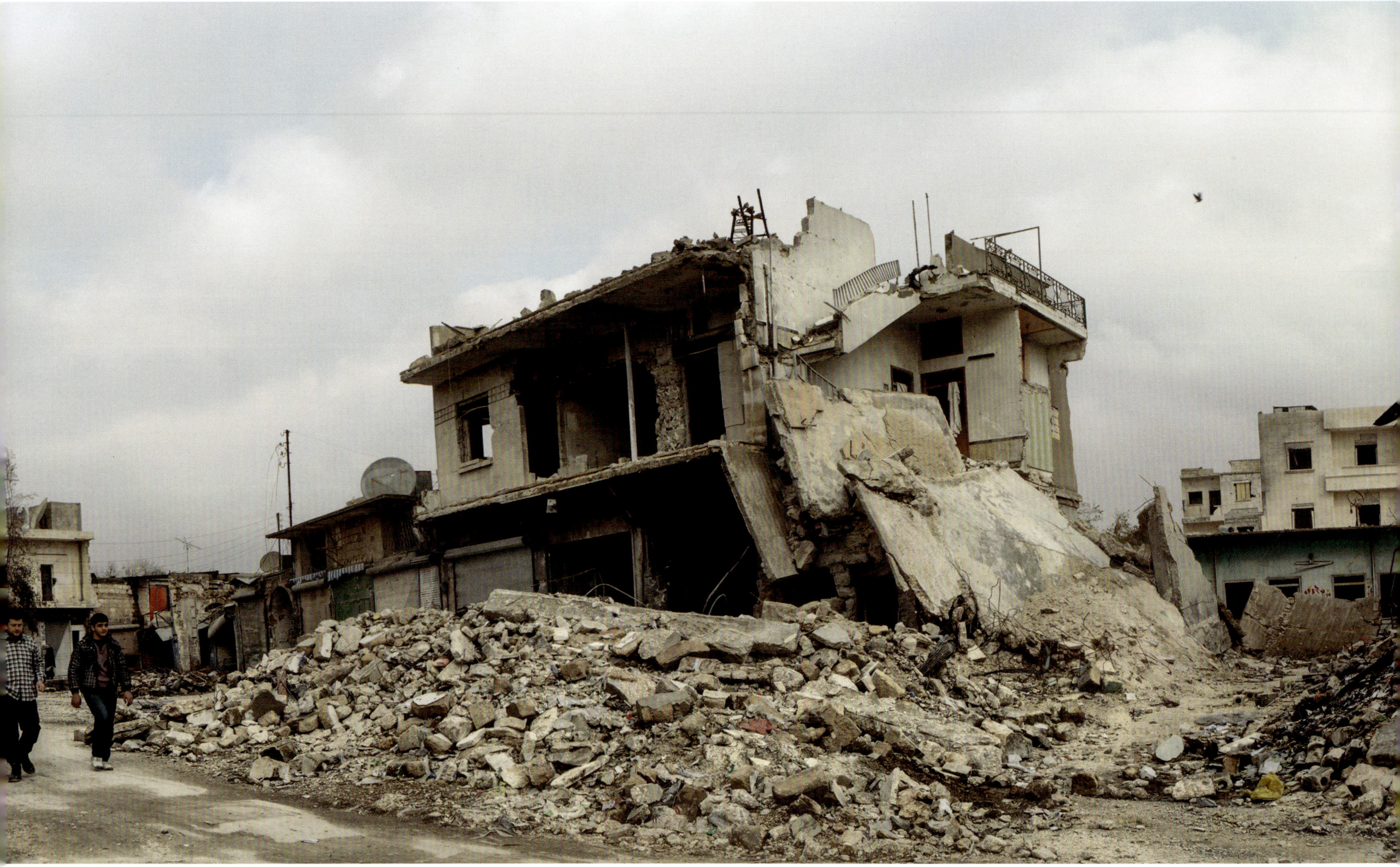

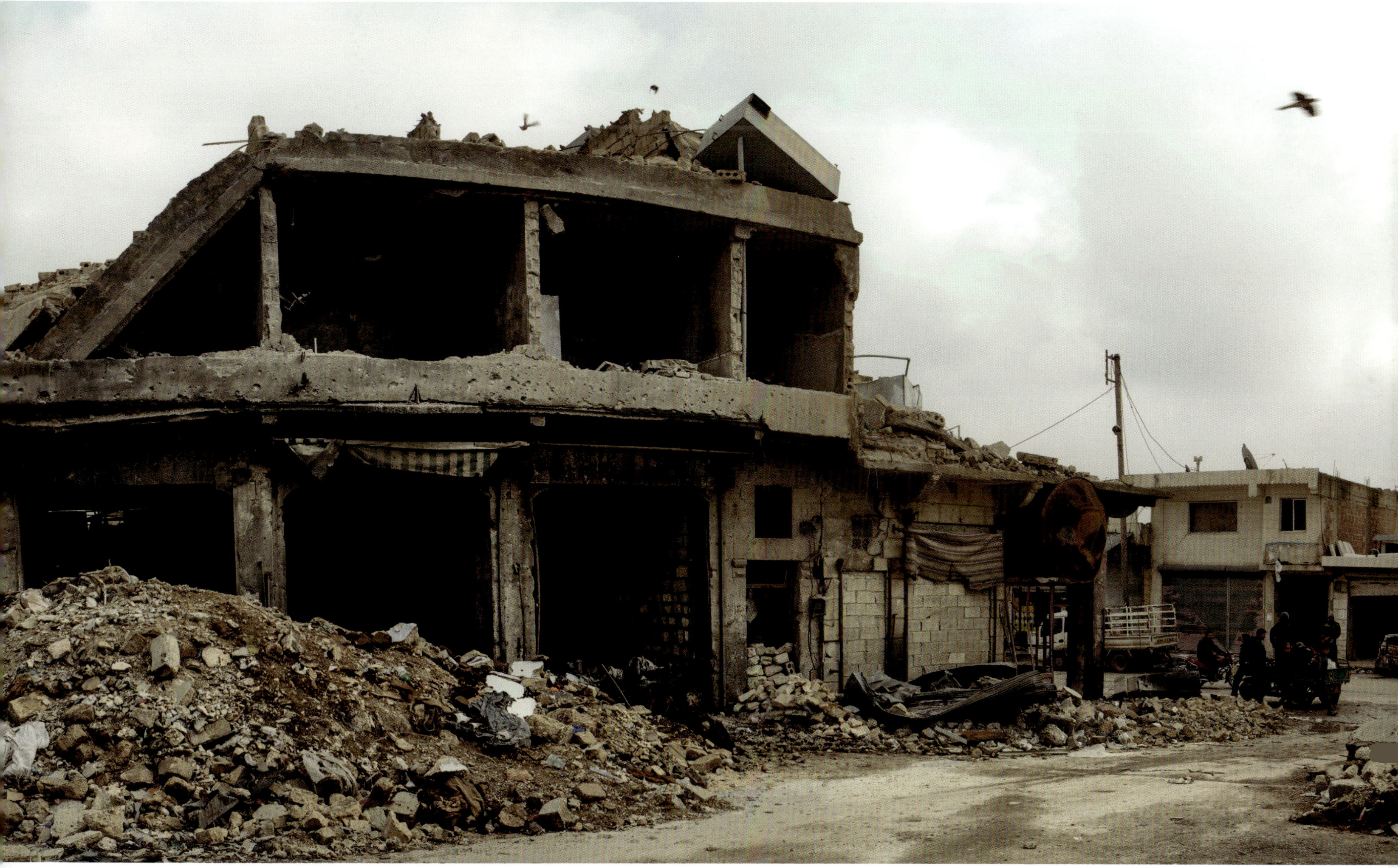

February 9, 2013, Azaz.

A Syrian Government battle tank destroyed by Opposition forces sits amid the rubble of a damaged mosque.

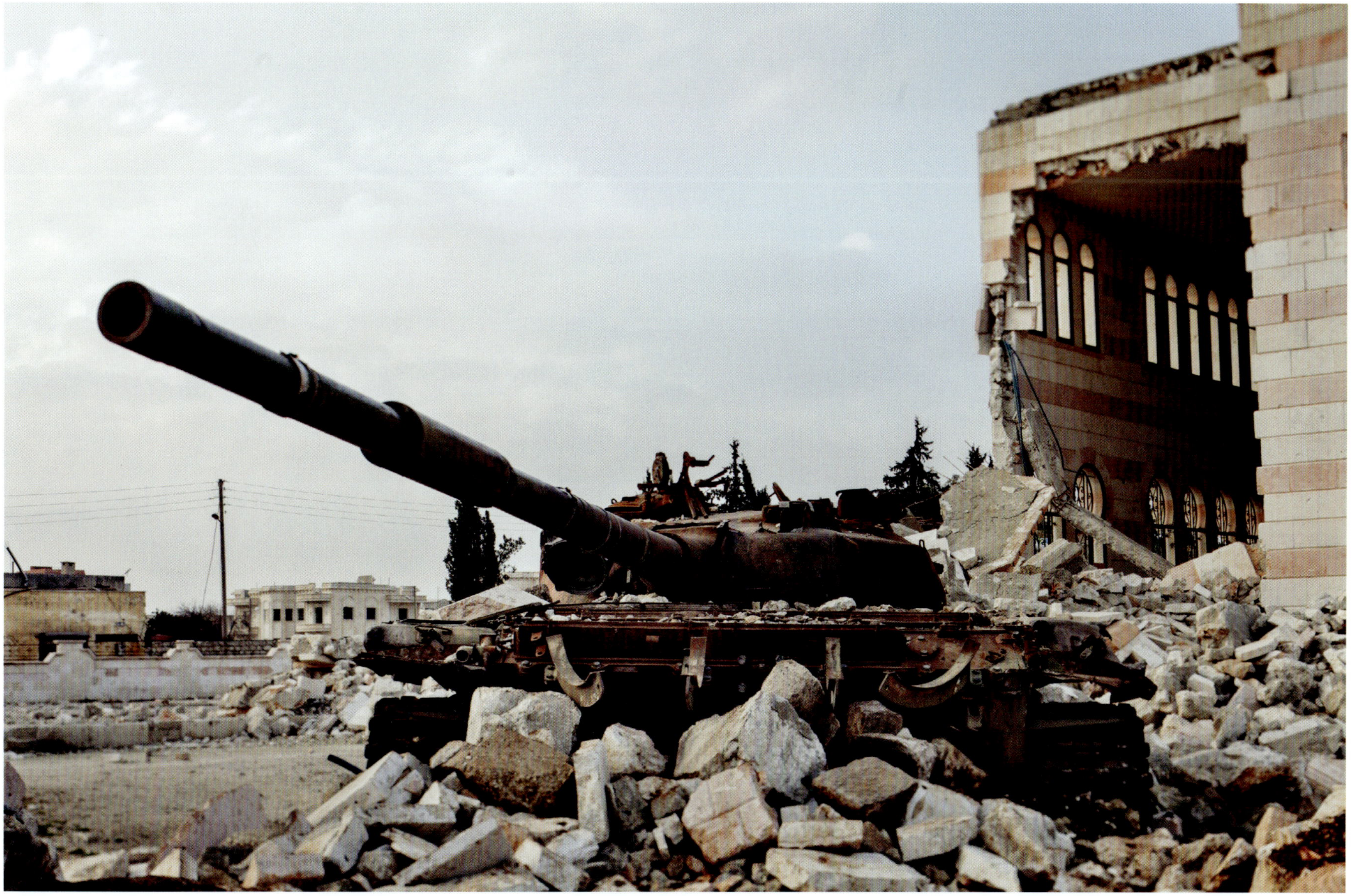

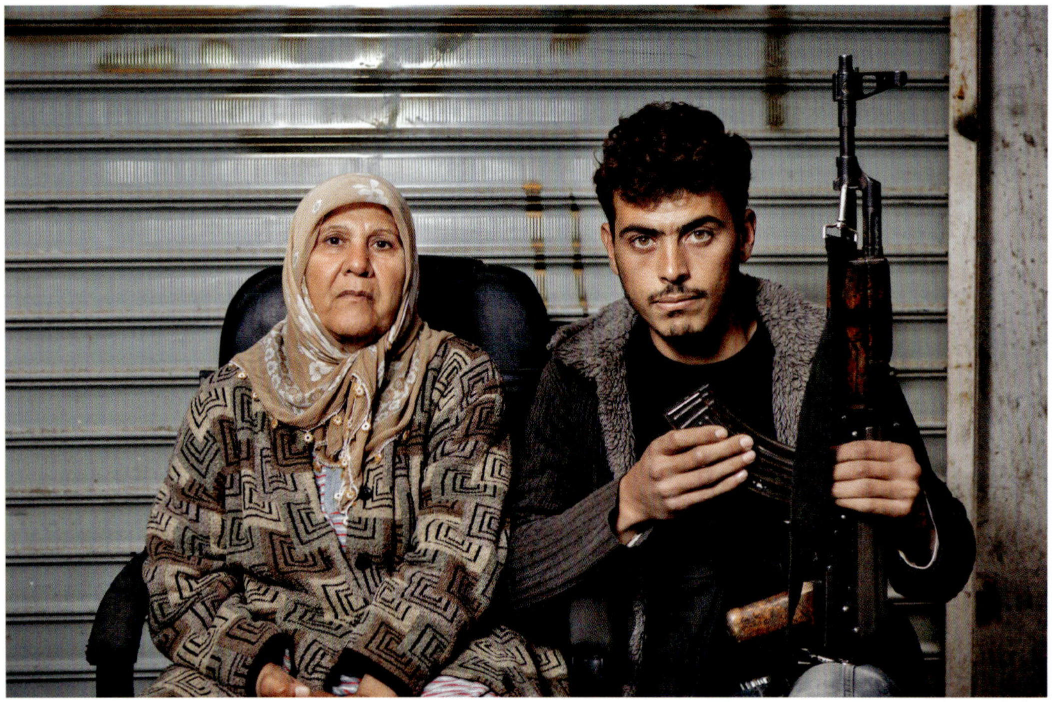

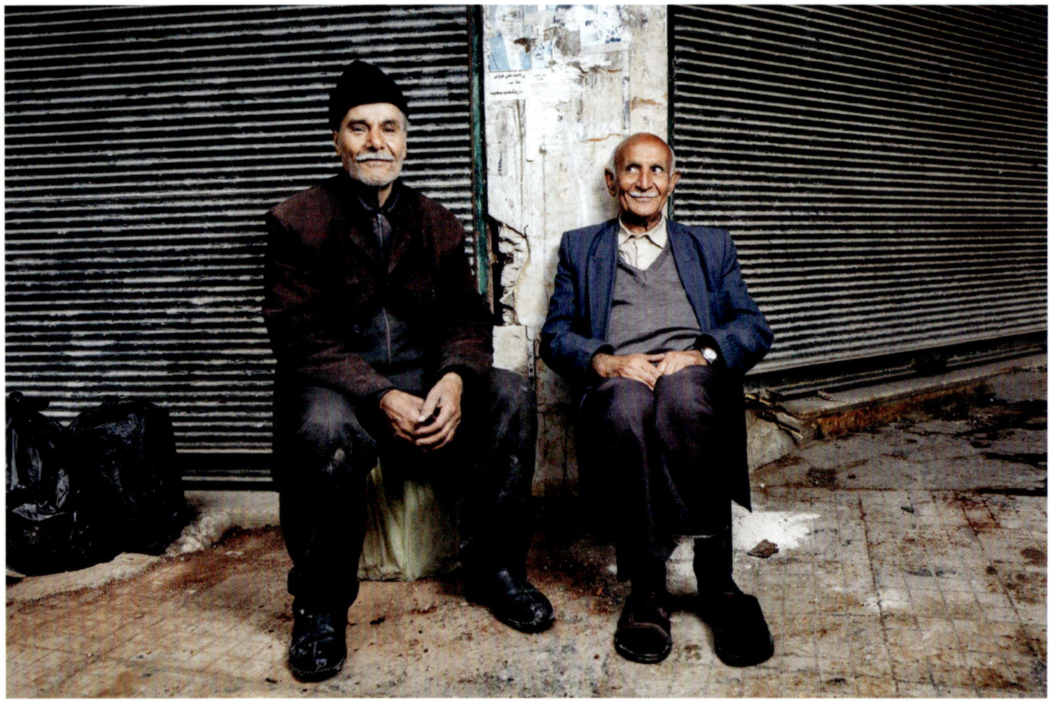

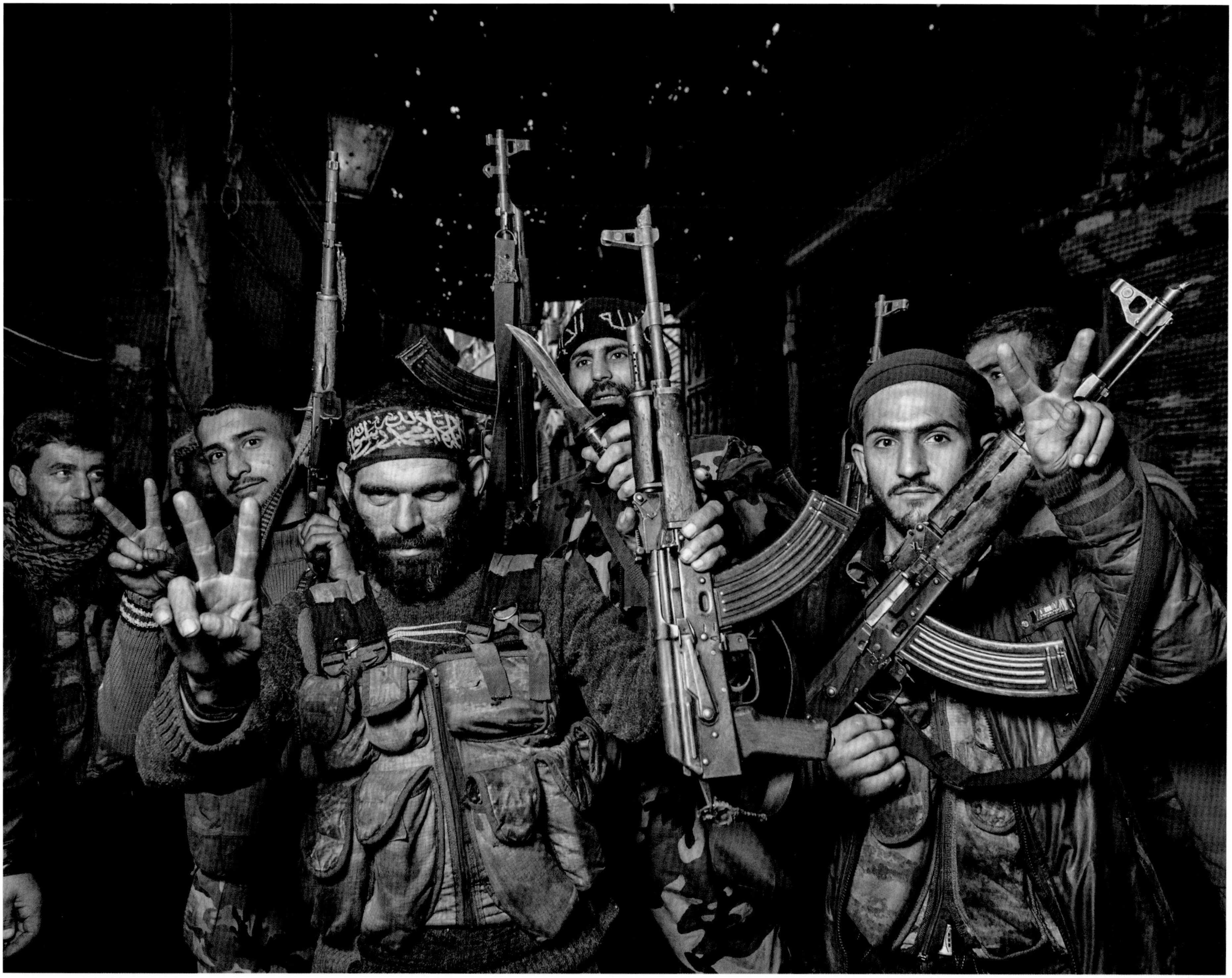

"FOR THE DEAD AND THE LIVING, WE MUST BEAR WITNESS."

— *Elie Wiesel*

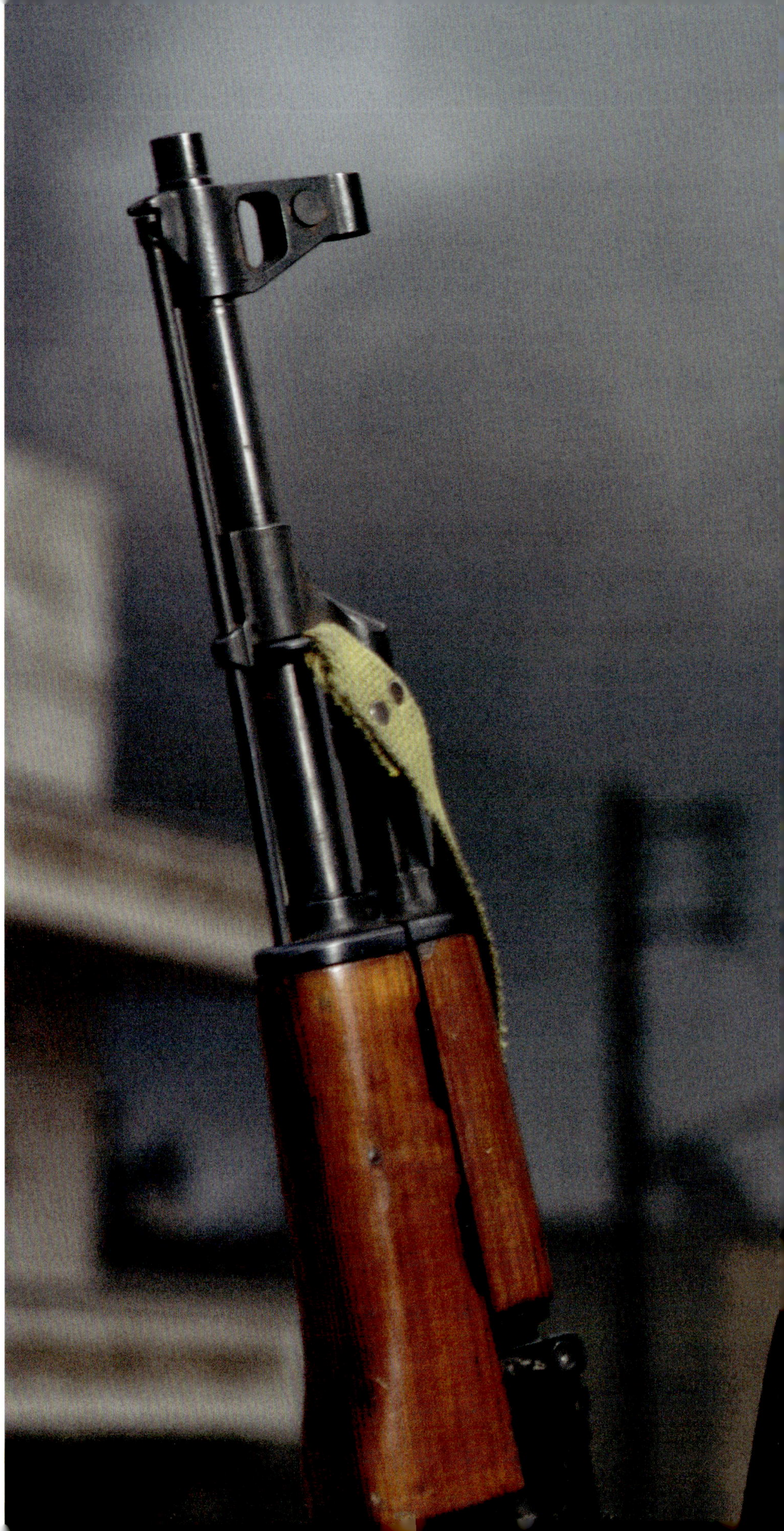

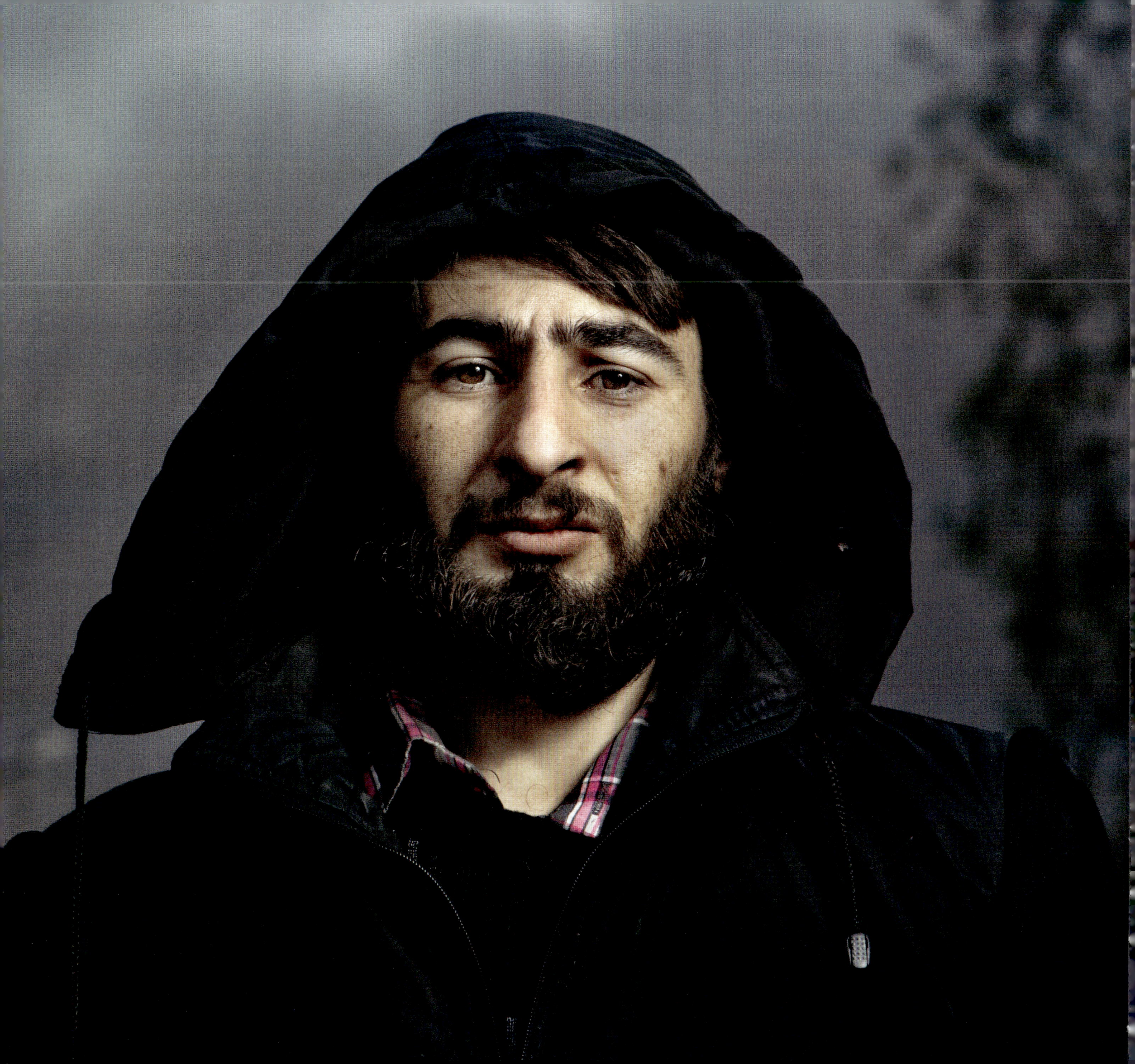

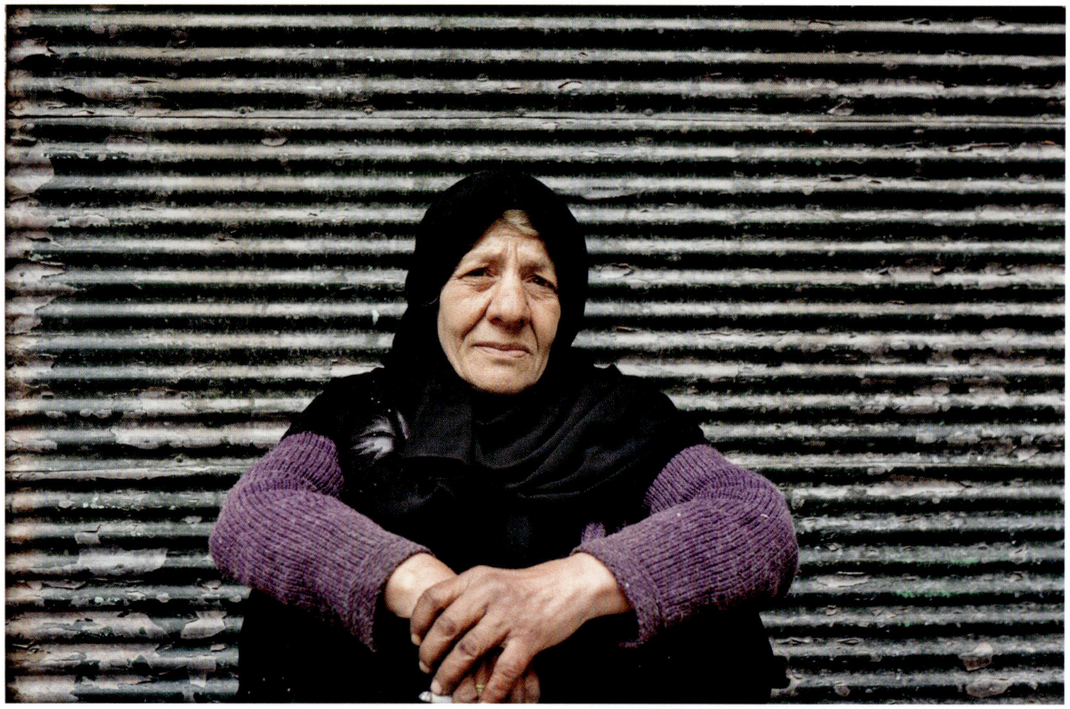

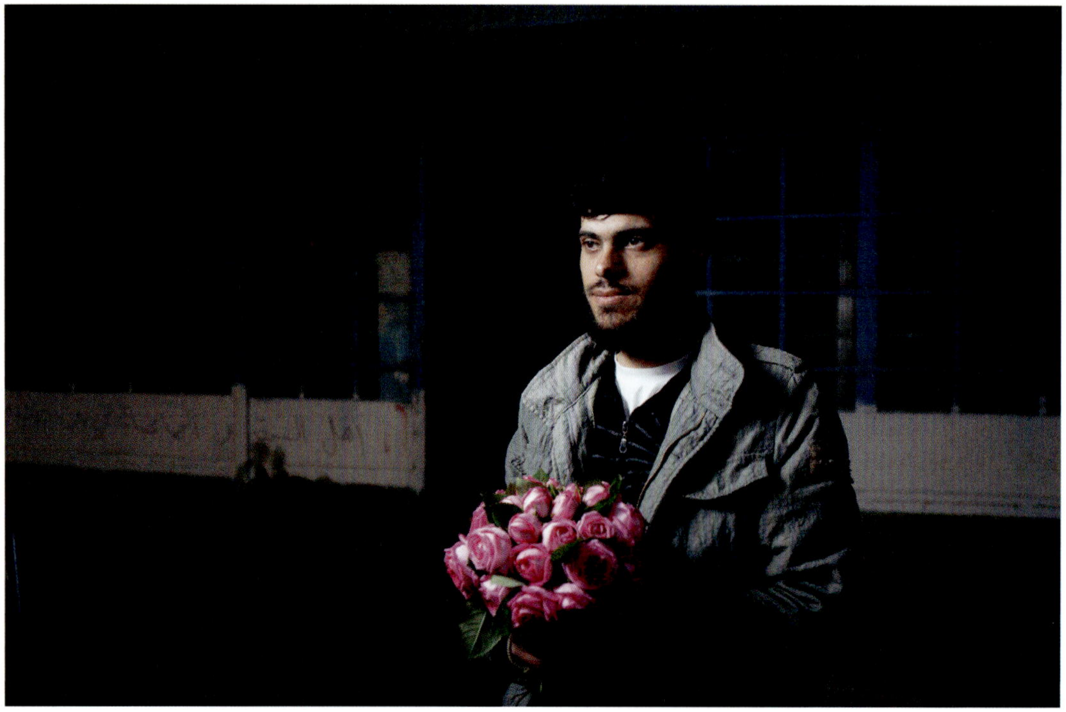

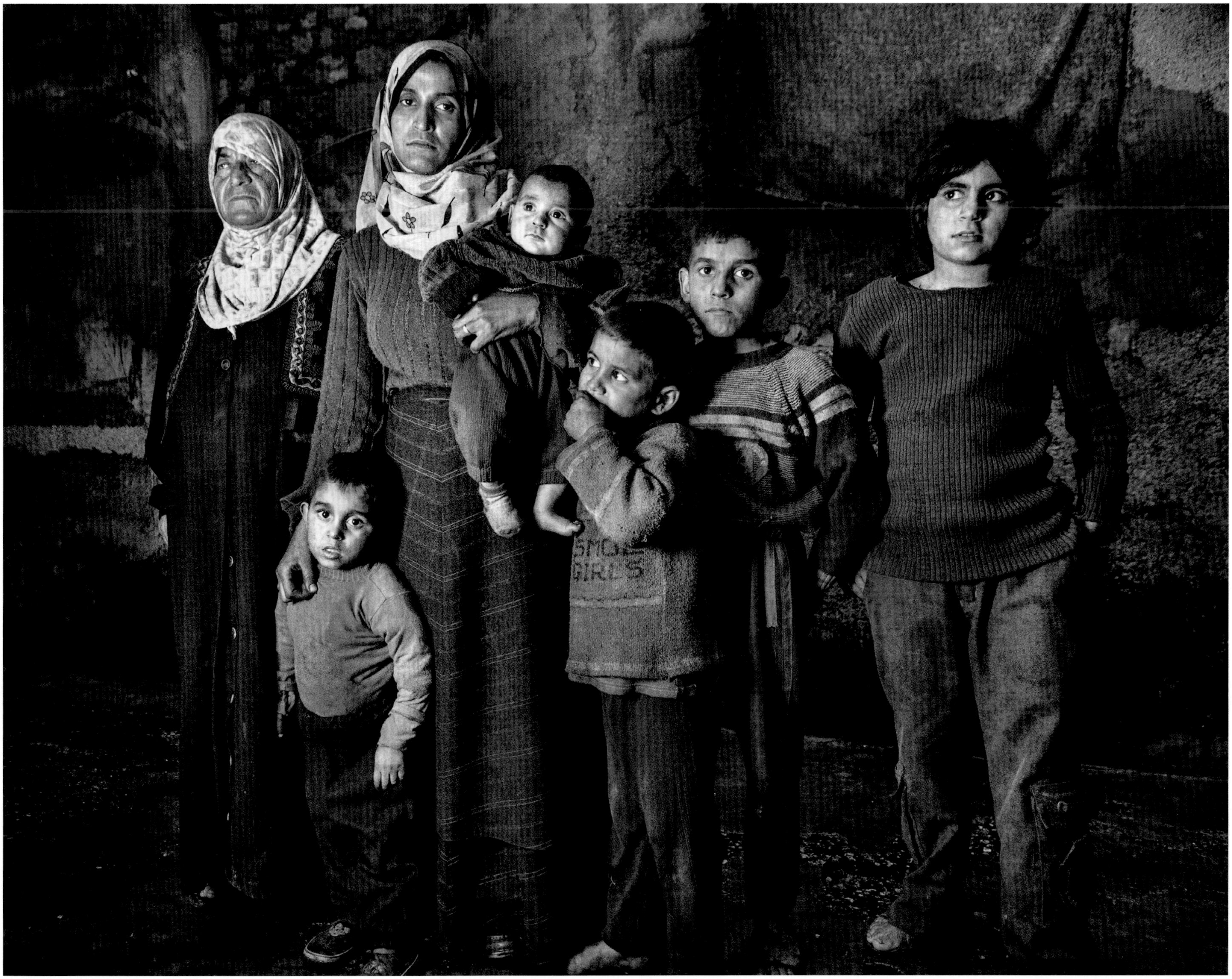

Early on, rebel forces scored lightning victories, and with the fall of much of Aleppo and the surrounding countryside, it seemed a tipping point had been reached. But soon, Islamist forces with agendas far removed from those of democracy and human rights crept into the country and began to choke the life out of the north.

The war continued. Rebel forces turned on the Islamic State, rejecting their brutal philosophies. But no help came. The regime's barrel bombings increased, raining down across the country to collectively punish the residents of "liberated" areas. And no help came. Whole suburbs were starved out in sieges. And still no help came.

Five years later, the war in Syria grinds on. Even ceasefires offer nothing in the way of long-term stability. The conflict and its aftershocks will last for decades to come. The country lies in ruins. Its people are now spread across the four corners of the world, many of them in camps just miles from the battle zones.

—Emma Beals

April 20, 2013, Masaken Hanano, Aleppo.

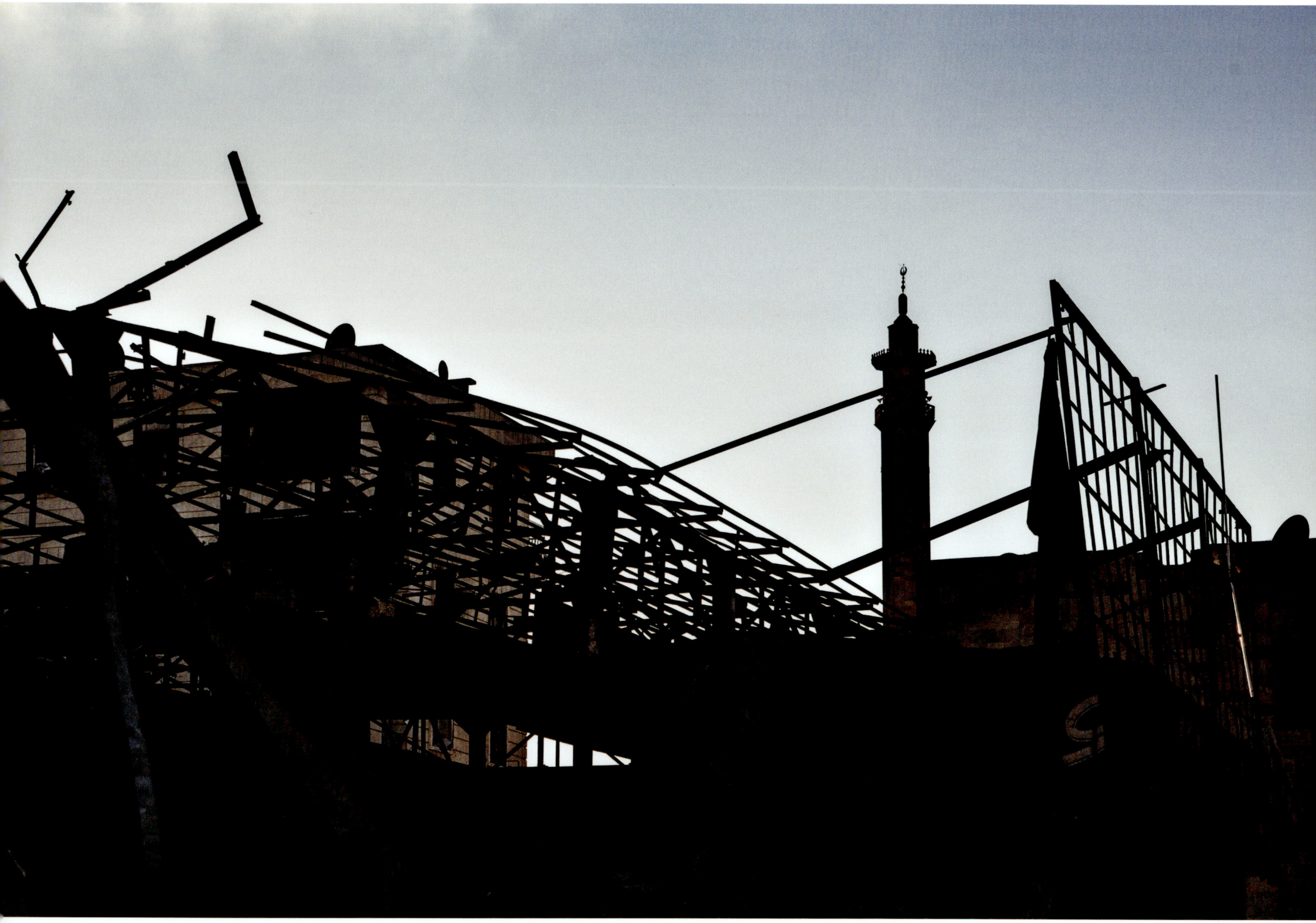

Even working in such an intense environment, you start to evolve a routine. In some ways this routine provides a sense of normality, and to a degree, reassurance. Relationships are heightened. The espresso seller you only met three mornings in a row greets you like a son, the kebab seller like a brother. A few hundred yards back from the front line, life continues as normal. In the air lingers a cocktail of freshly cooked kebabs and the stench of rotting rubbish Almond cake, ice cream, cold drinks, sportswear are all on sale. The scene could be set anywhere in the Arab world, until a Russian-made MiG fighter jet comes into view overhead, making menacing turns in the sky, safe in the knowledge that there is nothing below that can shoot it down. At street level, people run manically in all directions, fear written on their faces. A mother, holding her daughter's hand, runs for cover, the child struggling to keep up. Do you seek cover in a building that could be flattened, or stay outside and try to track the gray war machine above? What can the pilot see from up there? Does he see the city as a Westerner would flying over London or NYC, recognizing the streets and buildings below? After all, he is Syrian. Who does he think he is attacking? Has he no idea that there are women and children down here? This is something I've struggled to understand, at an elemental level: how can someone inflict such suffering so deliberately?

—Will Wintercross

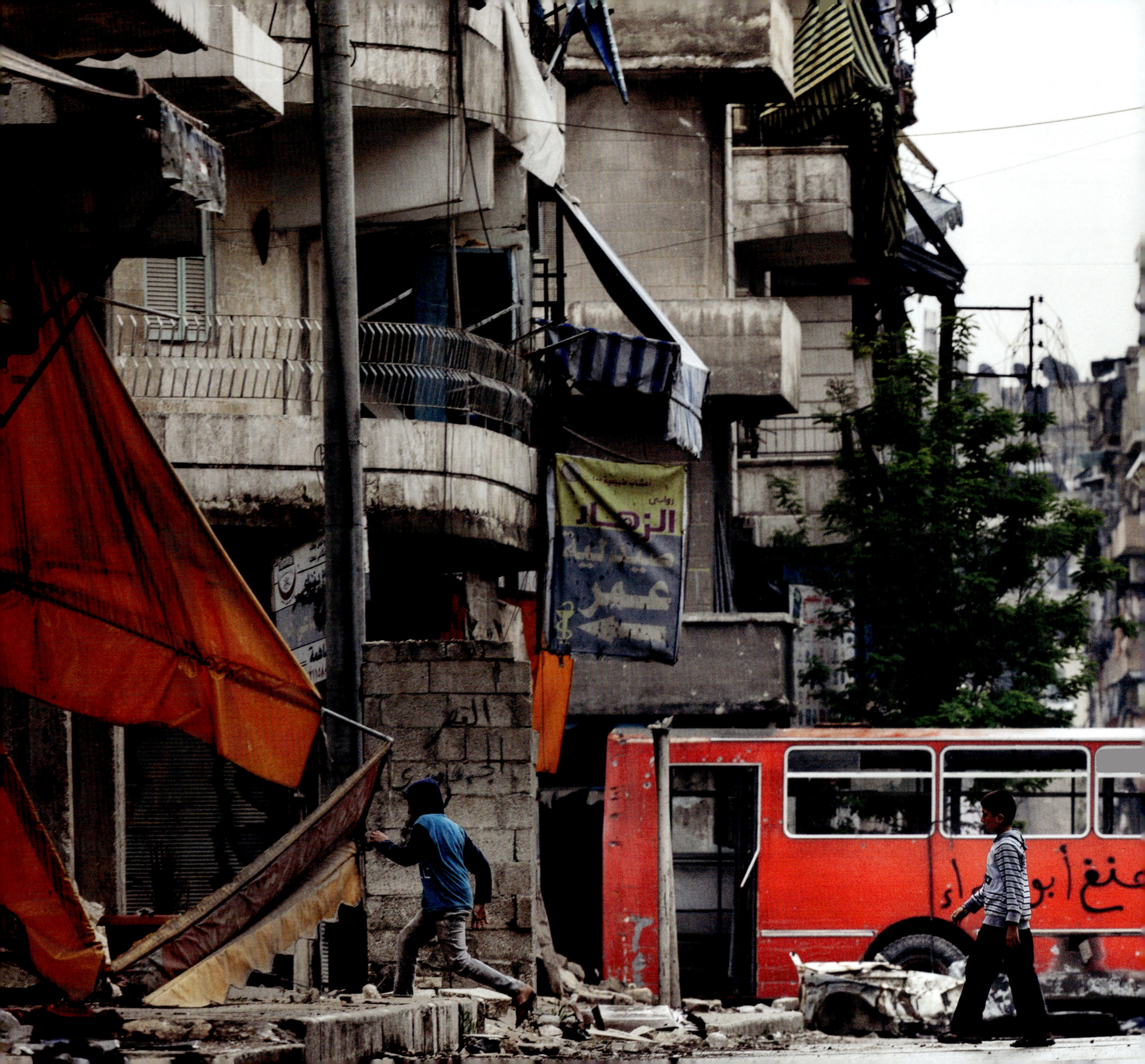

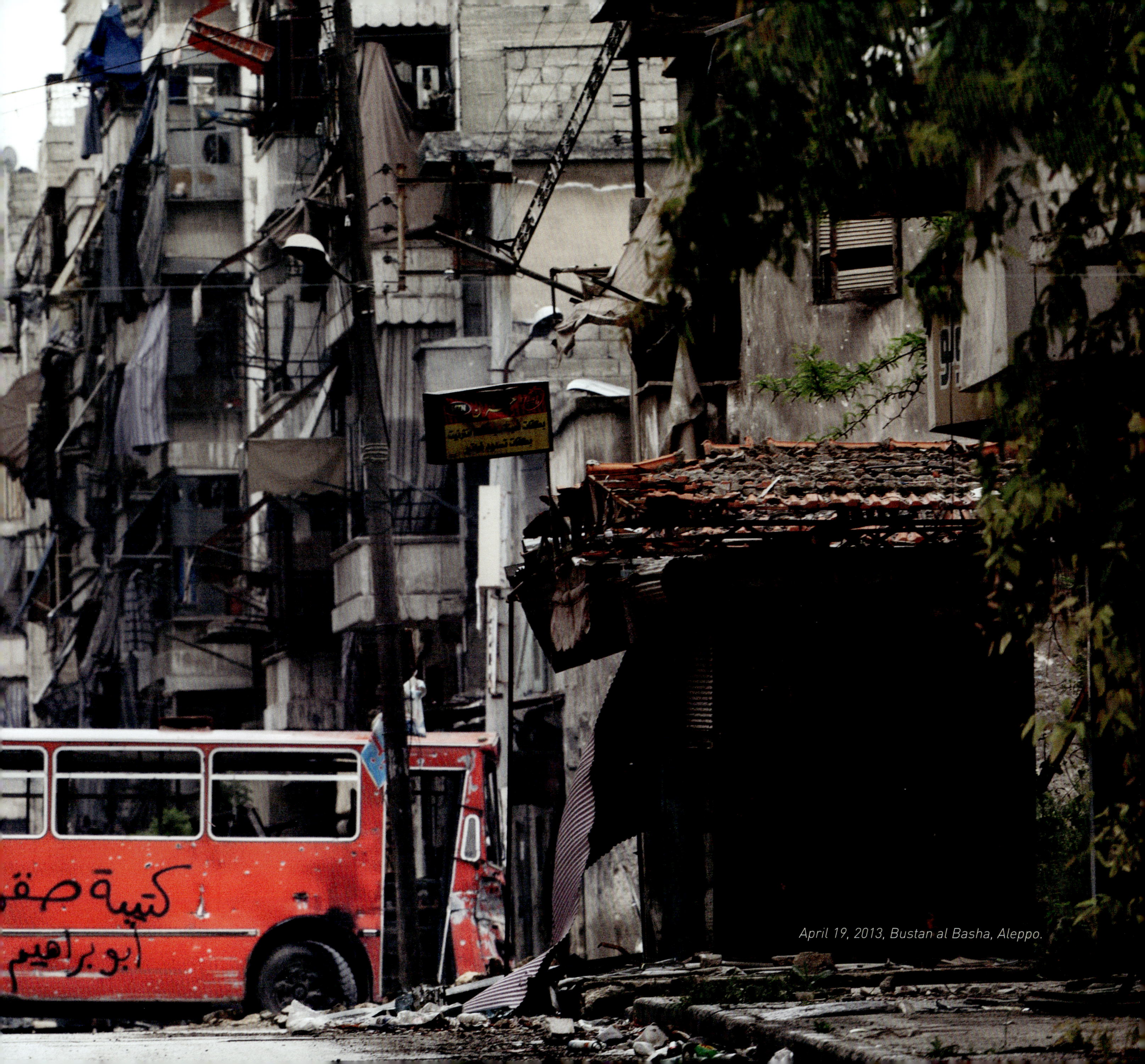

April 19, 2013, Bustan al Basha, Aleppo.

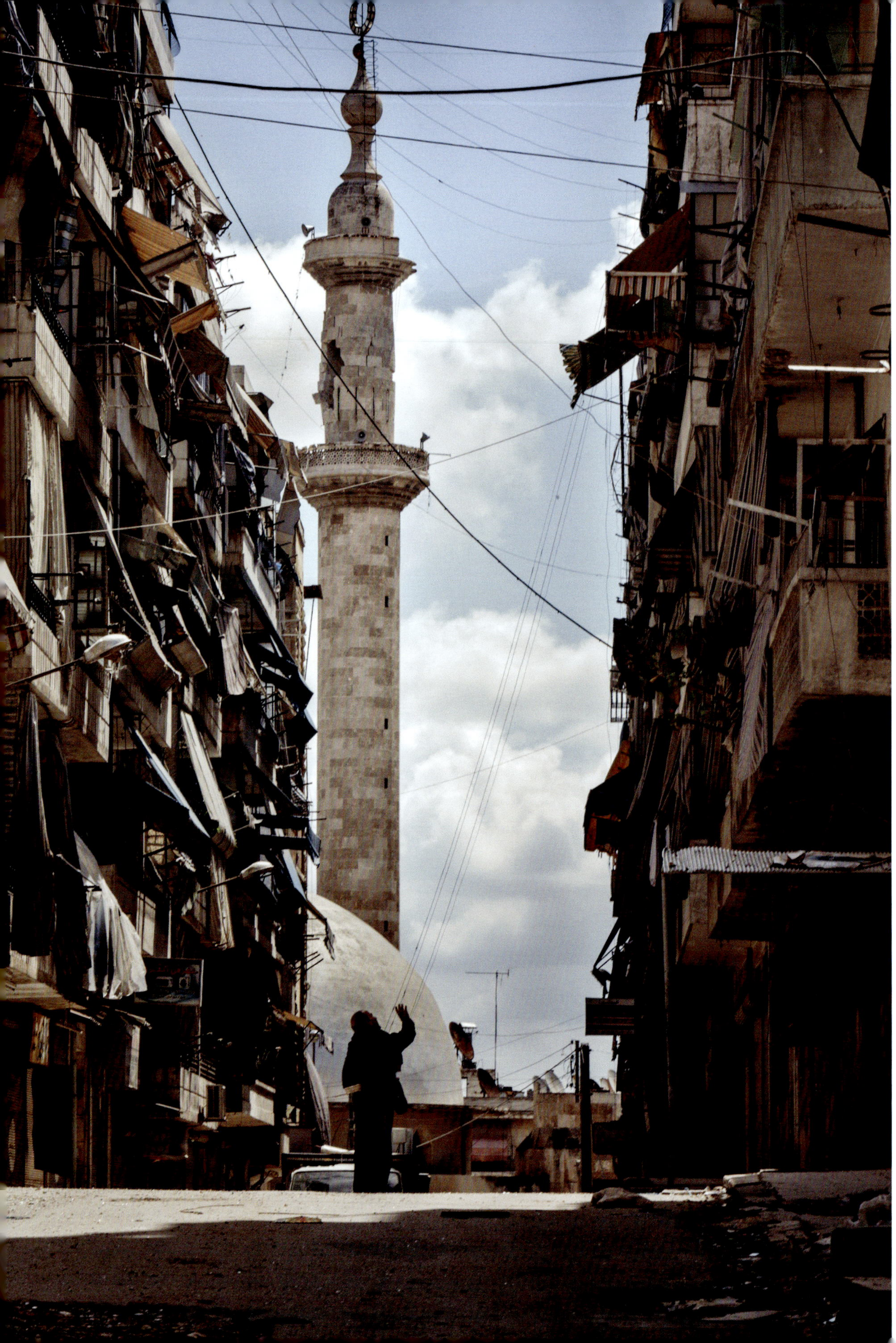

April 20, 2013,
Sheikh Maqsood,
Aleppo.

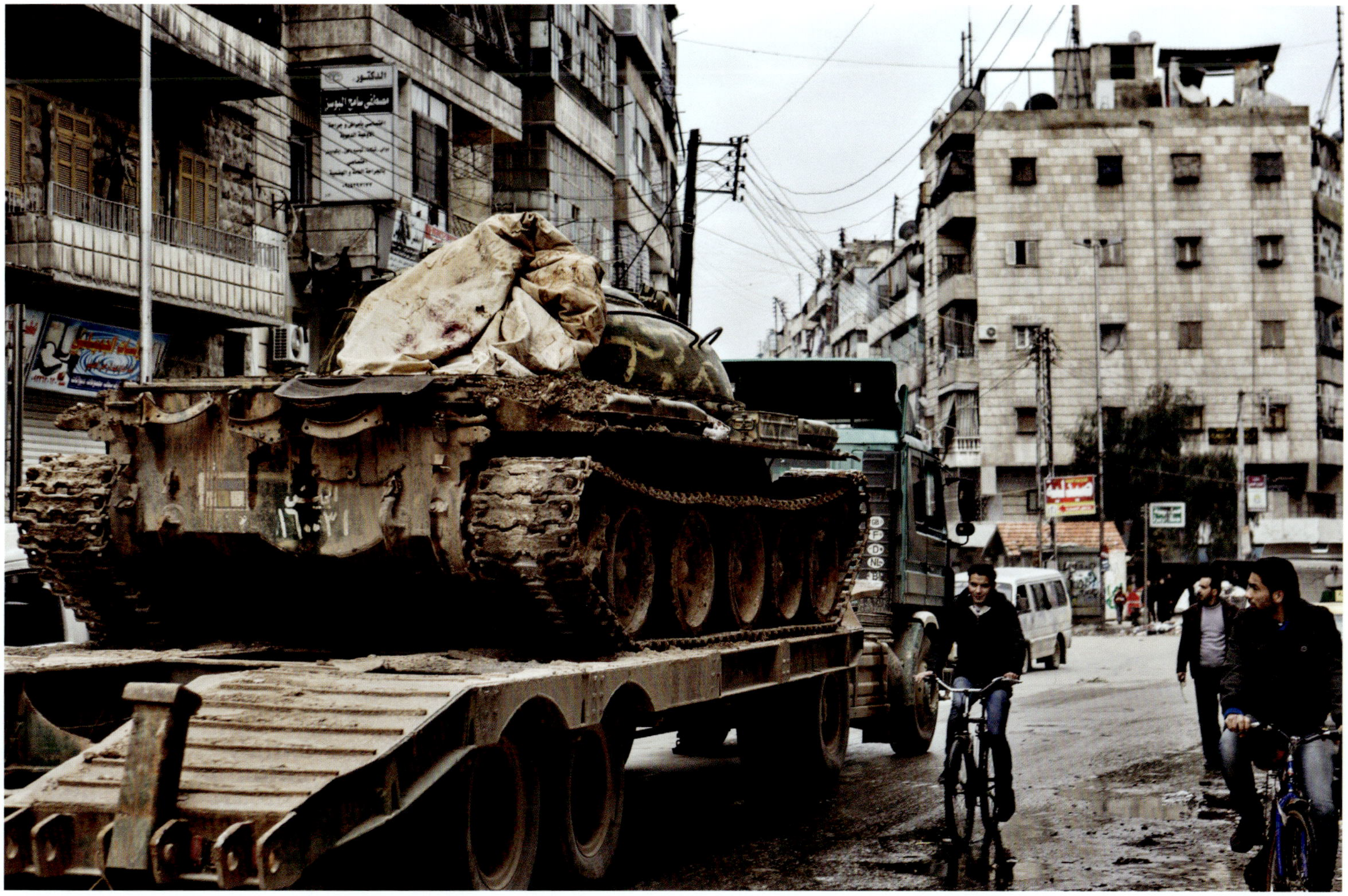

February 7, 2013, Tarik al Bab, Aleppo.

Opposition forces have relied upon captured weapons to combat the Syrian Government's greater military strength.

April 6, 2014, Maarat al-Numaan, Idlib Province.

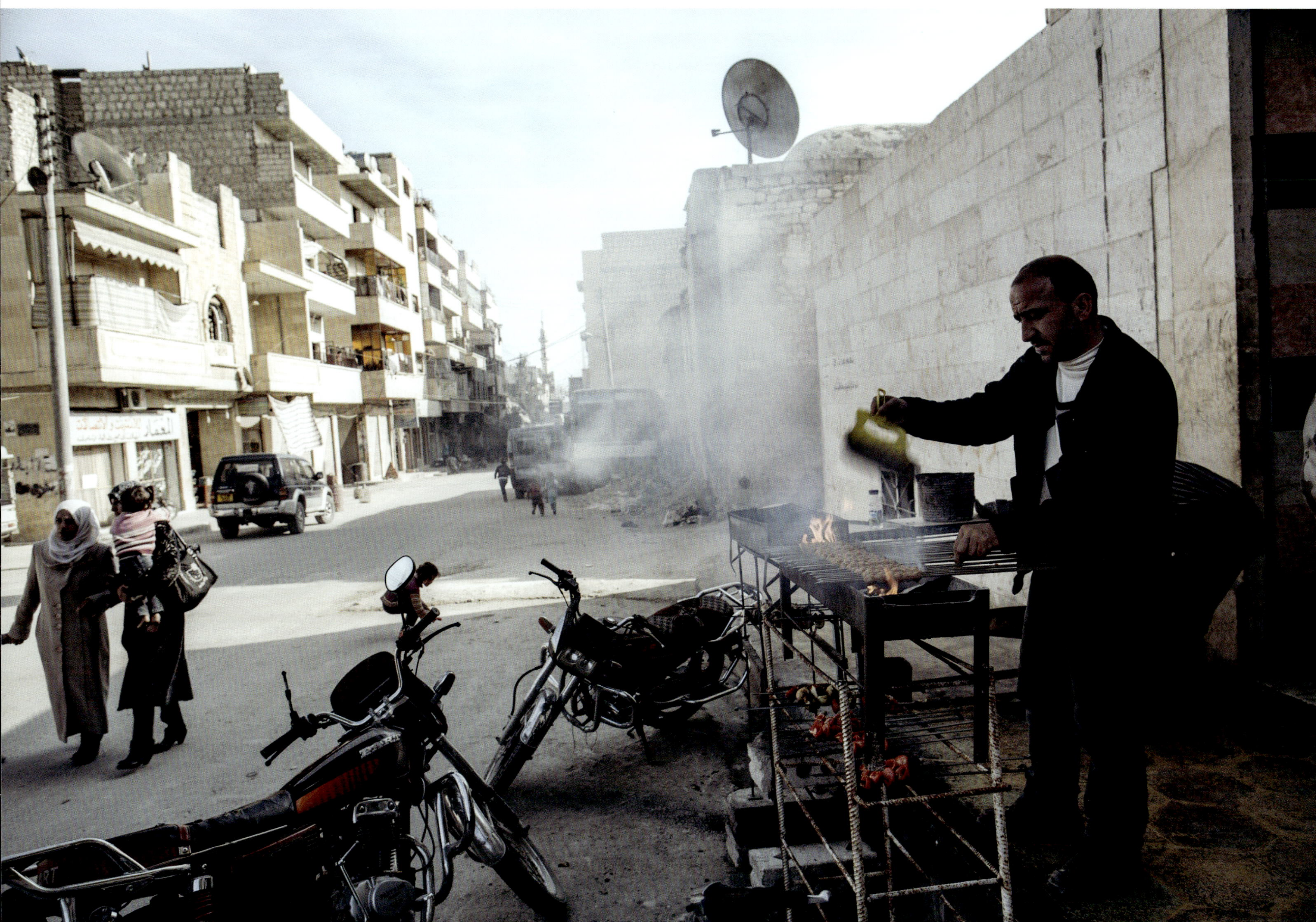

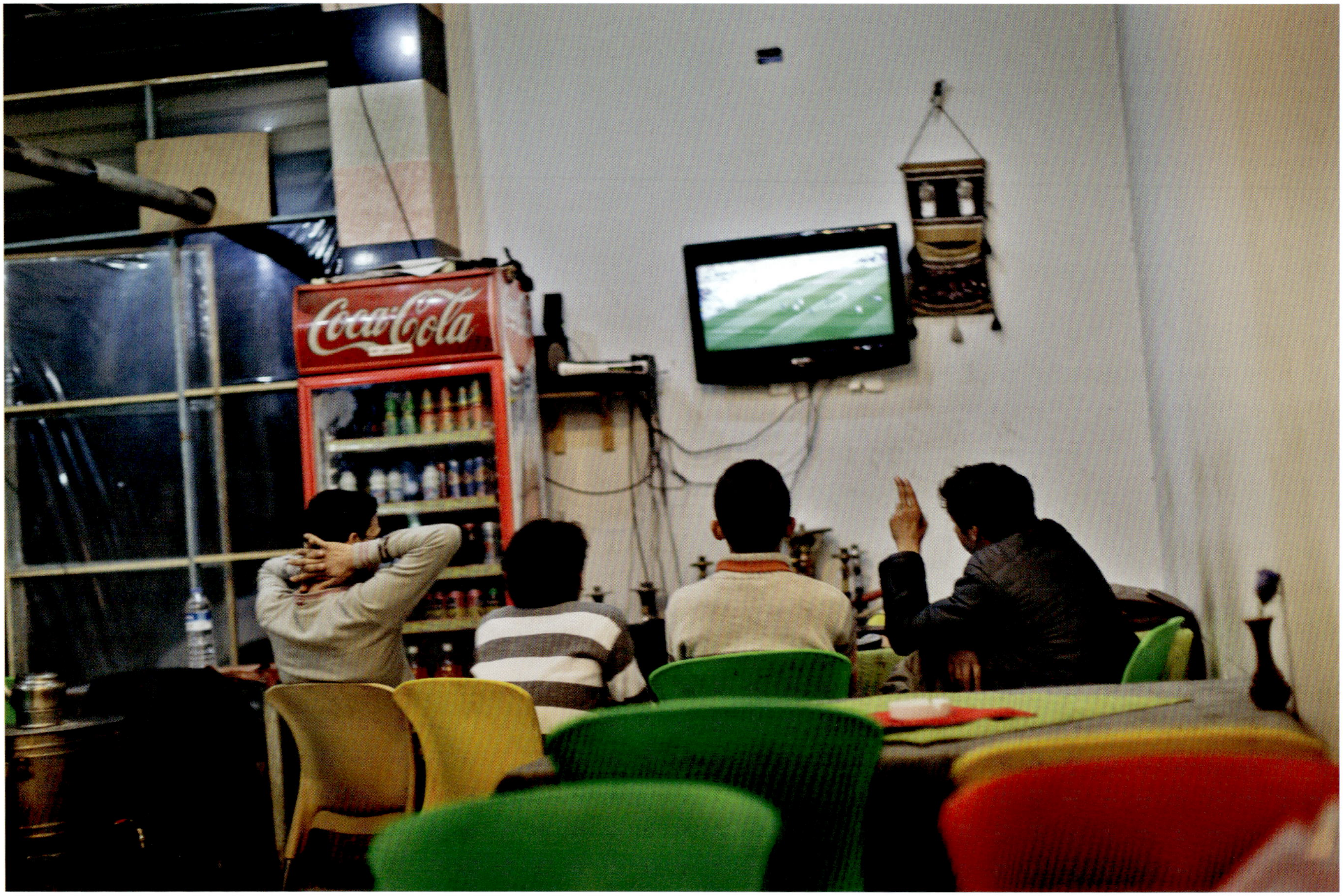

April 5, 2014, Maarat al-Numaan, Idlib.

Men watch an English League football match in a restaurant.

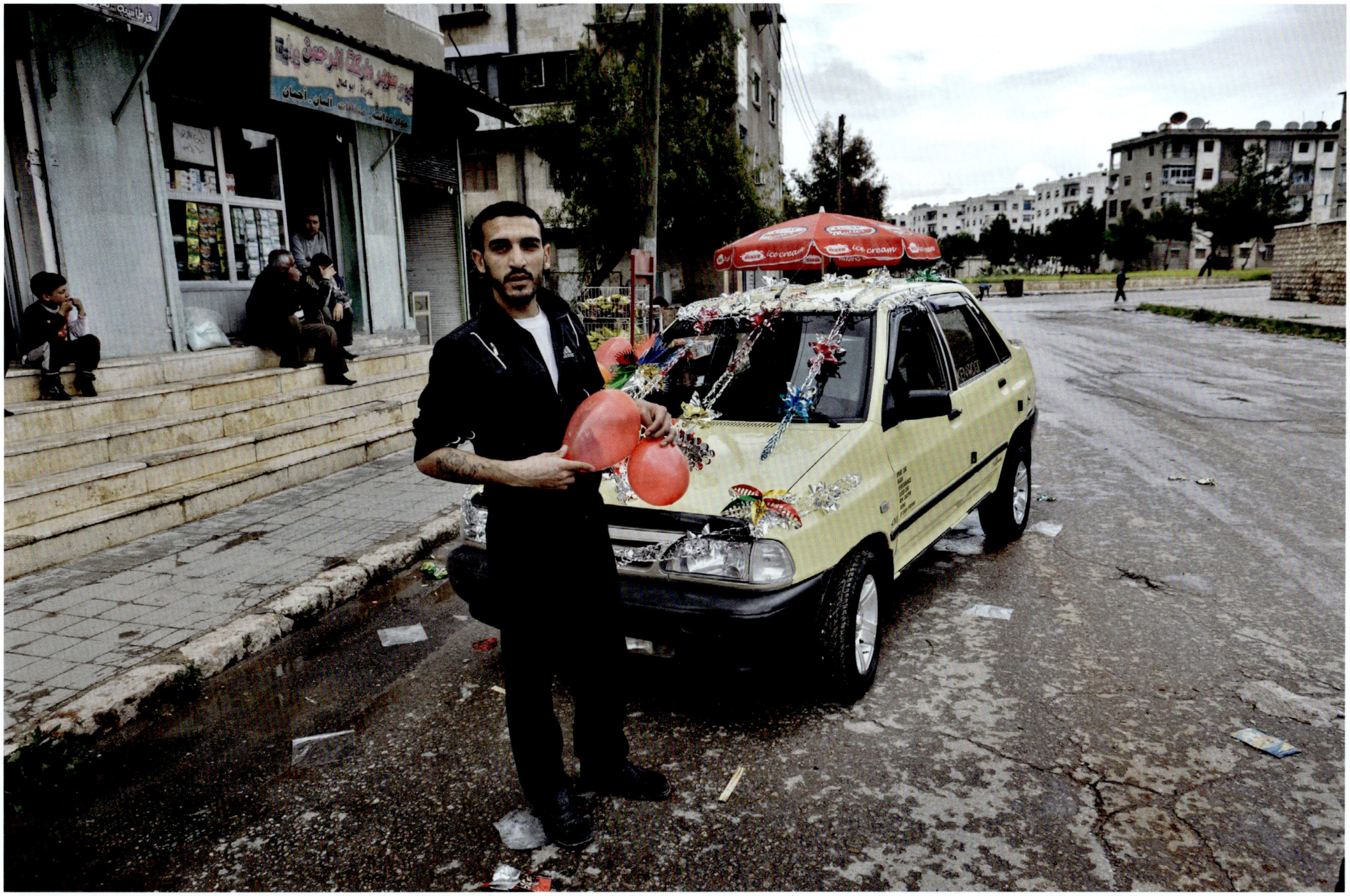

April 18, 2013, Masken Hanano, Aleppo.

A man decorates his car for his wedding later in the day. This neighborhood was the scene of fierce fighting just months previously, and despite the ongoing civil war, people continued to live there until the fierce Syrian Government barrel bombing campaign flattened the area in 2014.

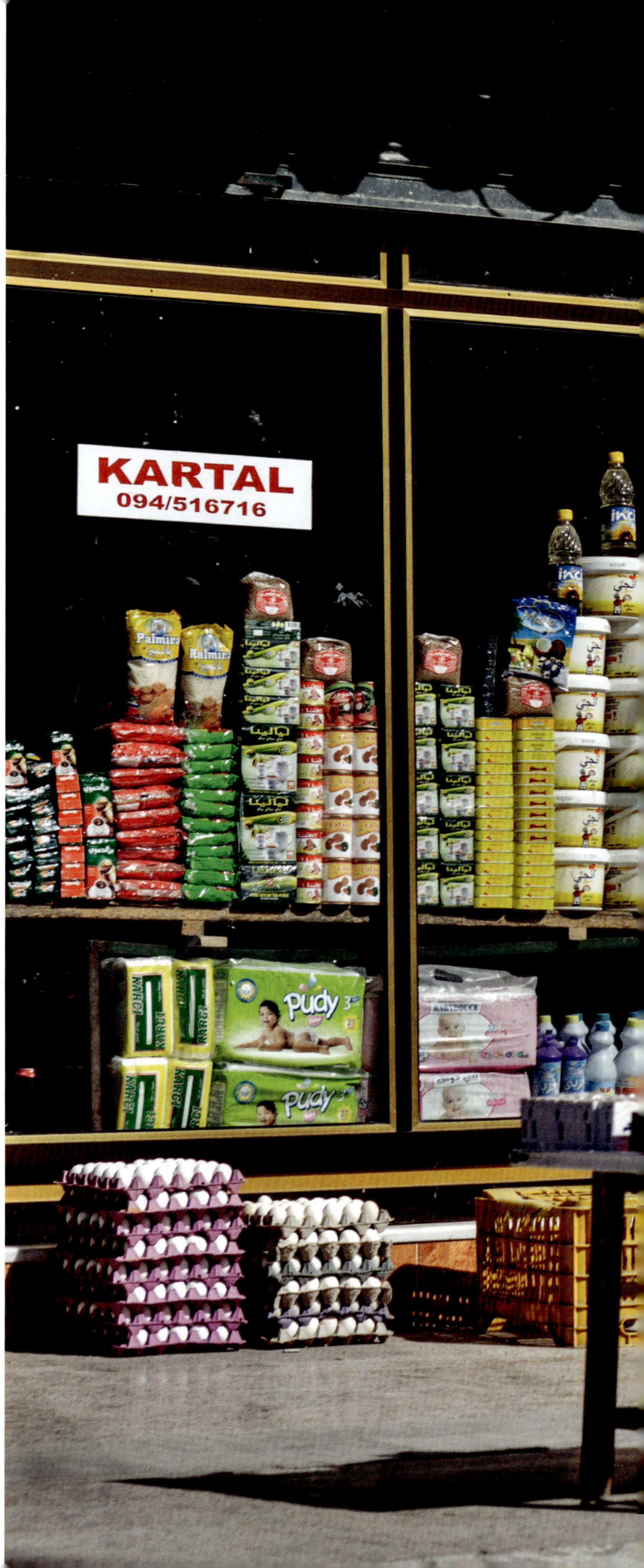

April 20, 2013,
Sheikh Khider,
Aleppo.

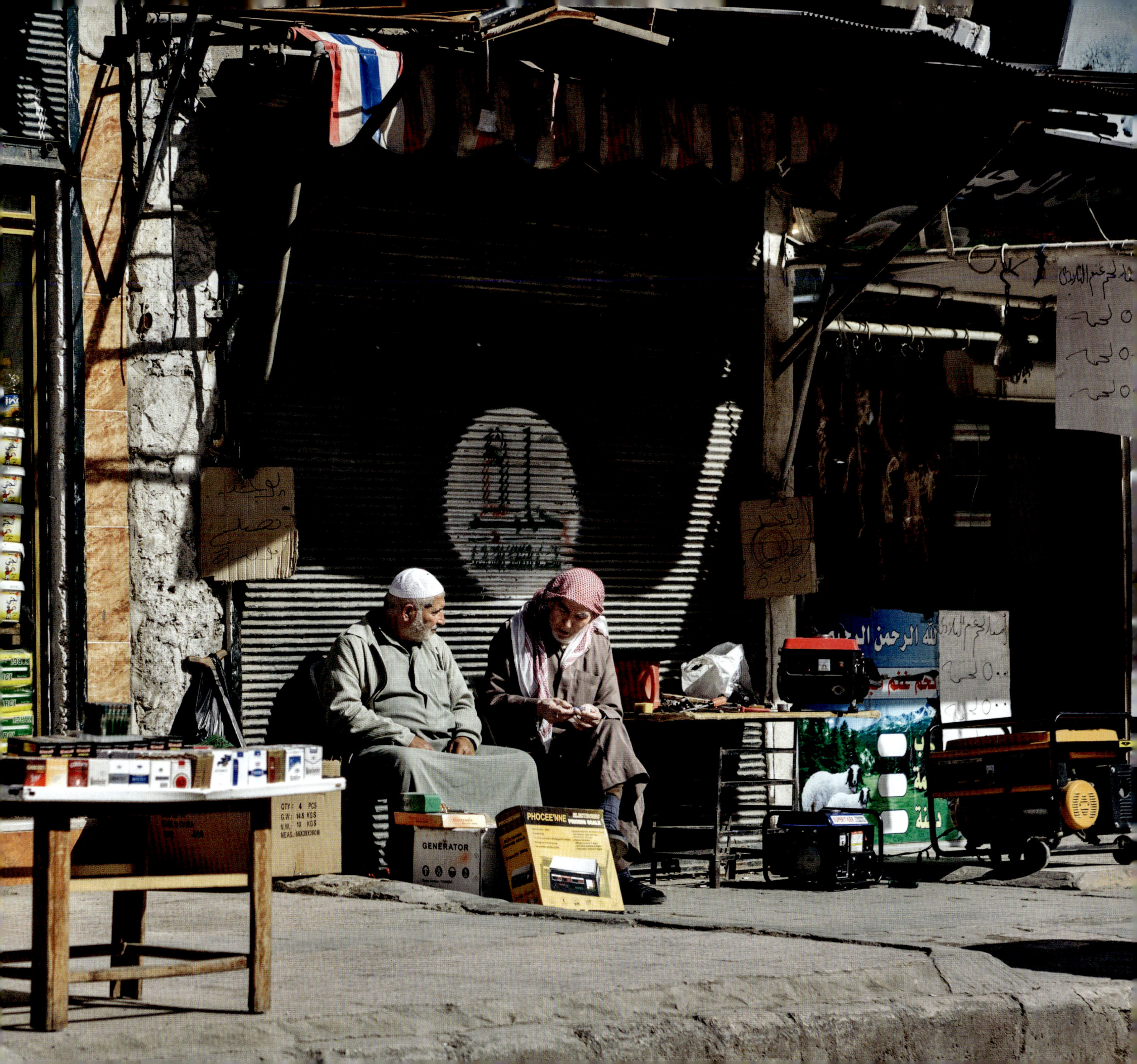
QTY: 4 PCS
G.W.: 14.5 KGS
N.W.: 13 KGS
MEAS.: 56X39X38CM
GENERATOR
PHOCEE'NNE

April 23, 2013, Jabal Badro, Aleppo.

Children play in the rubble of buildings destroyed by what residents say was a Scud missile strike launched by the Syrian government.

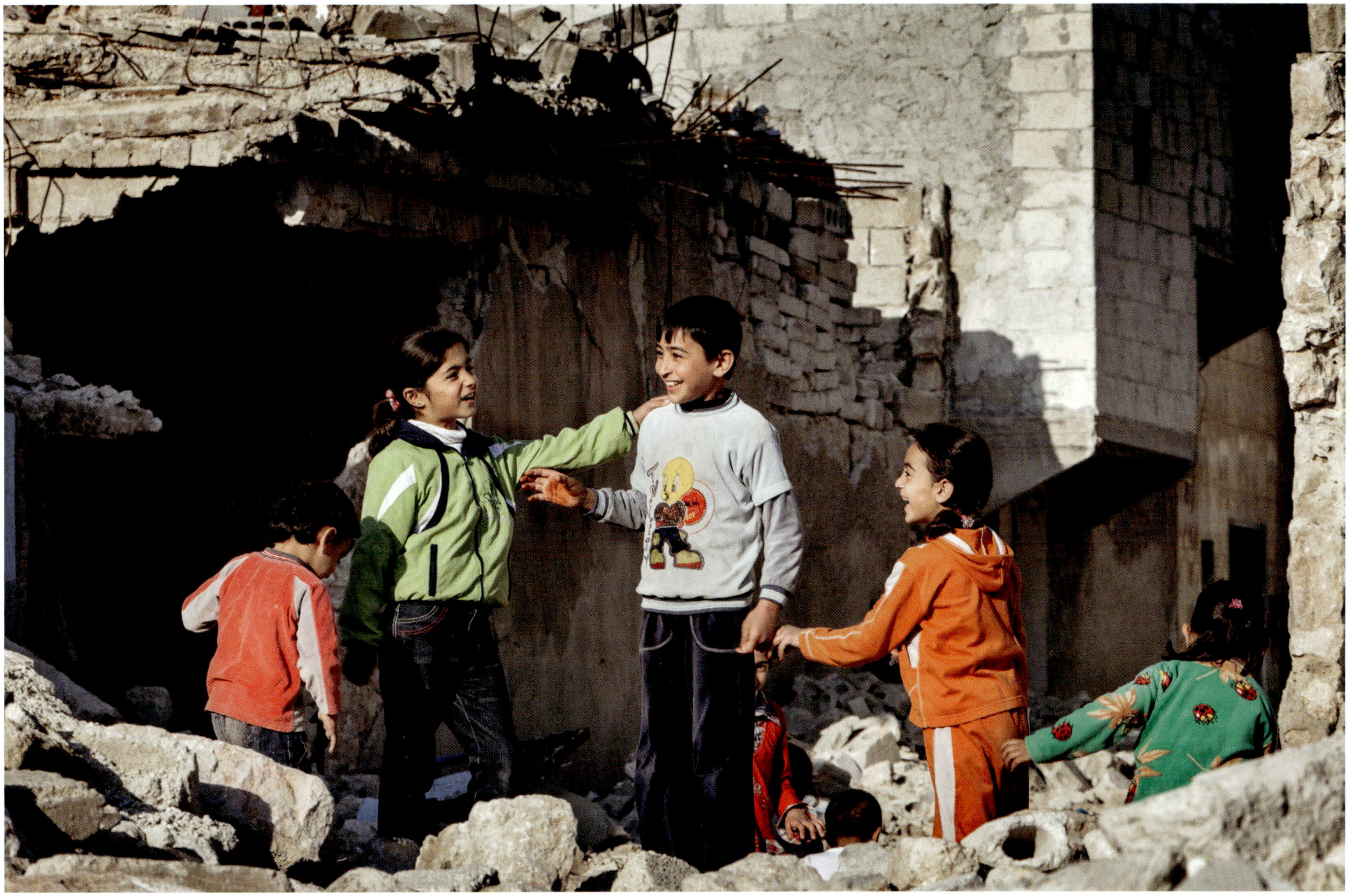

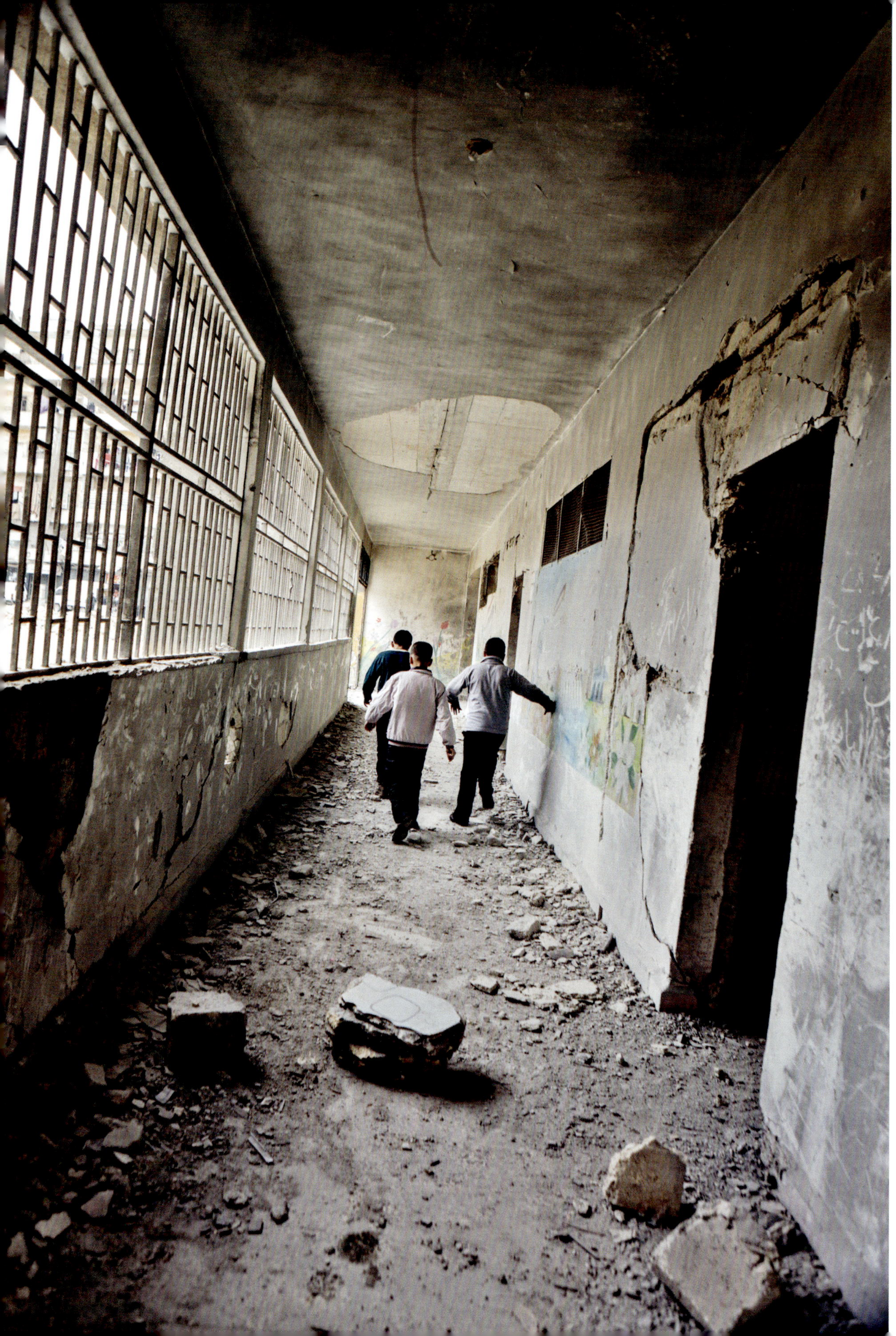

February 7,2013, Tarik al Bab, Aleppo.

Boys play in the hallway of a school damaged by shelling.

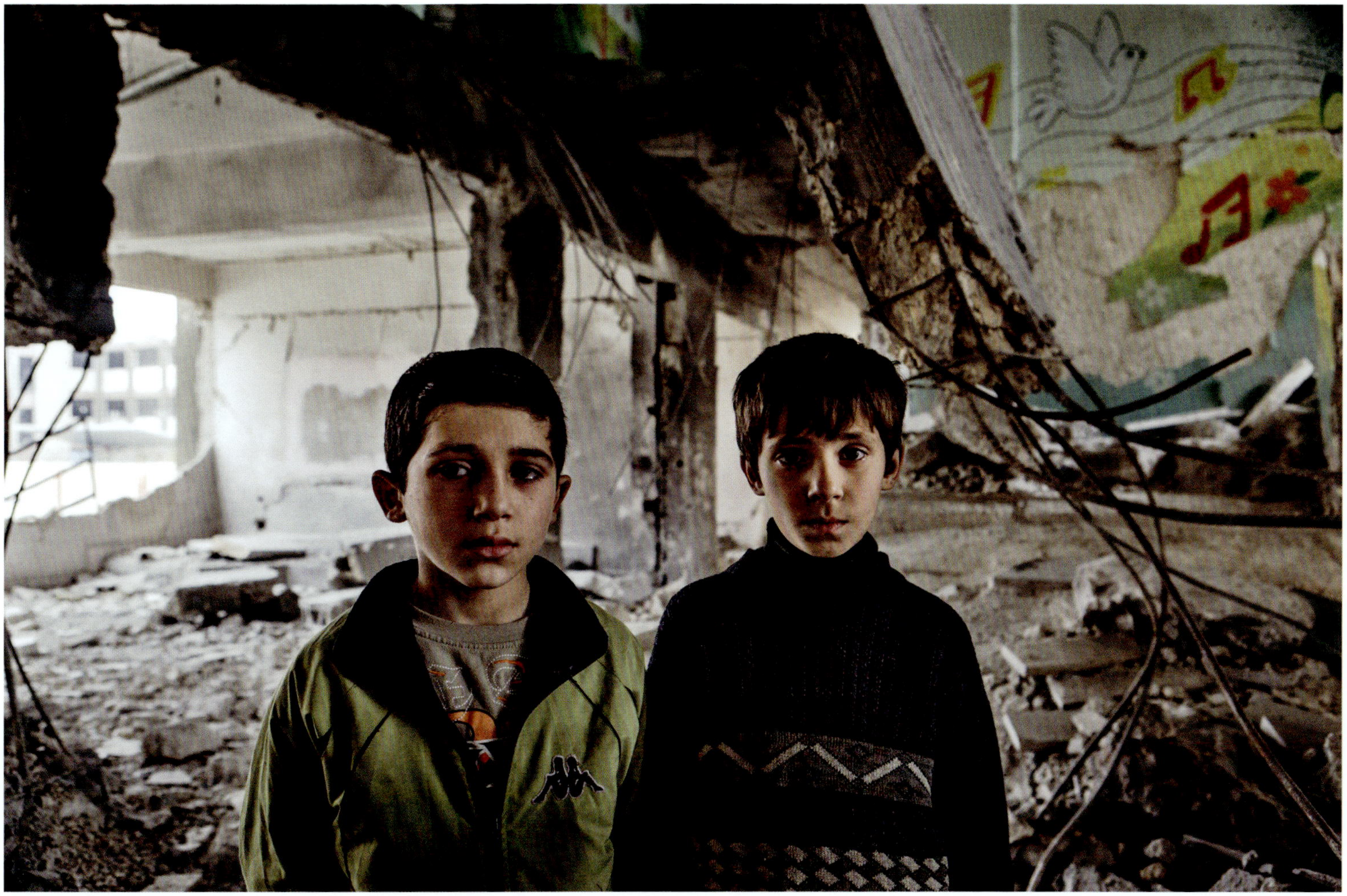

Febru ary 7, 2013, Tarik al Bab, Aleppo.

Two boys stand for a portrait in a damaged school building.

April 23, 2013, Sheikh Khider, Aleppo.

A classroom is in ruins after being damaged in heavy fighting.

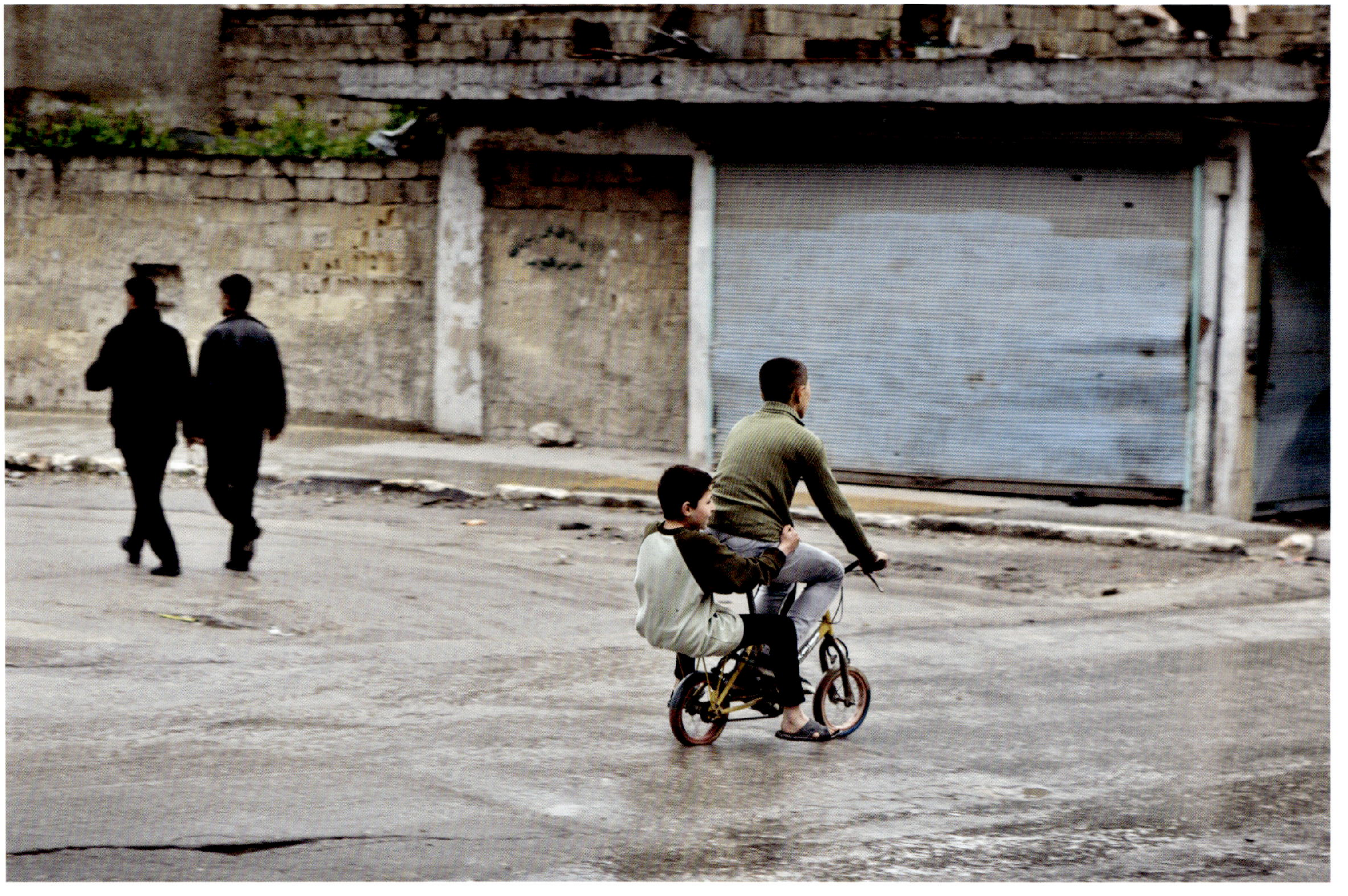

April 18, 2013, Sakhour, Aleppo.

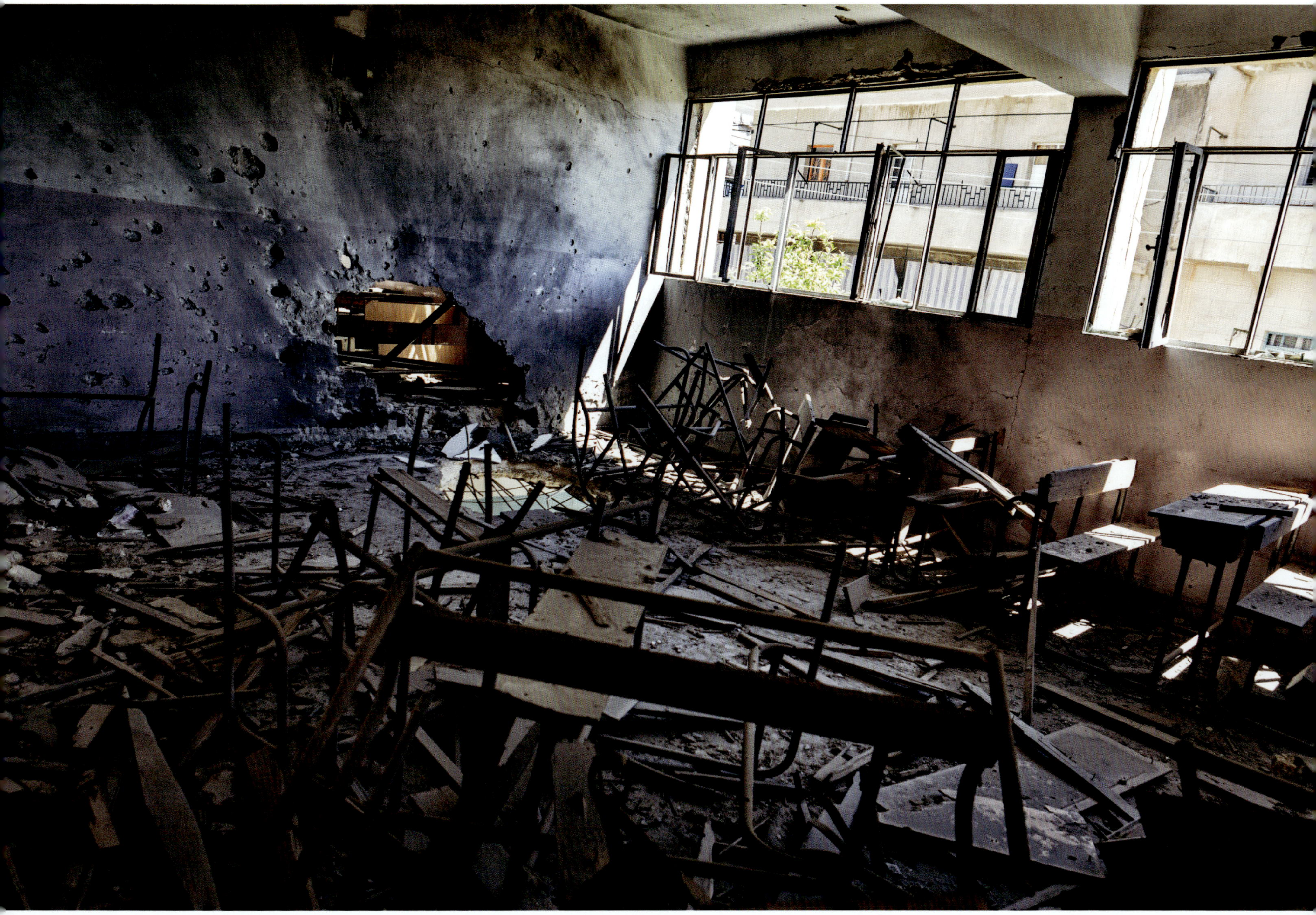

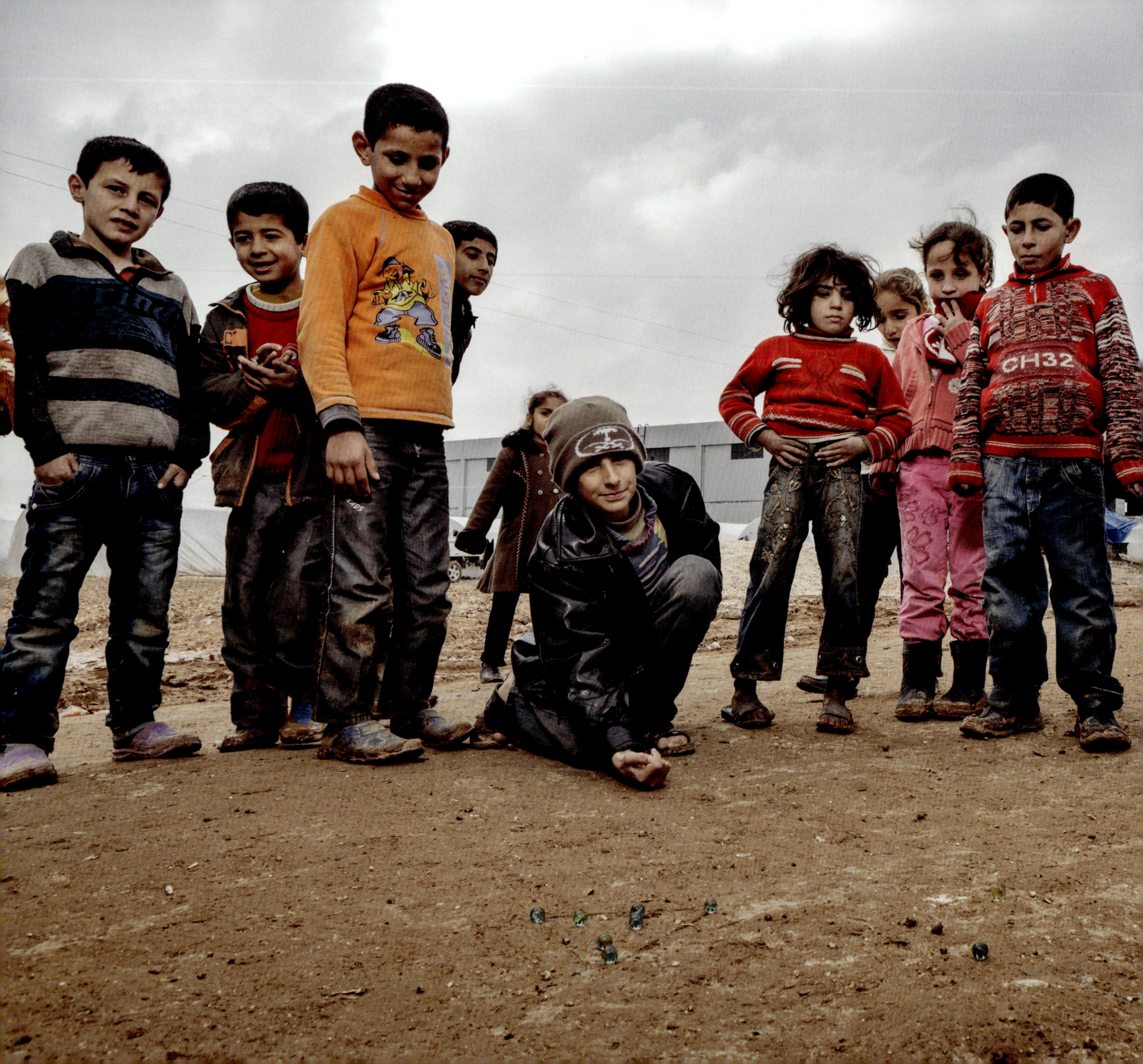
CH32

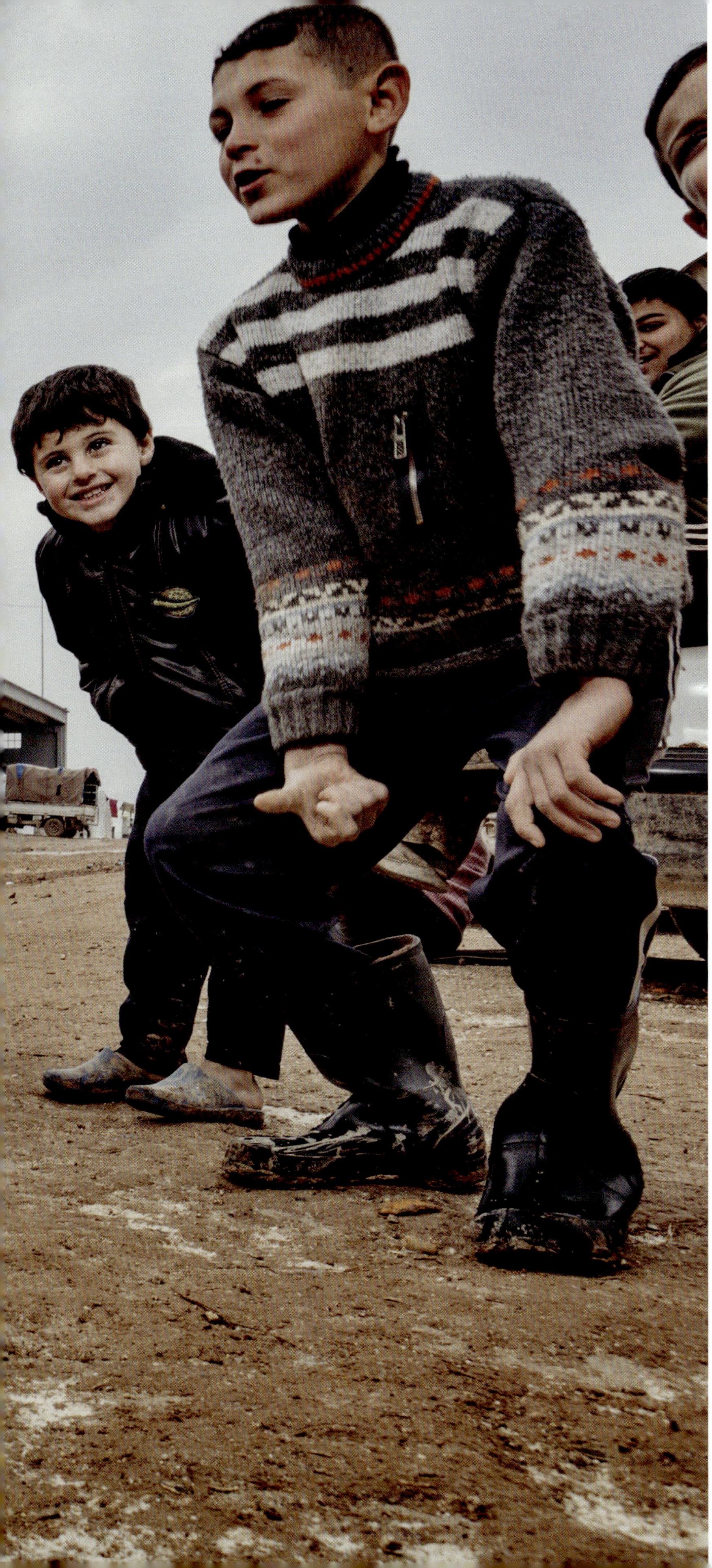

February 8, 2013, Bab al Salameh, Aleppo Province.

Kids play marbles in the Bab al Salemeh refugee camp next to the Turkish border.

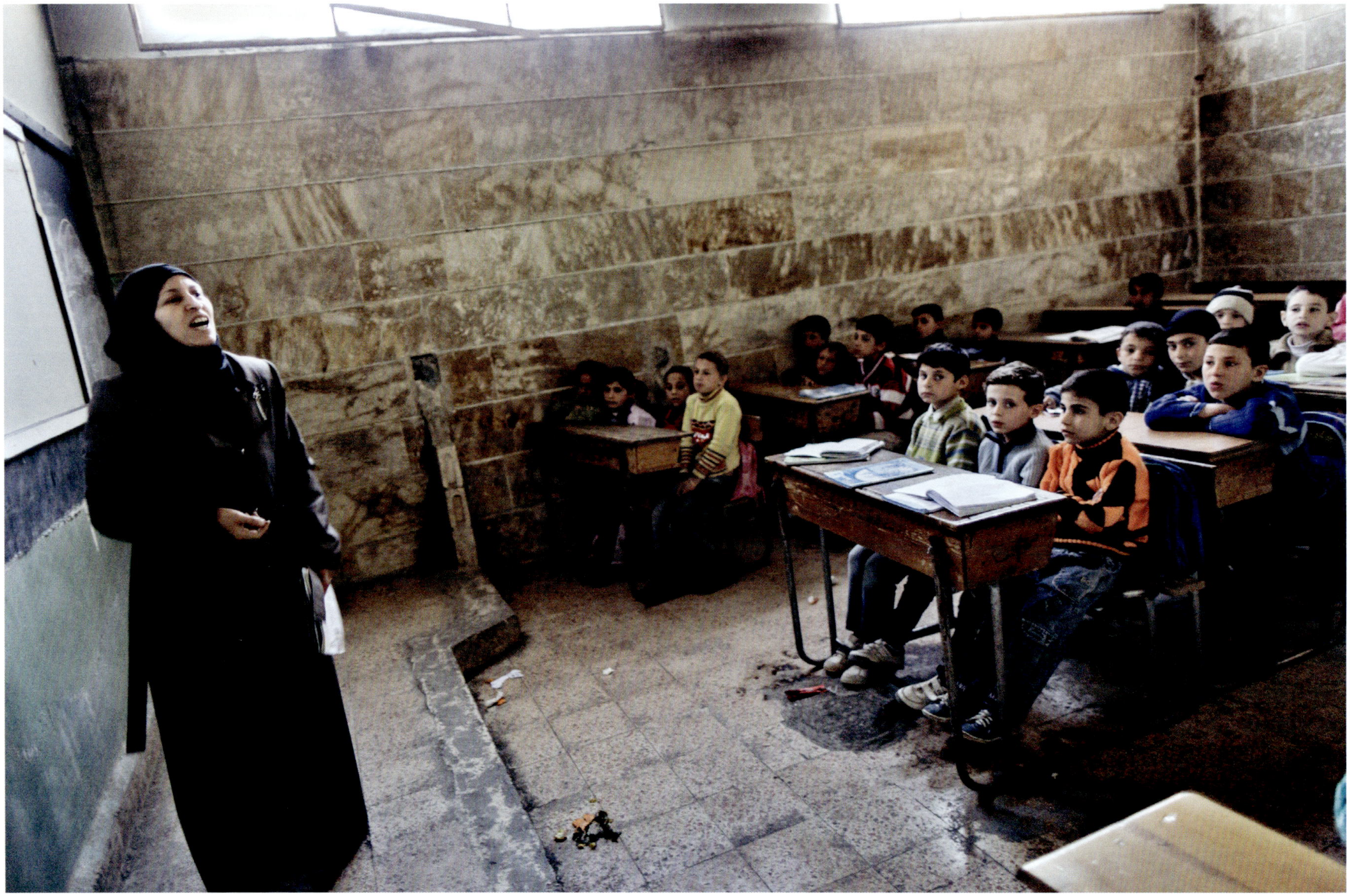

April 6, 2014, Maarrat al-Numaan, Idlib Province.

A teacher leads her class in English lessons. The local school, damaged by the fighting between Syrian Government and Opposition forces, was reopened in early 2014.

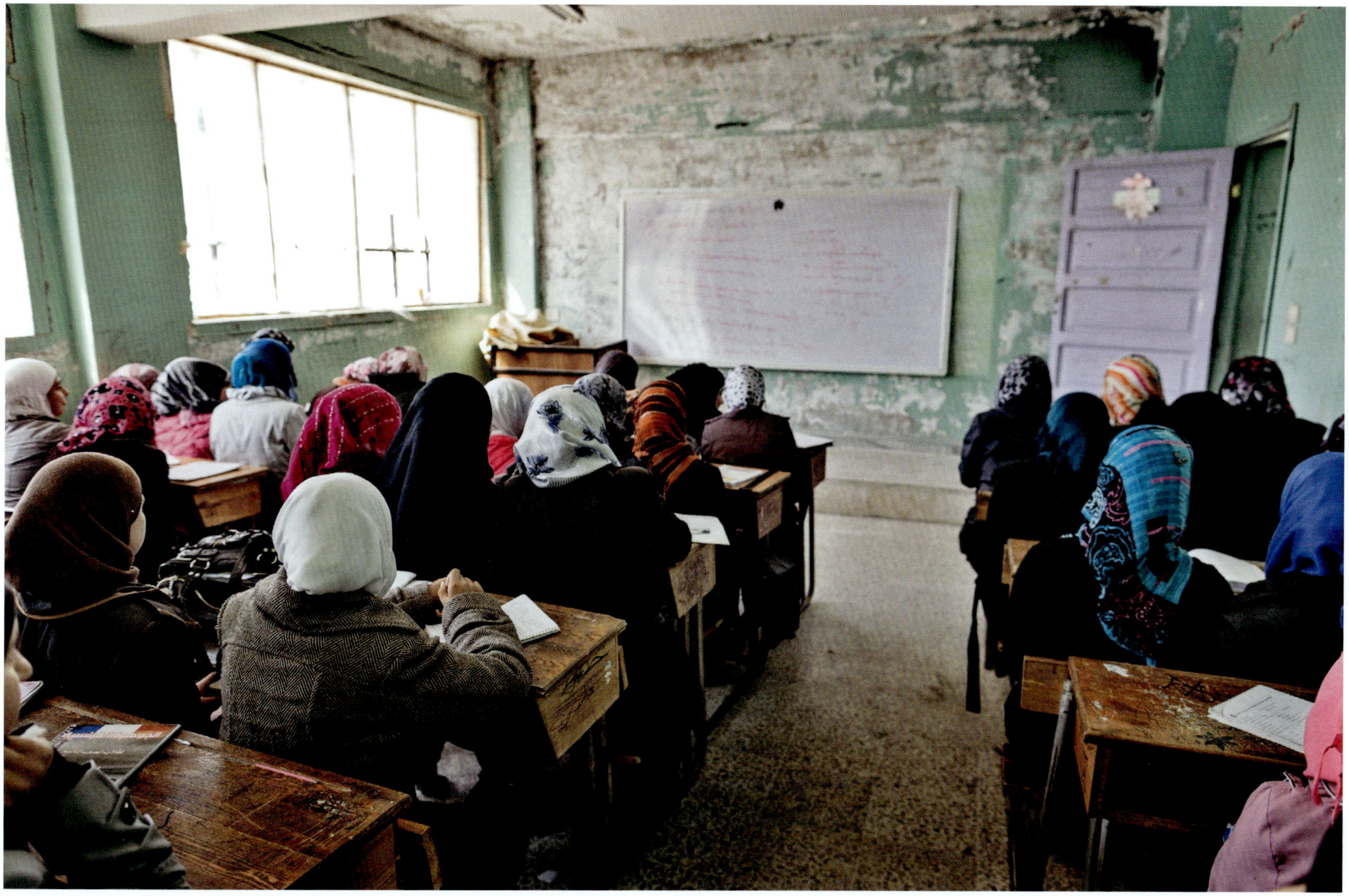

April 6, 2014, Maarat al-Numaan, Idlib Province.

Female students wait for their teacher.

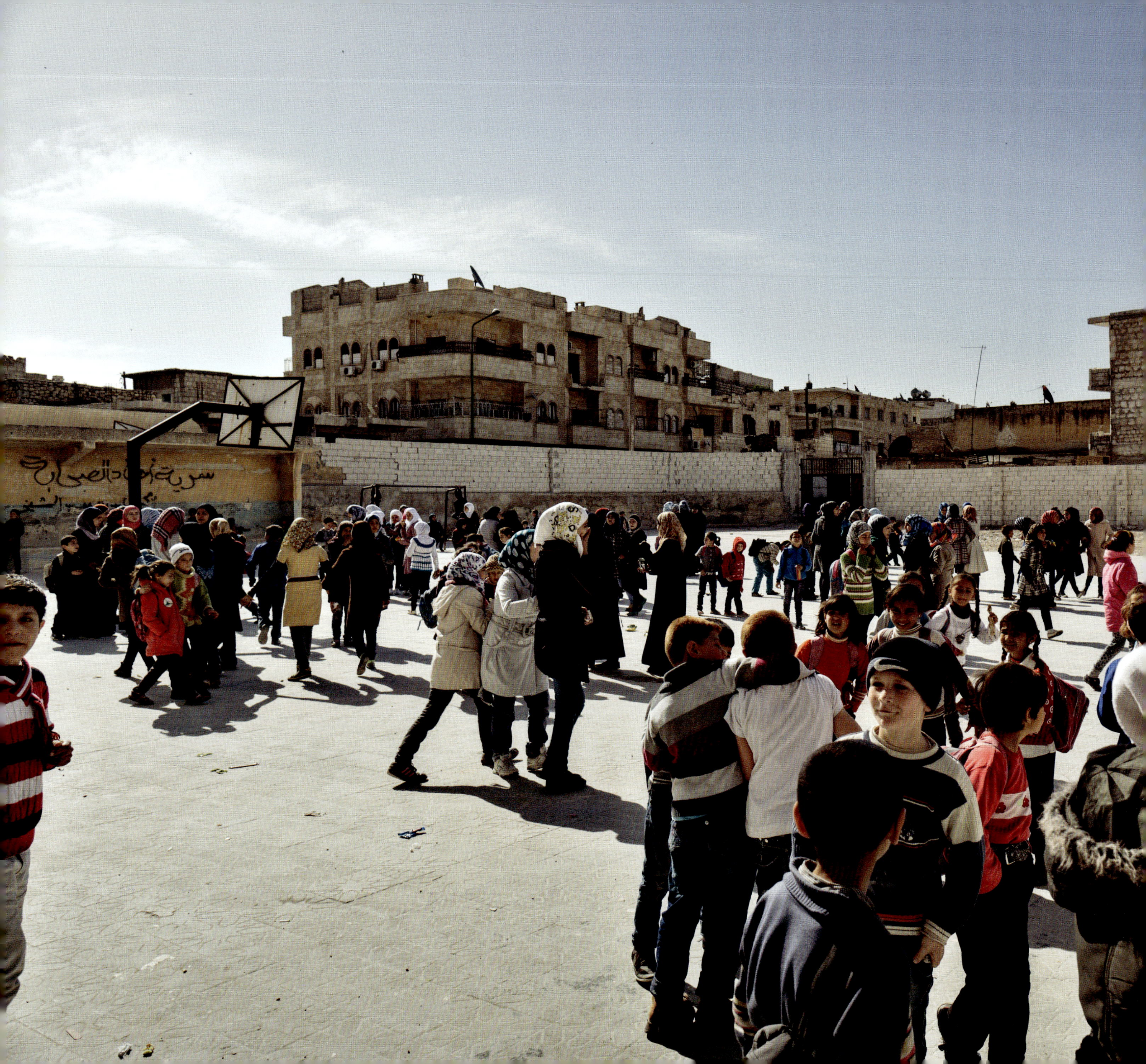

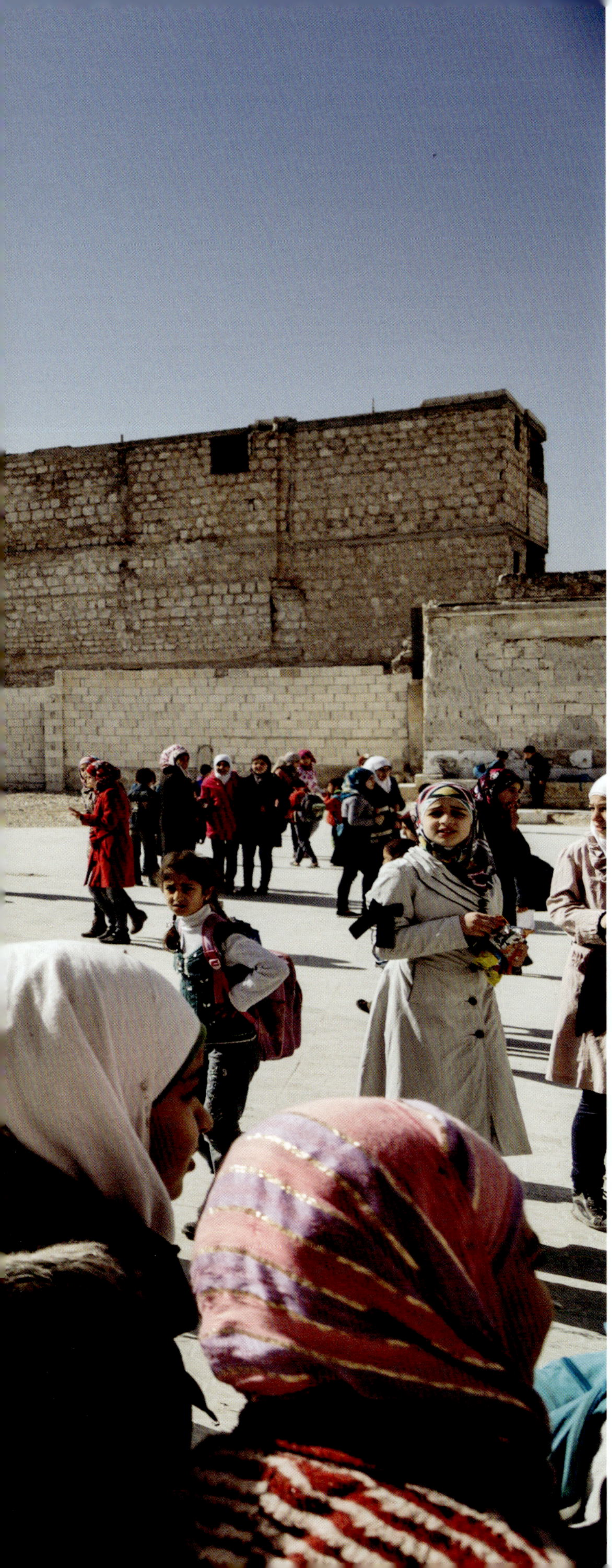

*April 6, 2014, Maarat al-Numaan,
Idlib Province.*

April 6, 2014, Maarat al-Numaan, Idlib Province.

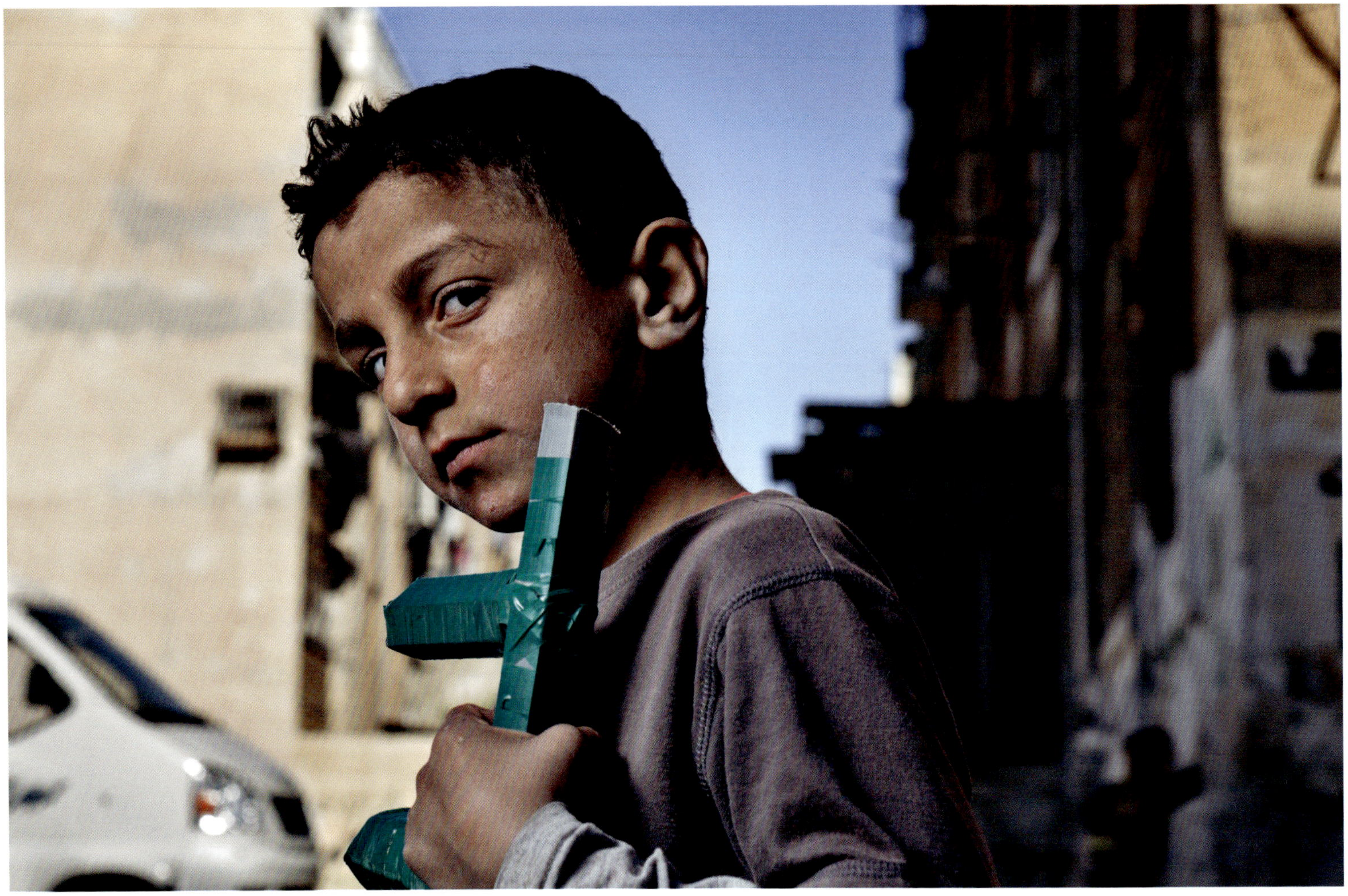

April 23, 2013, Masaken Hanano, Aleppo.

A boy holds a homemade toy gun. Millions of children in Syria have had their education and childhood interrupted by war.

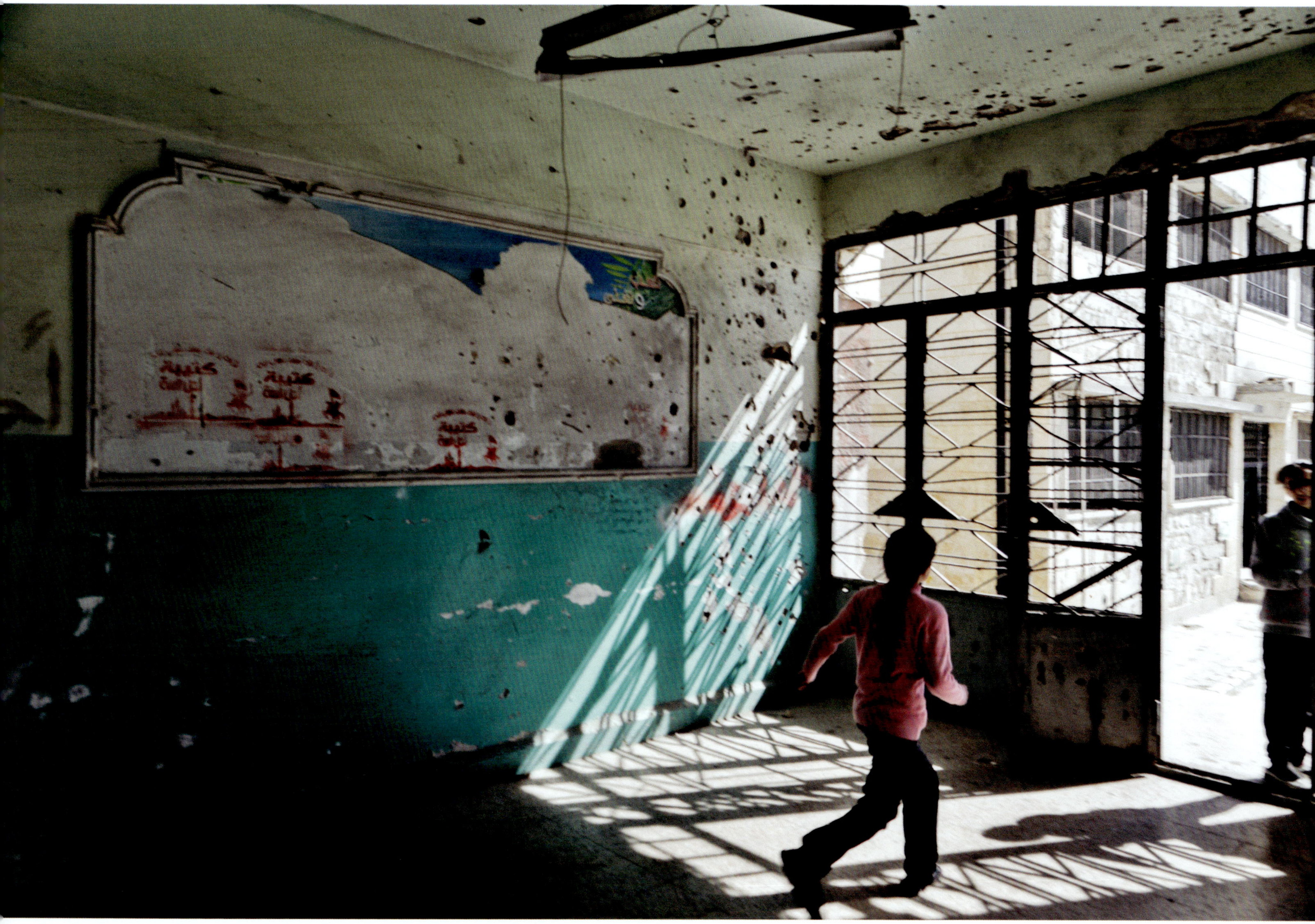
كتيبة
كتيبة
كتيبة

Breaking down the walls of prejudice or culture or ignorance is very important. To me, that means if I'm in a foreign culture, a foreign land, and I'm documenting a human condition there, I want to make it as human as possible. I don't want to objectify my subjects. I want to connect to my subjects. I want to try in some way to show that this parent crying over a sick child is the same emotion, the same feeling that you or I or your neighbor in America or Europe or Japan or China...the same kind of human emotions that we all have. We're all the same in so many ways. Ninety-nine percent of the world simply wants to have food, shelter, wants their children to do better than they did; they love their kids, and have the same feelings, emotions, goals and ambitions as we do. Often times, people in isolated worlds, whether it's in America or Europe or other places, think that these people on those boats or those people in those camps or those people in those bombed-out buildings are somehow different, not even human. They're not the same as me because I'm not in that situation and I'm healthy and I'm taking care of my children and shame on them for getting themselves in that place. Those are exactly the kinds of barriers we're trying to break down through our imagery. That's where, as photographers and filmmakers, if we can humanize these stories and show that if not for the luck of the draw that could be me, and someday it might be. Whether it's a hurricane like Katrina or earthquakes or other disasters, forest fires, or even gun violence in America, no people, no culture, no nation is immune from tragedy. How we, as human beings and as humanity, respond to that is going to be decided in great part by the imagery we see of those events and those people.

—John Rowe

April 18, 2013, Bustan al Basha, Aleppo.

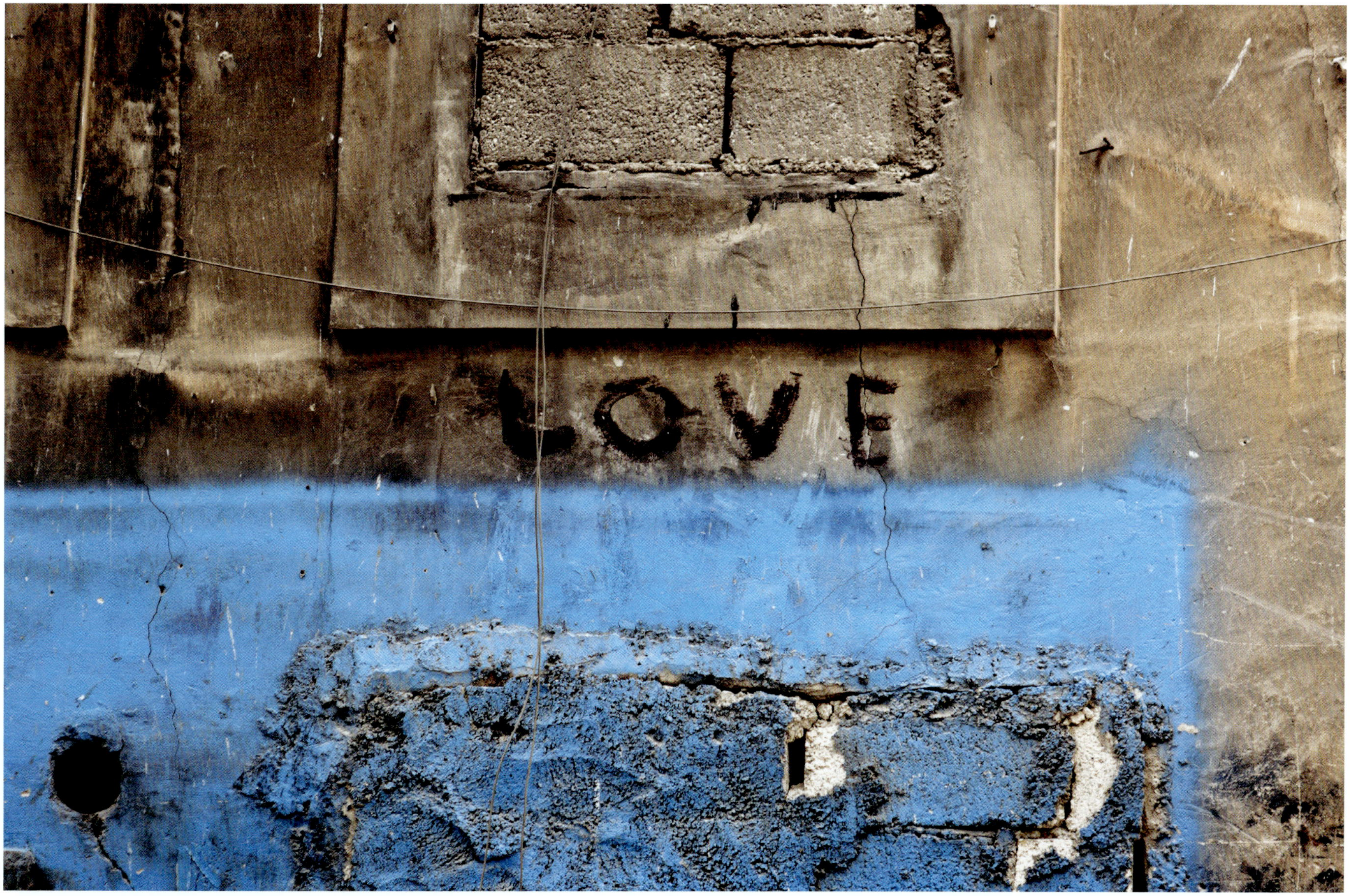
LOVE

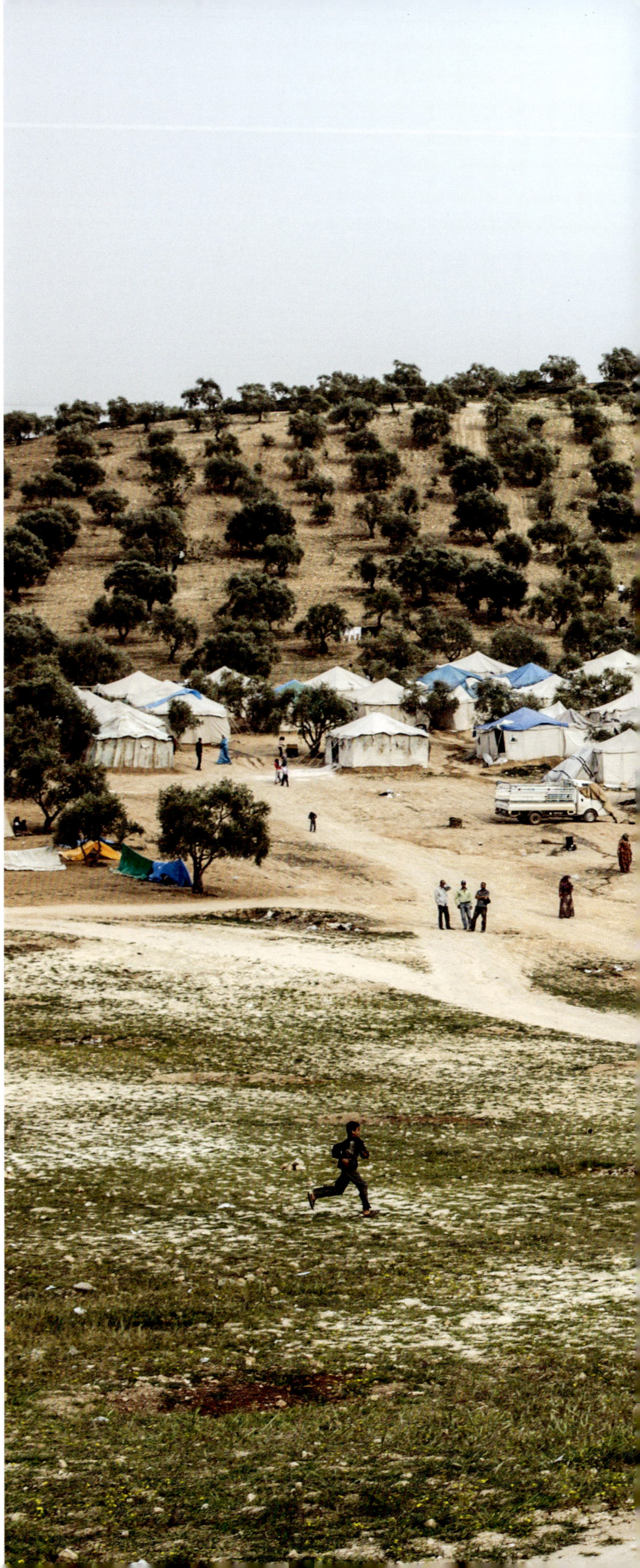

April 5, 2014, Atmeh Refugee Camp, Idlib Province.

Tent cities spread up into olive-covered hills at the Atmeh refugee camp. The camp sits just across the border from Turkey, inside Syria. It is not one organized camp, but a series of small tent cities that have sprung up since the start of the war as people began to be displaced by fighting. Estimates placed the total population of the camp at around 30,000 persons in 2014.

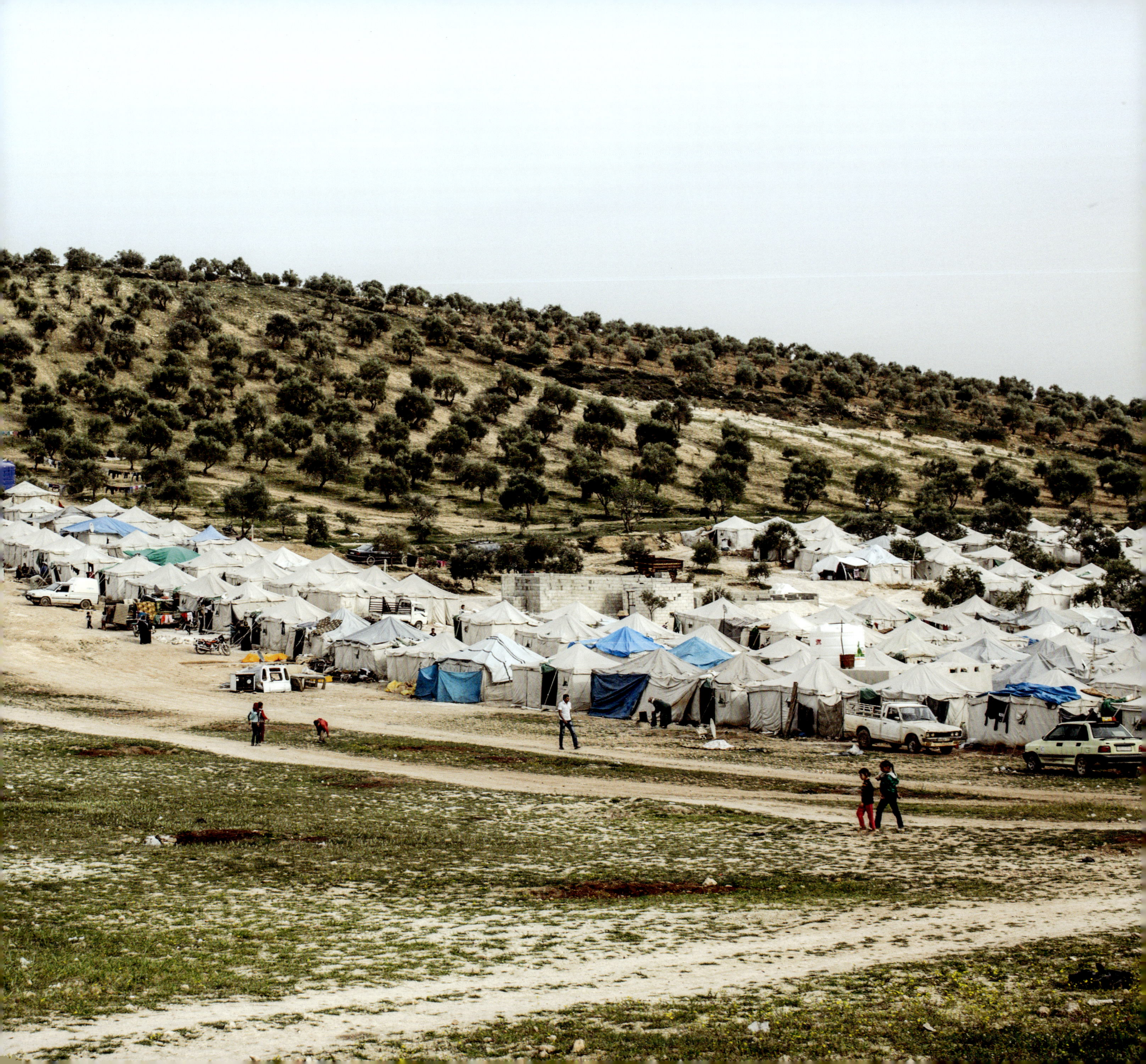

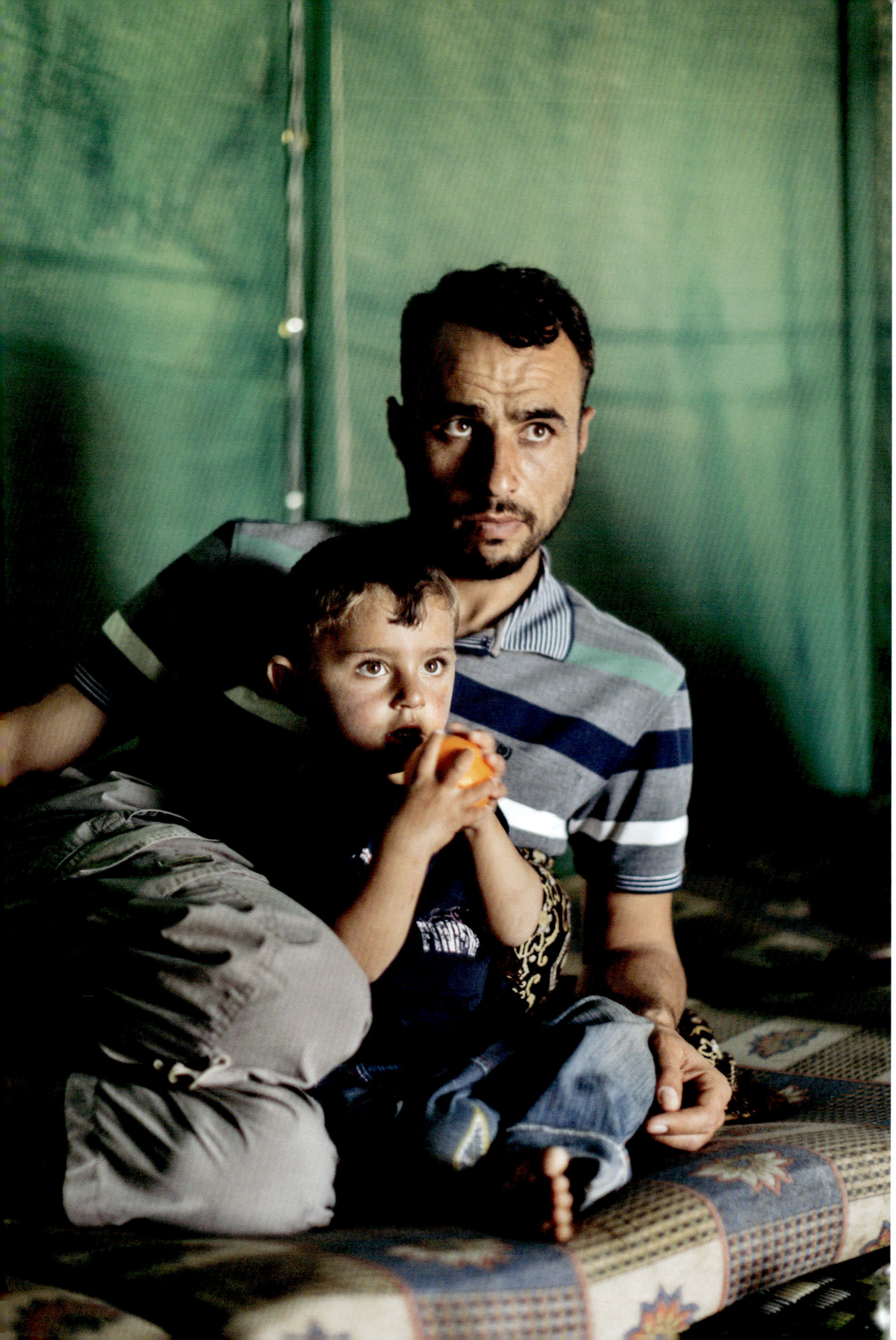

April 5, 2014, Atmeh, Idlib Province.

Walid Ibrahim, 36, cradles his nephew as he eats an orange in a neighbor's tent.

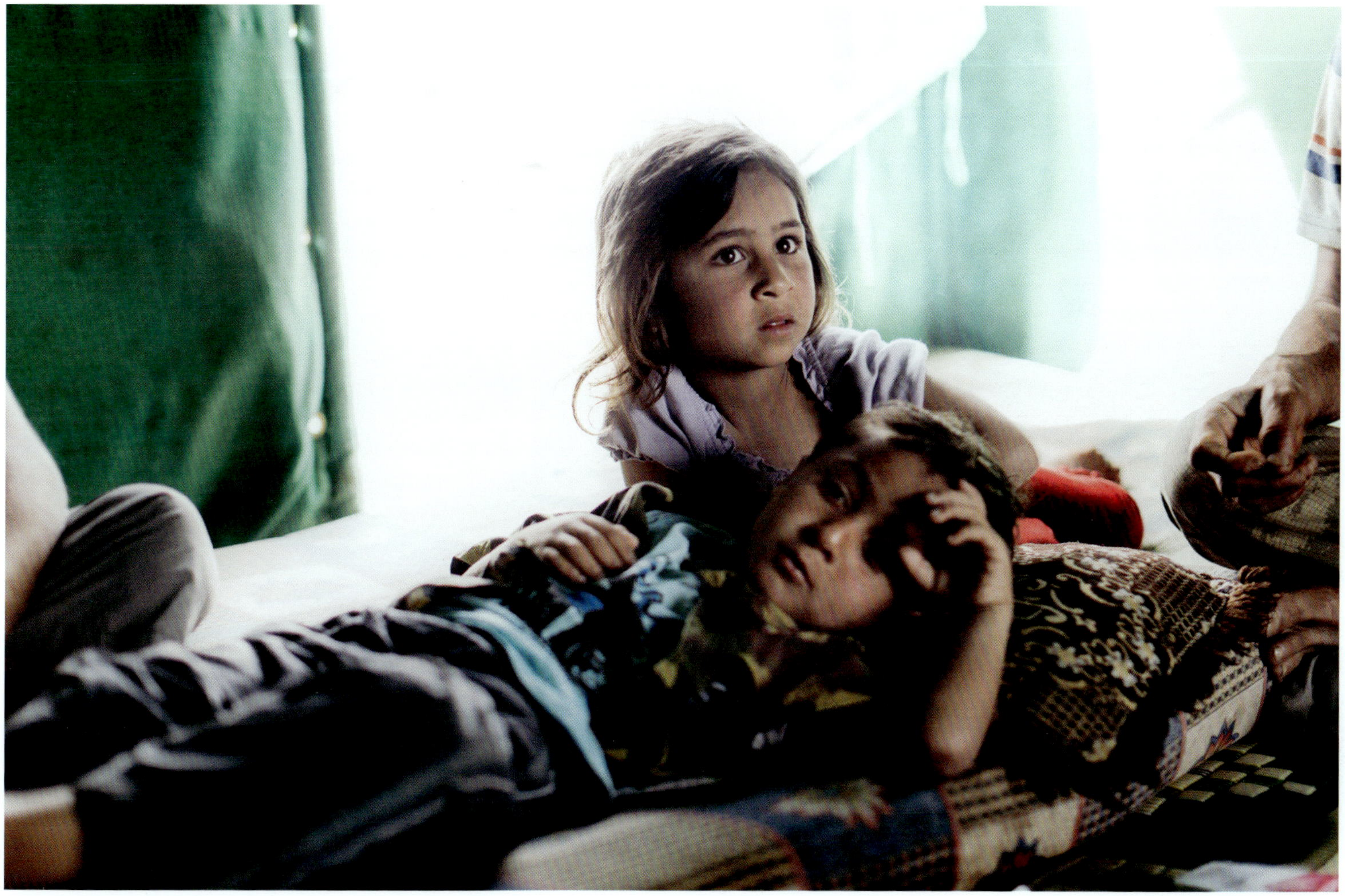

April 5, 2014, Atmeh, Idlib Province

Two of Abu Taha's children rest in the tent their 16 family members share. Abu Taha fights part time with the Free Syrian Army. His son Taha, 20, defected from the Syrian Army and also fights with the FSA; he was recovering from a wound suffered in a battle.

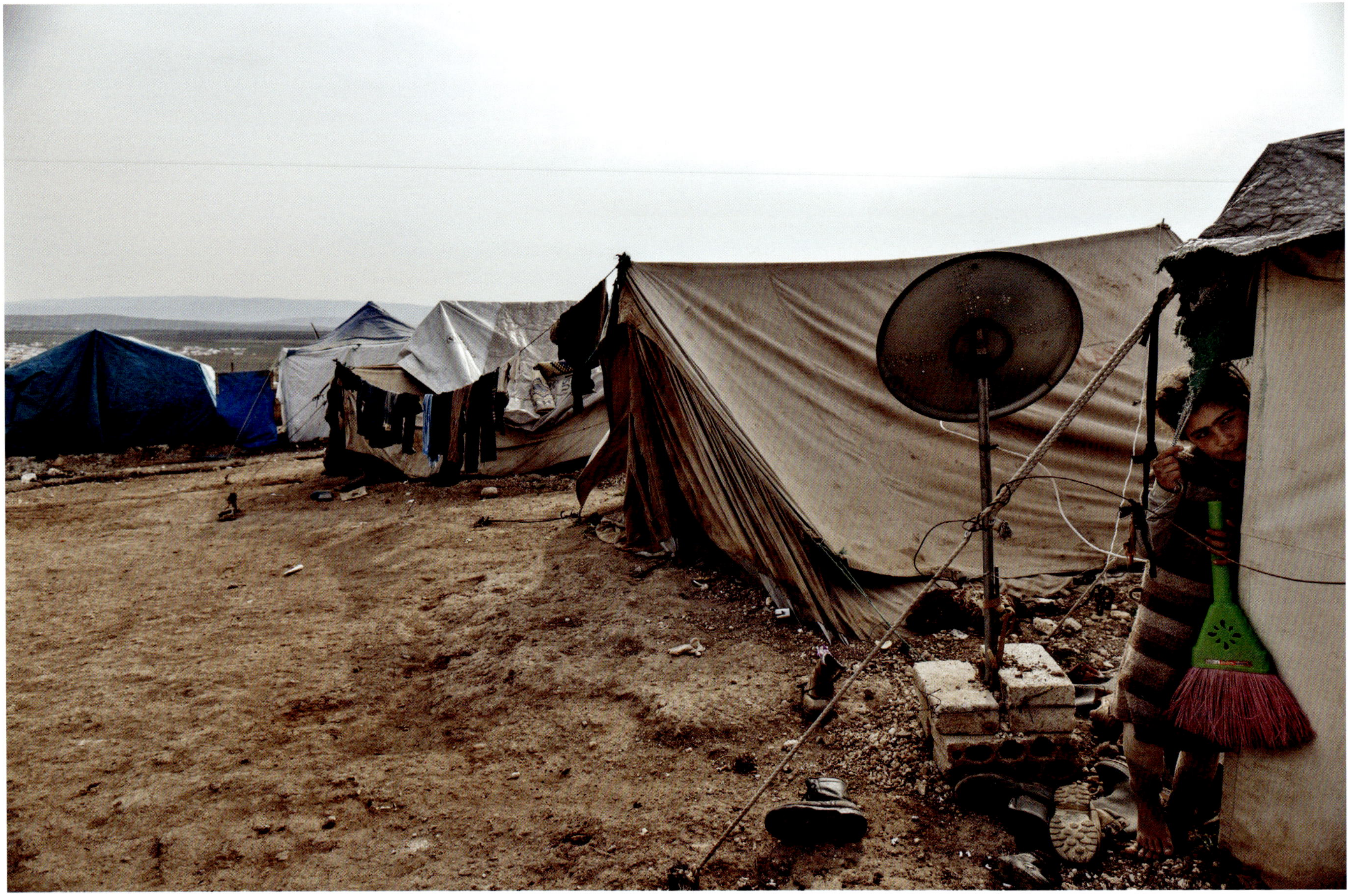

April 5, 2014, Atmeh, Idlib.

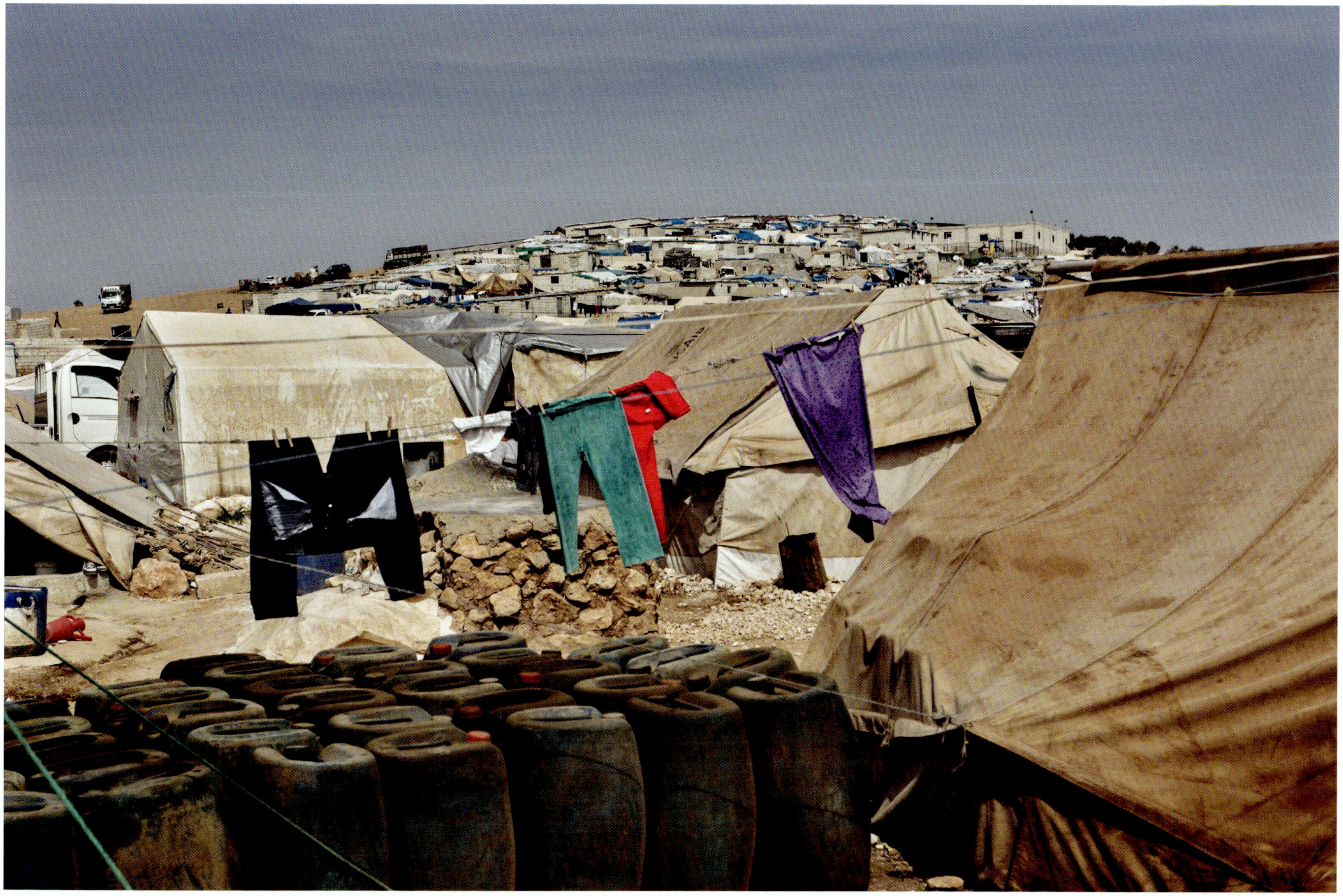

April 5, 2014, Atmeh, Idlib.

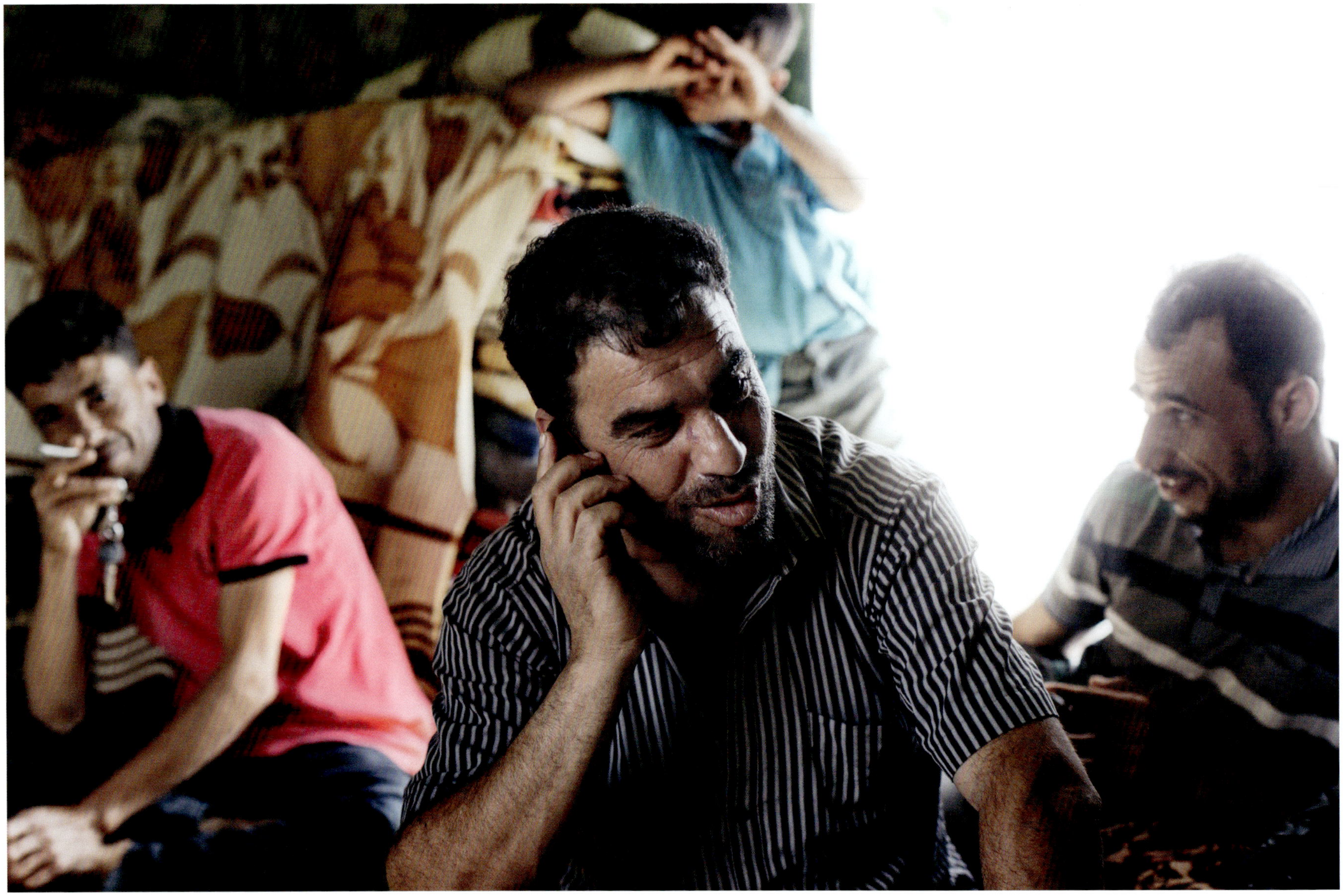

April 5 2014, Atmeh, Idlib.

Walid Ibrahim's brother talks on his mobile phone.

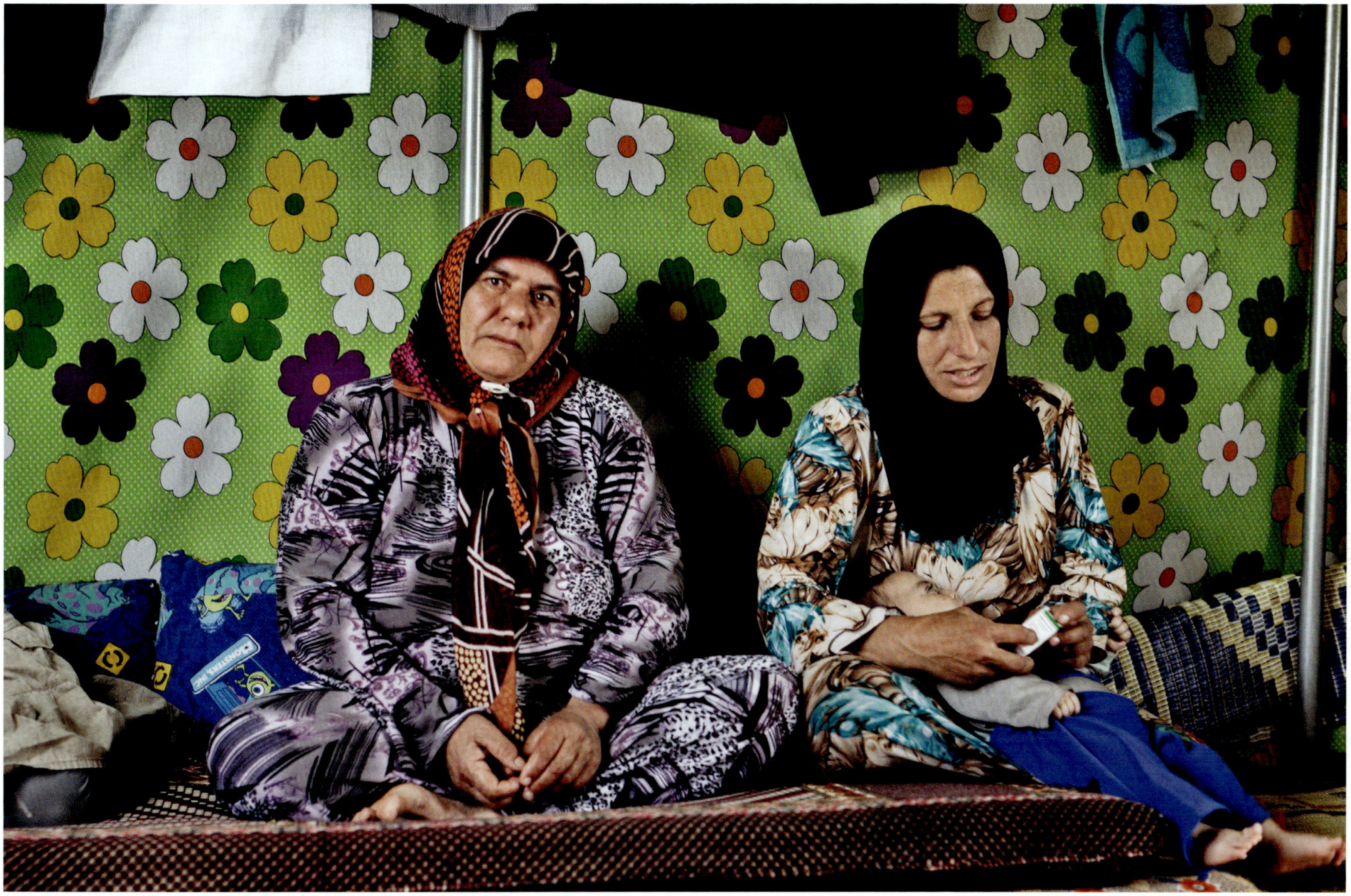

April 5, 2014, Atmeh, Idlib.

The wife of Hajji Kharim Ibrahim, 62, sits with one of her daughters inside one of the two tents they share with their four sons, four daughters, and their families. Kharim says, "We can live with hunger and thirst and heat and cold, but we can never live with the Regime. I want the West to understand this."

April 5, 2014, Atmeh, Idlib.

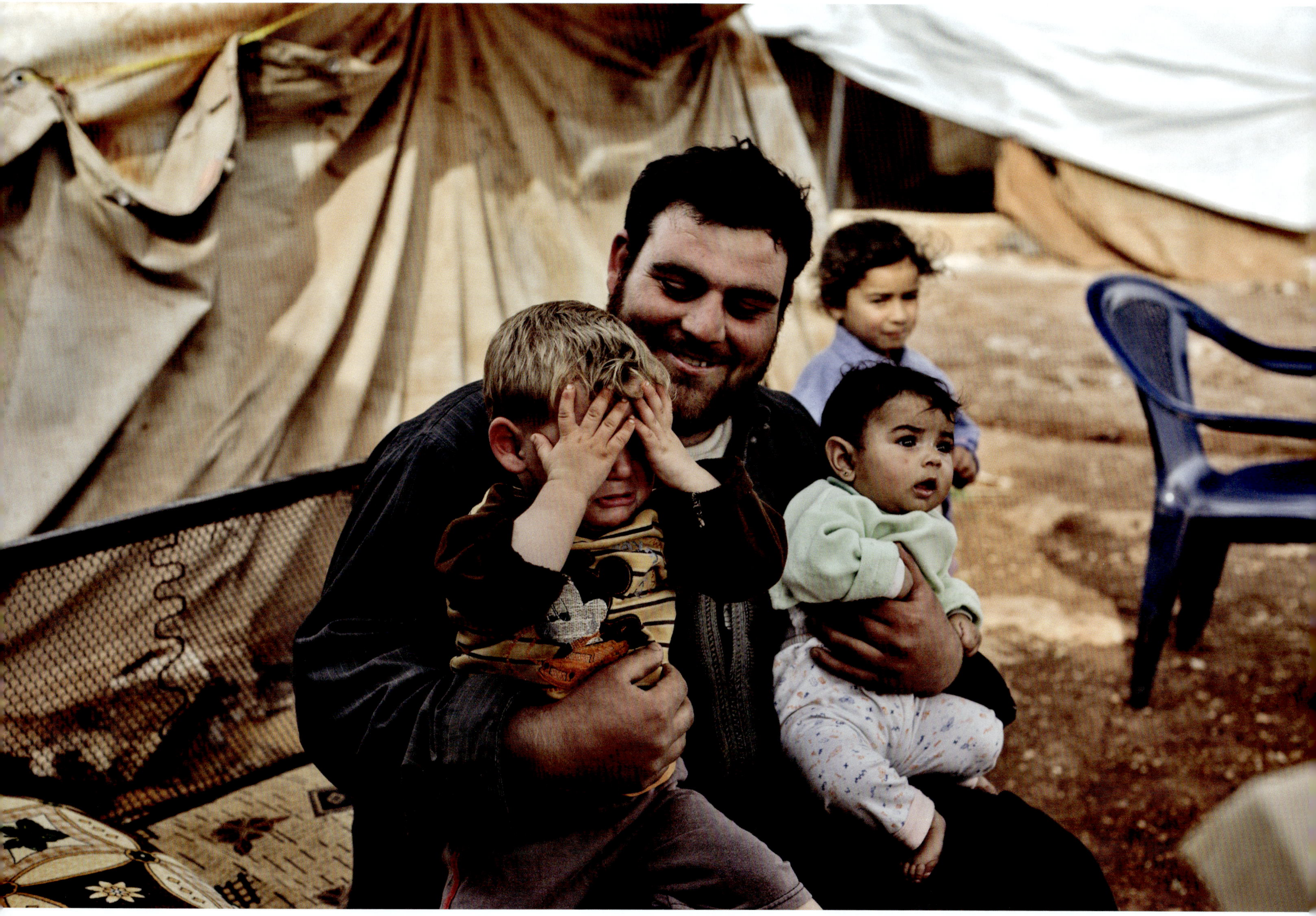

I think that now more than ever it's important to use all of your artistic abilities to create something really special. If you're in a situation where you're documenting human tragedy, number one, you have a responsibility to those people, those victims, the people you're photographing. To not give them the time or the respect or the effort to do it in the best way you know possible, to do that would be disrespecting them. I almost think that the more difficult the situation, the more serious the tragedy, the more important the responsibility the photojournalist has to show that tragedy in a way that that person knows will resonate with the audience, with the people who see that picture.

I think that tragedy needs to be photographed well. A photographer with experience and knowledge about composition and lighting and exposure and all of these things, really can help not only to tell the story in a single photograph but also elicit emotion. That's the difference between somebody holding up an iPhone and snapping a quick picture without giving any consideration to the composition or where the horizon is or where the sun is, and a trained photographer who sees a situation, wants to report it, wants to tell that story, has one picture to do it, and needs to include the right elements, the right composition and the right combination of ingredients so that it is seen. It would rise above the noise of the crowd, if you will, of all those phone photos that are being taken, into something really iconic and something really special.

—John Rowe

April 21, 2013, Aleppo.

Horses graze in a small plot of farmland between the Bustan al Basha and Sheikh Maqsood Neighborhoods.

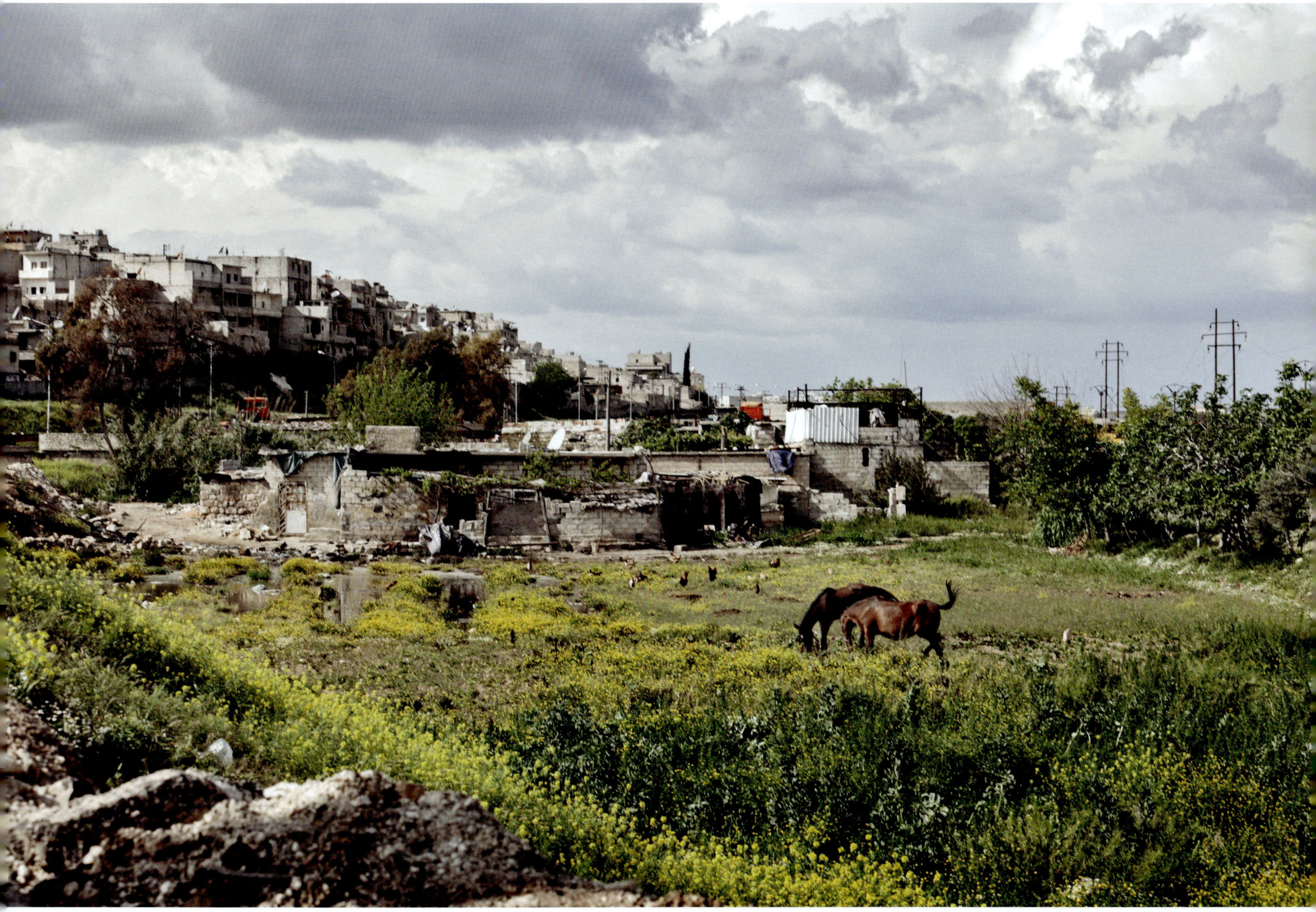

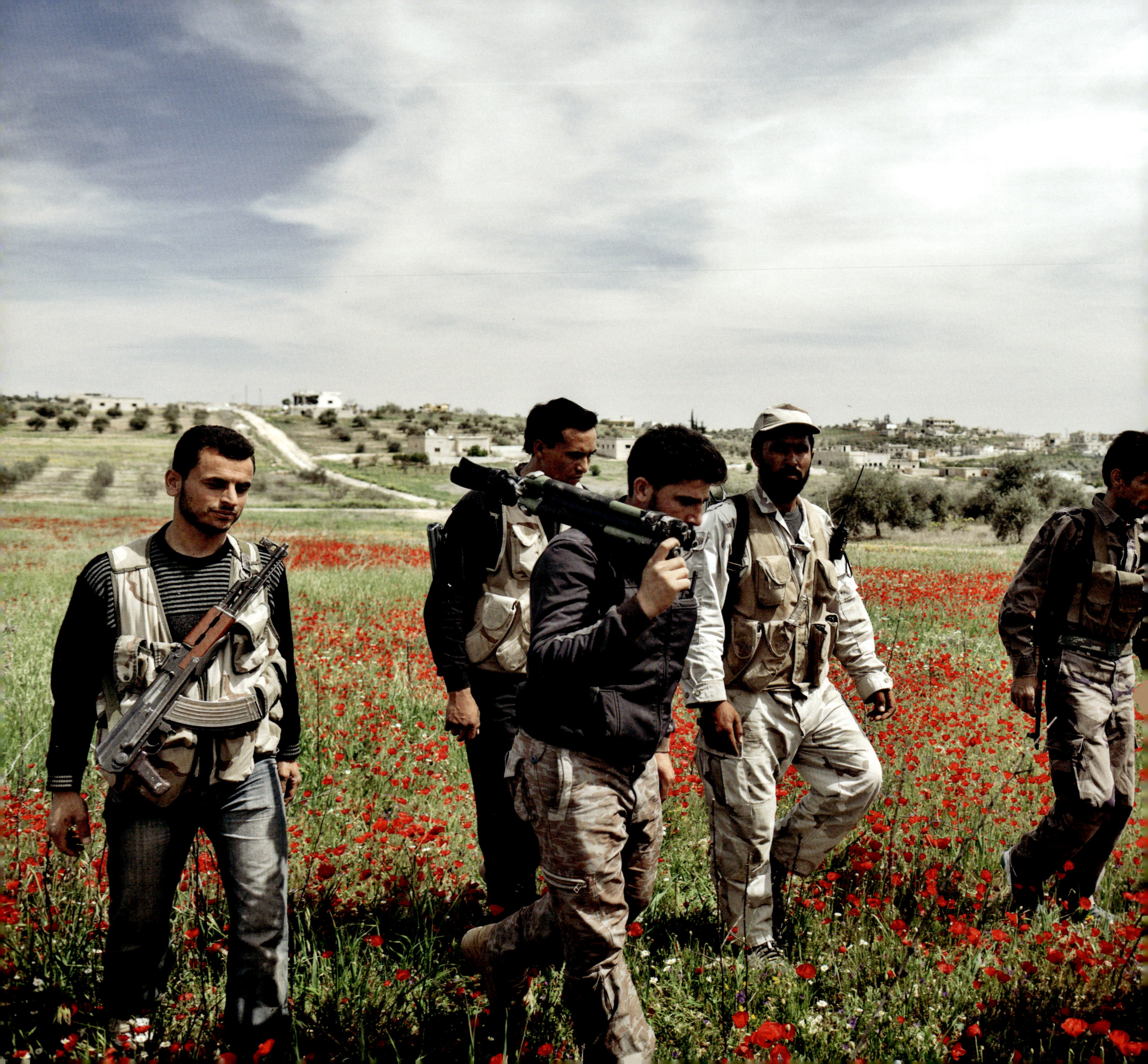

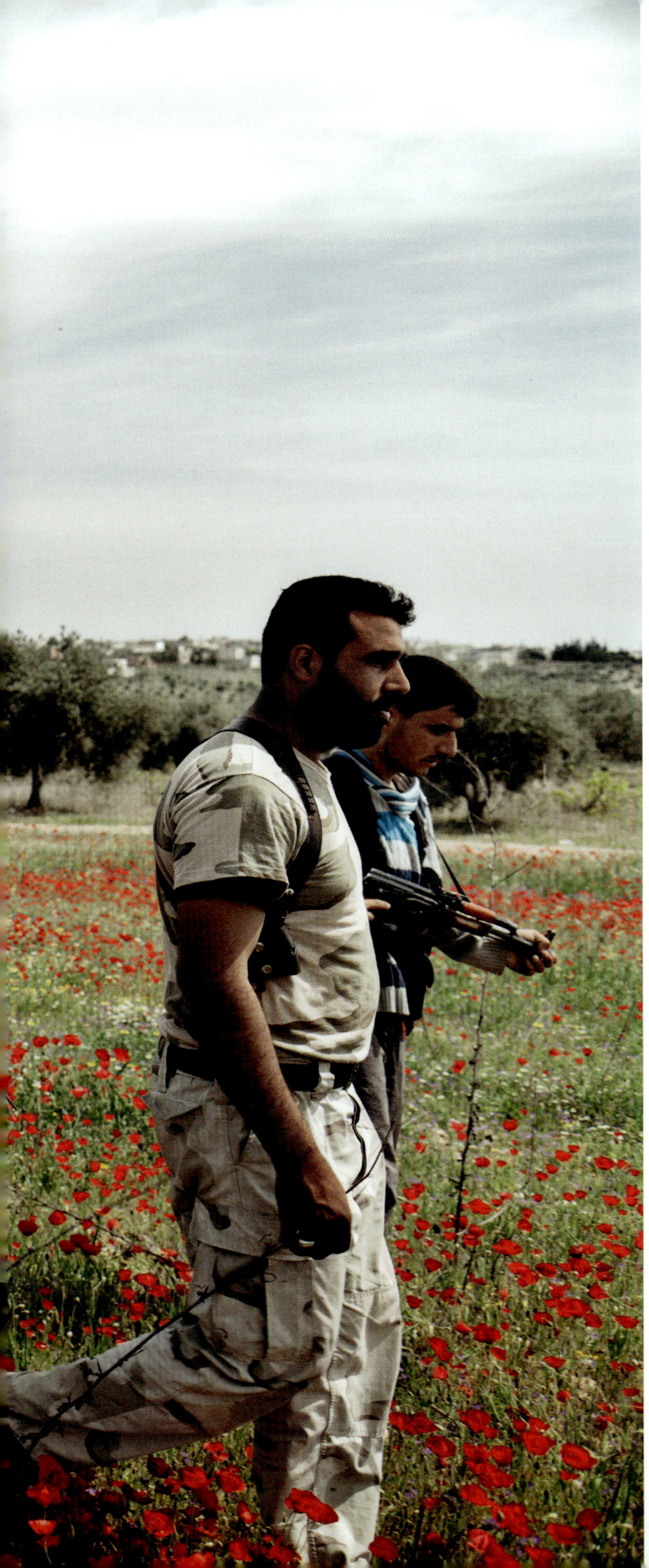

April 6, 2014, Hesh, Idlib.

Syrian Revolutionaries Front (SRF) fighters walk through a field near the strategic M5 Damascus-Aleppo highway during a battle near the town of Hesh.

Right: *April 6, 2014, Hesh, Idlib.*

SRF artillery strikes a Syrian Government position just off the Aleppo-Damascus Highway.

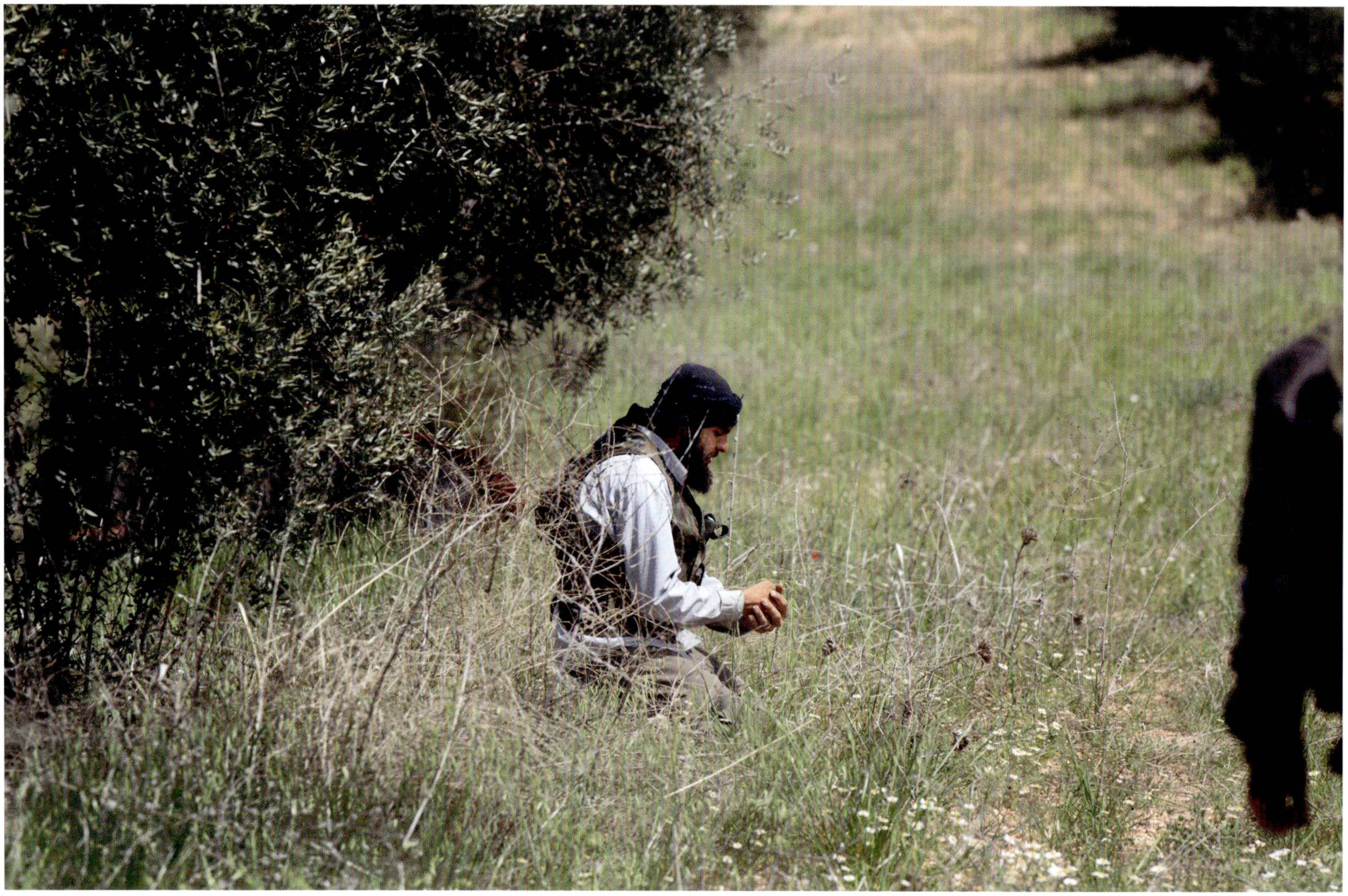

Top: *April 6, 2014, Hesh, Idlib.*

An SRF fighter prays in a field during the battle for Hesh.

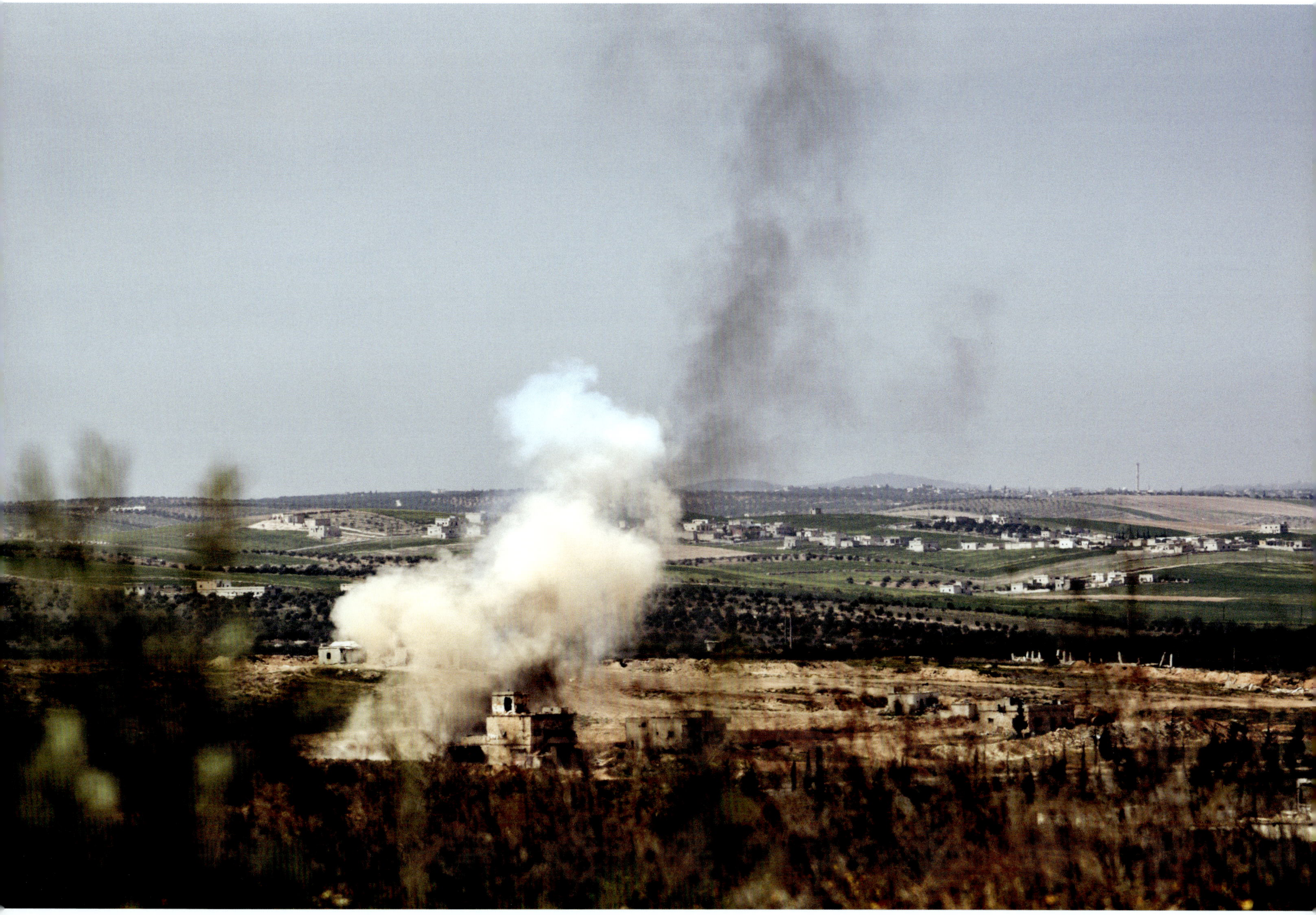

Right: *April 6, 2014, Kafr Nabl, Idlib.*

SRF fighters.

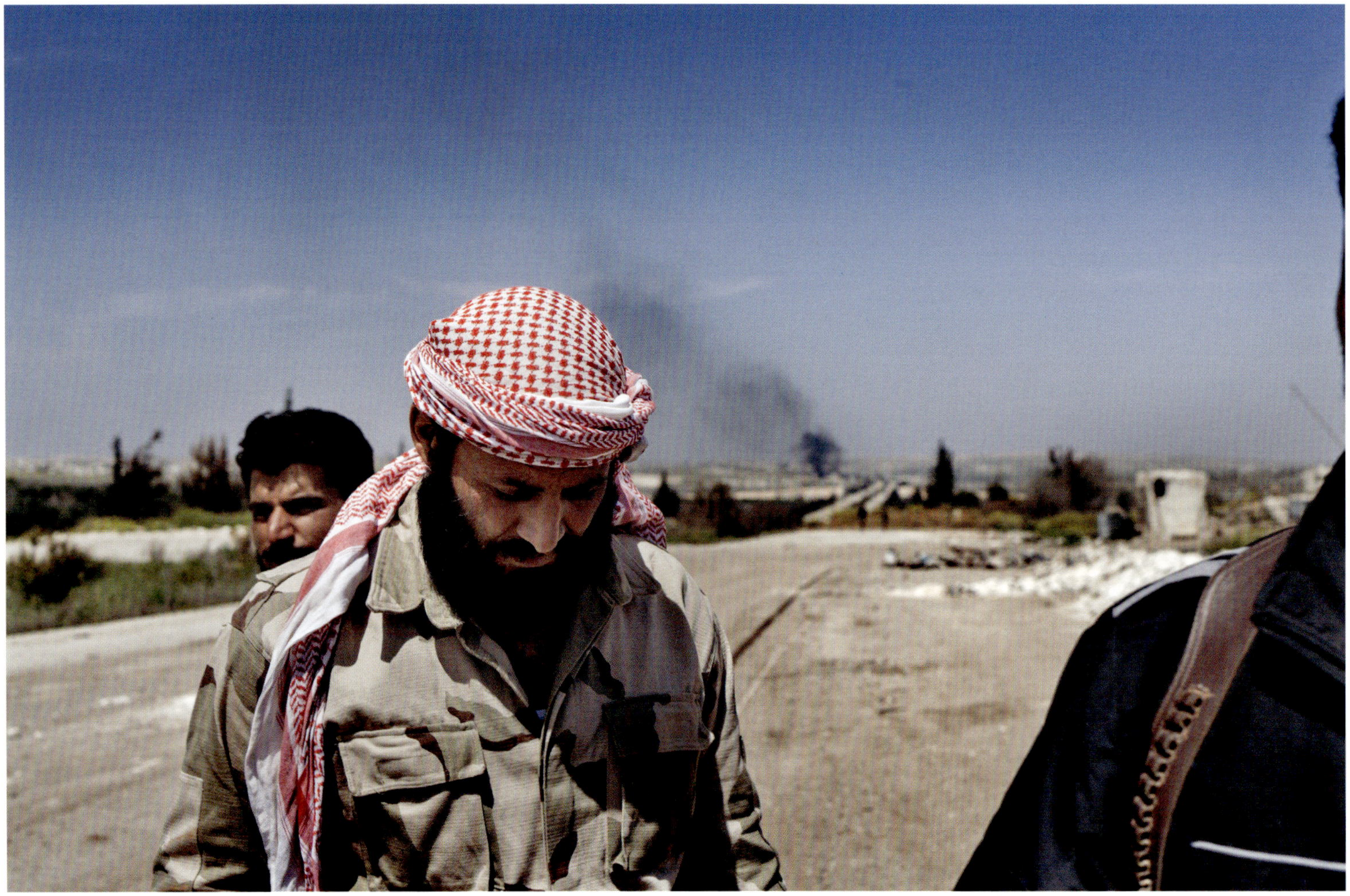

Top: *April 6, 2014, Hesh, Idlib.*

An SRF unit commander paces during a battle with Syrian Army troops as a Syrian Government battle tank burns in the background on the strategic M5 Aleppo-Damascus Highway near the town of Hesh. The SRF offensive started the night before and overtook several miles of the strategic road.

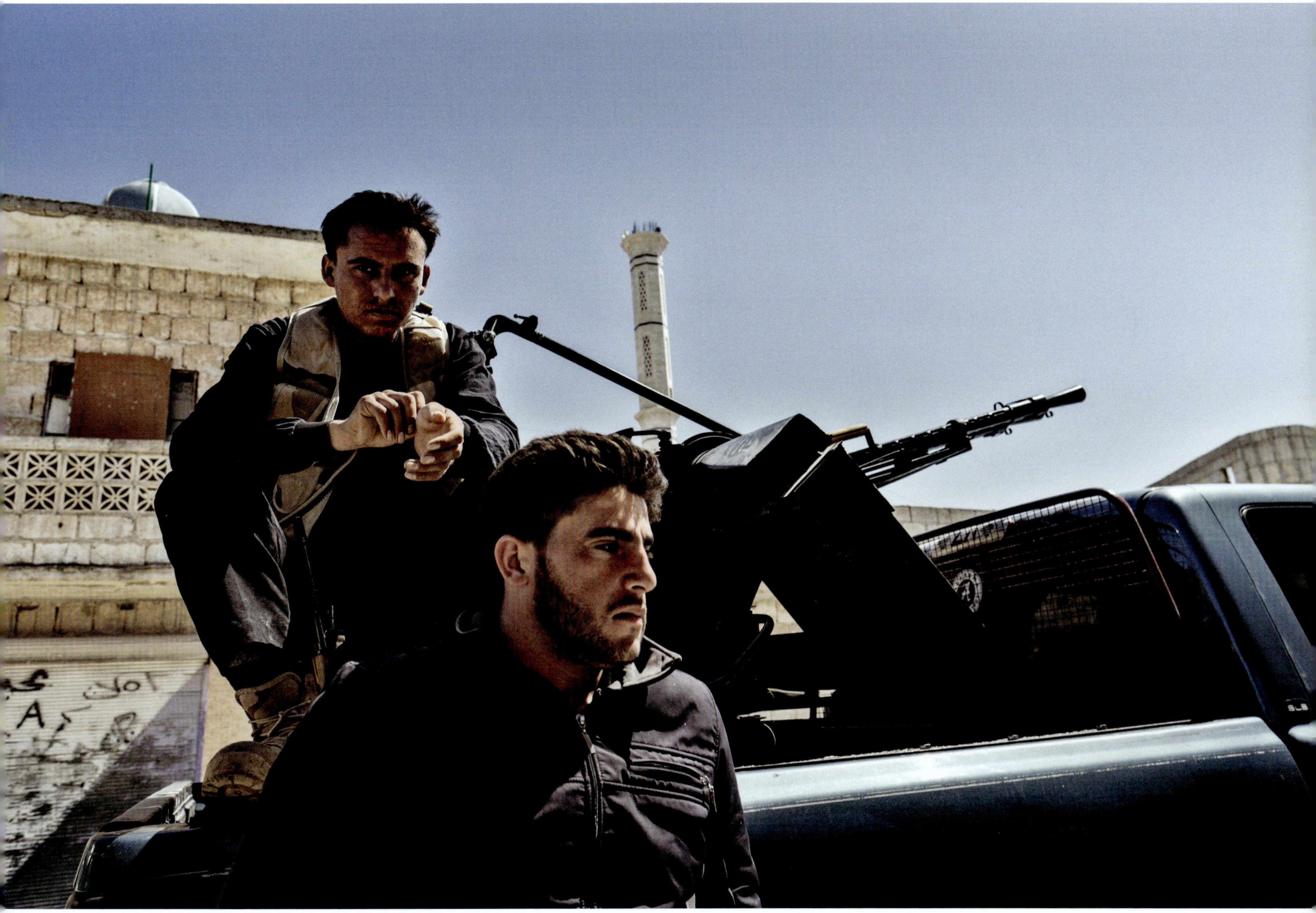

April 20, 2013, Masaken Hanano, Aleppo.

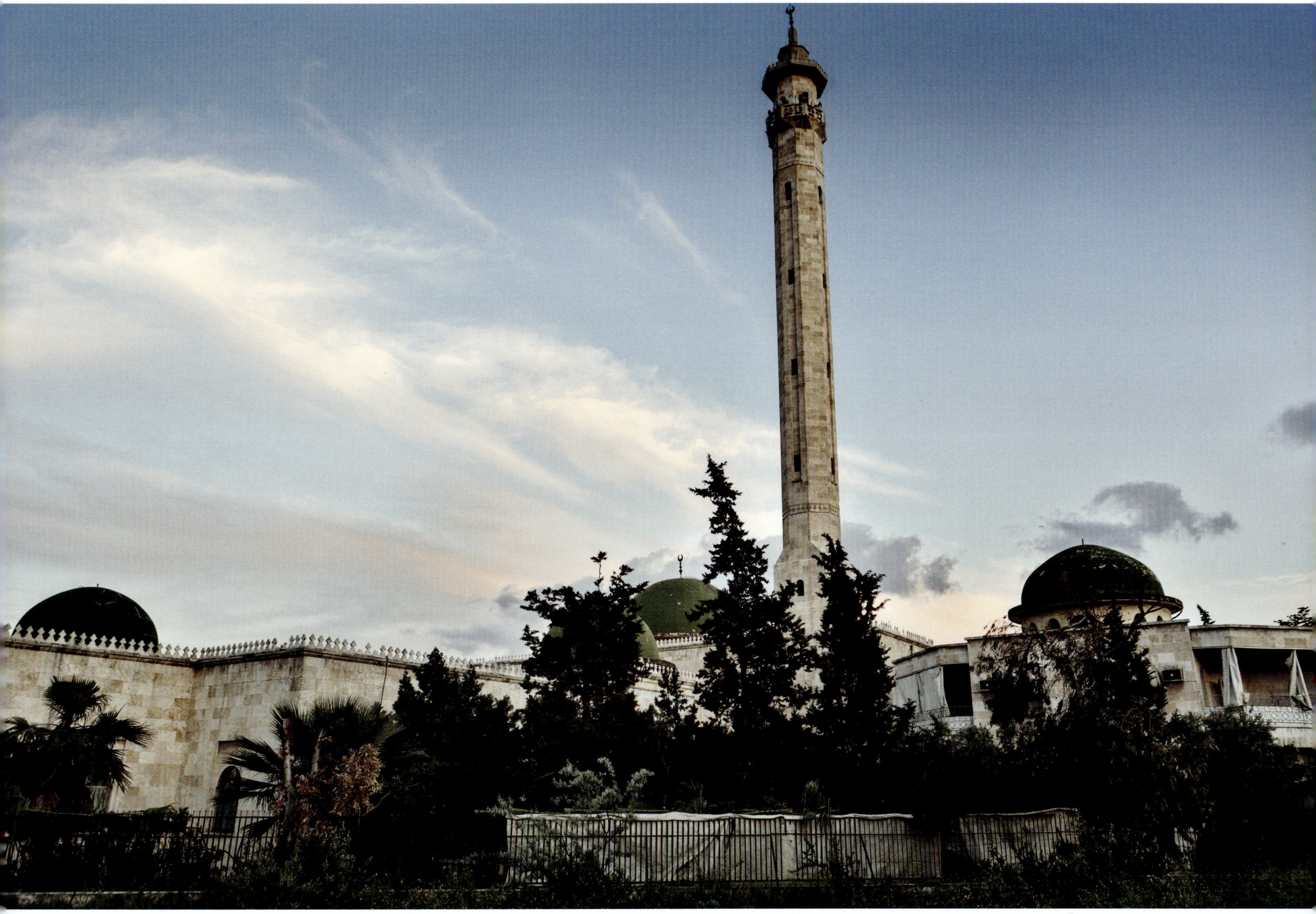

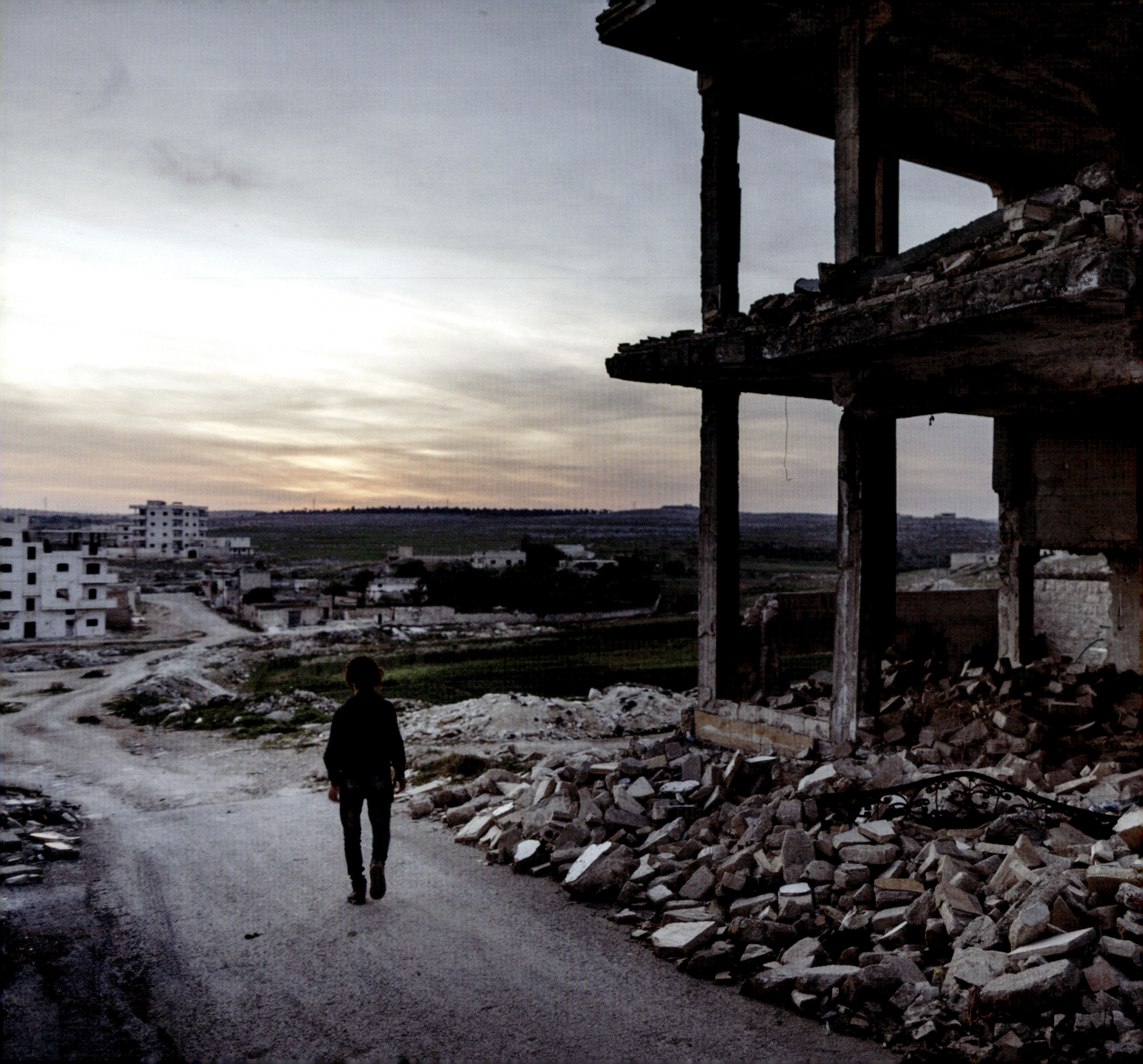

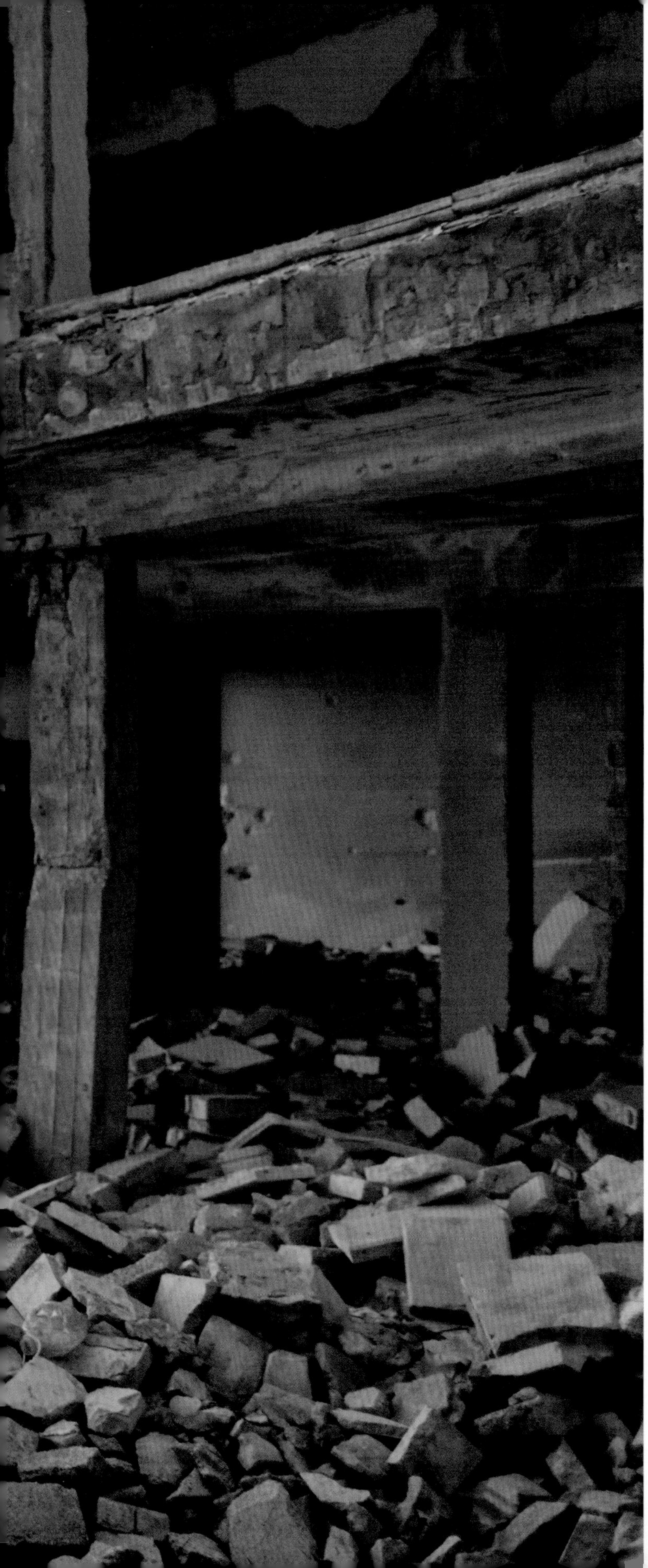

April 5, 2014, Maarat al-Numaan, Idlib.

كل العالم عميان

All the world is blind

ON THE IMPORTANCE OF PHOTOJOURNALISM

Greg Campbell

In a world where practically every human experience can be seen or shared with the tap of a finger on a smartphone, it's tempting to consider the art of photojournalism to be nearing its sunset. That's especially so when it comes to war reporting, which was already one of the riskiest facets of photography. The combatants themselves now photograph the fighting and share the images through Facebook, Snapchat, and Instagram. The risk of being intentionally targeted, either for kidnapping or death, is far greater now than at any other point in the history of documenting warfare, and so it's tempting to declare conflict reporting both redundant and unnecessary.

Nothing could be further from the truth, of course, but before getting to why, it's important to acknowledge just how dangerous this profession has become. The flood of cheap phones now available in even the farthest reaches of the globe, expanding global Wi-Fi, and free publishing platforms are the ingredients that make photojournalists unwanted by at least one major demographic: the armed groups fighting the very wars we need photographers to cover, whether they're traditional armies, grassroots insurgencies, or organized terrorist groups.

It was only a decade or so ago that impartial journalists could make the argument—often at gunpoint, standing at some tense checkpoint near a front line, far from help, rescue, or easy retreat—that allowing access to cameras was the only way combatants could explain themselves to the wider world. It was a nuanced argument made in a black-and-white environment, and it's never been easy to convinced armed men to see the logic in granting unfettered battlefield access to strangers openly promising to tell the truth about what they see and experience.

It didn't always work, but rejection didn't usually involve being executed on the side of the road. But that's exactly what journalists risk today, usually in the most gruesome way imaginable, and with the added horror of having their deaths broadcast on the Internet.

With all the trappings of their very own media apparatuses easily available, armed groups bypass journalists altogether and post their messages directly to the world, with no editorial filter but their own. Truth, always hard to define in conflict situations, becomes ever more elusive precisely due to the lack of impartial observers. To allow access to foreign reporters is to risk having your carefully crafted message—that a regime's bombing campaign is conducted with pinpoint precision to protect civilians, for example—contradicted by dispassionate observers. Who needs a fact-checker when you can tweet your own version of reality to millions of worldwide followers with just a few taps on a phone?

In truth, the need for objective and unembedded observers has never been greater. When the tools of media are as widely available as the tools of war to combatants, imagery itself becomes ammunition. Photos produced by actors in a conflict are rarely intended to objectively inform. They are made to inspire fear, stoke revenge, and justify atrocities. They are used to demonize and dehumanize enemies while presenting one's own cause in a positive light.

Without the balance provided by a free and unimpeded press, imagery that is authorized only by the ruling authorities on either side of the front line is nothing more than propaganda. That's always been the case, of course, but the sheer volume of images produced on a daily basis and the velocity with which they come at us tend to make it more difficult to separate fact from fiction and objectivity from spin.

But the importance of photojournalists to a fuller understanding of the world around us, and the forces that shape it, goes beyond just providing a balance and a counterpoint to competing narratives. The best photojournalism also serves to remind audiences that events occurring in distant lands are not happening to some strange and unknowable species. They are happening to people who could be our own sons, daughters, brothers, and sisters.

That we need to be reminded of this obvious truth is a sad enough commentary on the xenophobic fear-mongering and global upheaval being experienced as this book is being released—five long years after the start of the civil war in Syria. Absent humanizing images like the ones in this book, demagogues in Europe, the Middle East, and the United States have, with varying degrees of success, superimposed their constituents' darkest fears onto the amorphous terms "migrant" and "refugee," all for their own crass political gains.

Differences in language, religion, culture, and nationality have always been used to engender divisions. Those divisions lead to walls. Walls lead to massacres. Massacres lead to genocide. Look no further than the Balkans or Rwanda to understand the natural consequences of dehumanizing entire populations.

The very best photojournalists can undercut this insidious impulse. They can see through the differences, which are usually thin indeed, to illuminate the shared humanity beneath. As common as it is for dictators and demagogues to incite fear and violence over cultural or nationalistic differences, it's also common how quickly those specters are dispelled through the simple act of opening one's eyes to see below the surface.

All that is required to counter the poisonous rhetoric of demagogic candidates and zealot terrorists alike is a willingness to look for what's universal among all the peoples of the world rather than dwelling on differences. That's why the photos in this book are so important, especially in this day and time. Nish Nalbandian is among those rare photographers who cover war by covering the people who suffer through it.

In some ways, it's both the simplest and most powerful means of doing so. For when we see ourselves reflected in the eyes of those who have suffered unimaginably throughout the years of warfare, it becomes immeasurably harder to close our own eyes, and our hearts, to their plight. Photos don't always need to show the most gruesome aspects of warfare in order to remind us of how horrible it is; sometimes it just takes reminding us of the humanity of those who suffer through it.

The ability to do so takes more than a cell phone and Internet access: it takes professional photojournalists, whose skill, dedication, and bravery are more important today than ever.

Greg Campbell is a best-selling nonfiction author and a filmmaker. He is the director of a feature-length documentary about the legendary Getty Images photojournalist Chris Hondros, who was killed in combat while on assignment in Libya in 2011.

ACKNOWLEDGMENTS

I'd like to thank the following people without whom this book would not have been made:

All the people at Daylight Books—I hope that I have not been too difficult to work with!

My family, for worrying about me when I was in the conflict zone and surely thought I was insane.

Mike Shum, who supported me and helped me with my security planning.

Claudio Palmisano, for helping my images stand out from the crowd.

Saad Chouihna, Kawa Noman, and Mohammed Abdelazez for guiding me through Syria, being concerned for my safety, risking their own lives, and bring me back in one piece. I'm glad to call them friends to this day, and I'm glad they are all safe.

I'd also like to acknowledge all the Syrians I worked with or interviewed who stayed behind when I left. Special thanks to families who invited me to share intimate details of their lives.

Emma Beals, Will Wintercross, and John Rowe for providing their insight and writing for this book.

Finally, I'd like to acknowledge that I have only made pictures from one side of this conflict. I do not have access to the other side, and surely there is great suffering on the other side of the line as well.

The images in this book represent a snapshot in time, and as of late 2016 the situation in Northern Syria is much different.